FUND-RAISING EVENTS

FUND-RAISING EVENTS
Strategies and Programs for Success

Ralph Brody, Ph.D.
Marcie Goodman
Federation for Community Planning
Cleveland, Ohio

 **HUMAN SCIENCES PRESS, INC.**
72 FIFTH AVENUE
NEW YORK, N.Y. 10011-8004

Dedicated to Phyllis, Lisa, Mike, and Diane
and to Geri, Ben, Cor, Lisa, Mark, Kacie, Ann, and Lou

Printed in the United States of America
987654321

Library of Congress Cataloging-in-Publication Data

Brody, Ralph.
  Fund-raising events.

  Bibliography: p.
  Includes index.
  1. Fund raising—United States. I. Goodman,
Marcie. II. Title.
HV41.9.U5B76 1988   361.7'63'0681   86-27433
ISBN 0-89885-362-1 (hard)
    0-89885-390-7 (paper)

CONTENTS

PREFACE

This book is written for professionals and volunteer leaders who want to increase their financial ability to carry forward important programs of their nonprofit organizations.

Increasingly, nonprofit organizations must deal with a highly turbulent and competitive funding environment. Federal, state, and local government funding is being severely reduced. United Way funds, while generally growing, are not fully able to keep pace with the needs of community agencies. Appeals to foundations for grants are mounting in volume and in amounts asked. Charitable giving is increasing, but contributors are complaining more and more about the burgeoning requests for their voluntary dollars. Truly this is an era in which nonprofit organizations must find more effective and sophisticated methods to meet the challenge of their financial survival.

The focus of this book is on fund-raising events, which is only one aspect of funding for nonprofit organizations. By fund-raising events, we mean activities that are designed to provide contributors with something in return for their financial support of an organization. We purposely do not cover other aspects of funding, such as proposal writing, direct solicitation, defered giving, or membership campaigns, because there are a number of articles and books on these topics.

Writing this book has been a tremendously rewarding and challenging undertaking. It has been rewarding because it has brought us in touch with outstanding professionals and volunteers who are interesting, competent, intelligent, enthusiastic, and dedicated to raising money for their charitable causes. It has been a joy to encounter dozens of people who, despite frustrations, receive such satisfaction from their work. The preparation of this book has also been challenging because, while we did want to make a special contribution to strengthening the capacities of nonprofit organizations to achieve their goals, we did not want to duplicate fund-raising event books already in existence. Having conducted in-depth interviews with over 70 professionals and volunteers, we think that the scope and comprehensive review of current strategies and programs make this book a useful tool.

This book is divided into two major parts. The first part describes generic principles and concepts that will guide your strategic thinking for all events. This part will provide you with information about fund-raising events in general, including selecting, planning, promoting, implementing, and evaluating events, as well as managing their funds and maximizing their profits. We think that careful attention to this section will save you much time, energy, and money. It will also prevent considerable aggravation. The second part, which is divided into 21 major program categories, describes actual fund-raising events. We have provided sufficient detail about the events so that you can feel confident in making the decision to carry them out, while at the same time we have not overloaded you with more detail than is essential.

We hope that you will use the book as a handbook to gain knowledge that will help your organization function better and as a reference book to focus on particular issues and types of events. Both the table of contents and the index will assist you in identifying topics of special interest to you.

We trust that after reading about these strategies and programs you, too, will join the ranks of those who successfully plan and implement fund-raising events in your community.

Enjoy!

Ralph Brody, Ph.D.
Marcie Goodman

ACKNOWLEDGMENTS

We acknowledge with appreciation the following individuals who devoted their invaluable time and expertise to the preparation of this book:

Fund-Raising Event Experts—Gloria Abrams, Terry Adelman, Bruce Akers, Gloria Aron, Carol Bailey, Cathy Barber, Betsy Beckwith, Ella Becton, Kul Bhushan, Ben Bonanno, Anita Brindza, Isabelle Brown, Betsy Brzozowski, Marjorie Carlson, Russ Catanese, Kathleen Cerveny, Stephen Chamides, Mary Jane Christyson, Beverly Coben, Lana Cowell, Evelyn Croft, Lois Davis, George Delmoro, Georgia Drake, Judith Dworkin, Morris Everett, Jr., Dorothy Faller, Judy Fleming, Chet Foney, Daisy Ford, George Fraser, Barbara Galvin, Sandi Gerena, Cheryl Goggans, Susan Golden, Jon Goldman, Sis Gottlieb, Marietta Gullia, Charles Habjan, Marilyn Helf, Marty Hiller, Jay Hoffman, Elizabeth Horrigan, Fred Issacs, Marilyn Isler, Coleridge Jones, Gloria Pace King, Jo Anne Lake, Teri Levine, Julian Lewis, Gail Long, Priscilla Luce, Paula Mays, Gregory McGrath, Carolyn Miller, Paula Mindes, Lindsay Morgenthaler, John Opperman, Kim Pesses, Ray Pianka, Angela Primm, Jerry Rauckhorst, Sharon Robinson, Roselle Rush, Mary Sanders, Sara Sato, Diann Scaravilli, Harriet Schwartz, Janet Shipman, Robert Silverman, Ray Simmons, Don Slocum, Walter Smith, Jr., Avis Sonchez, Altha Mae Spates, Mickey Stern, Dave Talbott, Mary Tekavec, Judy Thistlewood, Michael Walker, Mikelann Ward, Judith Weiss, James Williams, Michael Wolf, Walter Zborowsky; *Manuscript Advisors*—Rena Blumberg, Phyllis Brody, Polly Clemo, Gigi Fein, Nancella Harris, Renee McGee, Carol Olson, Patricia Pasqual, Janet Shipman, Marlene Stoiber, Neal Szpatura, Joyce Wallace; *Tax Consultant*—Mark Volsky; *Research As-*

sistants—Rose Alexander, Dorothy Mikita, Gautam Yadama; *Editor/Proof-reader*—Roslyn Bucy; *Correspondence Center Staff*—Viola Chapman, Marta Camargo, Audrey Ice, Nick Santone, Ann Vargo.

Finally, we would like to express our gratitude to Seth C. Taft, President of the Federation for Community Planning, for his support and encouragement.

RB
MG

PART I

STRATEGIES FOR SUCCESS

Chapter 1

SELECTING AN EVENT

FITTING AN EVENT WITHIN THE OVERALL STRATEGIC PLAN

Before you organize an event, you should go through an intensive four-step examination process to determine whether to undertake a fund-raising event in the first place and, if so, to choose the one that is right for you. In step one, fit the fund-raising event within an overall strategic plan. In step two, review the negative and positive aspects of conducting an event. In step three, list ideas for fund-raising event possibilities that suit your needs. And, in step four, narrow your selection by conducting a feasibility analysis.

In developing an event, an organization should prepare a strategic plan that shows how an event fits within a larger analysis of the organization and its goals. The ingredients of an organizational strategic plan include the following: a mission statement that reflects the basic concept and character of the organization, the organization's general goals; the specific program objectives to be accomplished within a year by the organization, a plan of activities the organization must pursue to achieve its program objectives, the financial objectives for not only the coming year but the next two or three, and the plan of activities the organization must undertake to achieve its financial objectives. Hence, consideration of a fund-raising event is not separate from the overall strategic plan of the organization—it is an integral part of that plan.

In planning strategically, the organization should carefully determine its financial objectives based on needs identified for the upcoming fiscal year. Of the total amount to be raised, the organization must determine

15

how much will be derived from solicitation drives, endowment funds, grants, and other special fund-raising programs. In determining an organization's financial objectives, some members may be tempted to concentrate only on increasing revenue. But it is important to be as disciplined as possible about reducing expenses as well. If the revenue needed is set too high because of excessive expenses, then you set in motion unrealistic expectations for fund raising. This in turn might lead to later frustrations if the fund-raising efforts do not produce the desired revenue. The objectives should be based on both reasonable financial needs and reasonable expectations for raising funds.

As part of your strategic plan, you will want to analyze the role of the event in the organization. The fundamental question facing the organization is a "chicken or egg" situation: Should the organization strive to strengthen itself before planning an event, or should the organization plan an event as a means of enhancing its capacity to achieve its objectives? There is no simple answer to this means-end issue. Under some circumstances you may need to strengthen the capacity of the organization as a precondition to undertaking an event. For example, you may want to add certain corporate leaders to your board of trustees or work on small-scale projects to promote team efforts before taking on an ambitious event. Under other circumstances you may purposely launch an event to strengthen the organization. For example, you may want to stimulate a renewed spirit of commitment or enhance the leadership capabilities of your board of trustees and members. The important factor is your ability to think through these questions: Do we have the preconditions to pursue a successful fund-raising event, and will the event strengthen the organization?

In the strategic planning process, determine whether a fund-raising event complements other fund-raising approaches. For instance, as part of your strategic thinking, you might consider an event as a way to promote your organization's cause and to heighten its name recognition, which could then make responses to direct membership solicitations or endowment contributions easier to obtain. An event could also identify people who might want to become involved in the organization. Hence, as part of your strategic planning process, you will want to determine how a particular event fits with your other fund-raising activities.

The strategic planning process must also consider whether an event is more or less preferable than other fund-raising approaches. If your sole purpose is to raise money, conducting a fund-raising event may not be the best approach. Your organization might just as well conduct a solicitation drive. Appealing for funds directly can often result in greater profit in relation to time, energy, and money expended. For example, you may decide that rather than organizing a rummage sale to raise a few thousand dollars, you would be better off conducting a solicitation campaign for the money needed. Or you may decide to concentrate fund-raising efforts on endowment gifts, if you feel that obtaining one large gift will take less effort and have greater results than planning a number of fund-raising events that will each net a small amount. Of course, one approach does not necessarily preclude another. You could organize both an event and a solicitation drive. The important point is that all fund-raising decisions should be part of a strategic analysis and emerge from a general design rather than from impulse or happenstance. Any fund-raising event should not be undertaken as an isolated episode resulting from fiscal desperation; it should be part of an overall plan.

If an organization already has one or more events in its repertoire, the strategic planning process should include a careful examination of the fund-raising events portfolio. Just as pension fund managers review their investment portfolios from time to time and add or subtract from them, by analogy, an organization should critically review its events portfolio and make hard decisions about the future of its events. In the business world, some products are called "cash cows," because they bring in considerable money, while others are designated as "dogs," because they have clearly run their course. You may want to review carefully your own situation with these terms in mind to determine whether to keep what you have or make changes. To enhance your strategic analysis when you have been organizing a number of events over several years, consider these approaches:

> Conduct a detailed review of the financial performance of each event. You will want to see whether any pattern of increases or decreases in net revenues emerges.

> Establish a long-range planning committee, perhaps consisting of all former event chairpersons, that would meet to focus on what fund-raising events should be considered during the next 2 to 5 years and how to modify current events. Presumably there are experienced people who are not currently involved in the day-to-day planning of this year's event. Involve them in a strategic planning process.

> Conduct a review of what has happened since each fund-raising event was initiated. Have the market, the competition, or the values of the community changed, warranting a shift in fund-raising events? Have members' attitudes about fund-raising events changed? Are members as enthusiastic now as they were in the past or do they feel burned out? The assumption here is that external and internal changes are certain and often accelerating. Therefore, organization members need to be

continuously reviewing and adapting to the particular situation.

In summary, a strategic analysis requires you to study your overall financial picture, to assess how an event fits in with other methods of raising funds, and to review your current portfolio of events.

CONSIDERING THE NEGATIVE AND POSITIVE ASPECTS OF AN EVENT

Before embarking on an event, which can be a demanding enterprise, you should first consider reasons why you might not undertake an event. Weigh these negative factors against positive aspects in determining whether to conduct events to raise organizational funds.

Negative Aspects

One negative aspect is that the expenses involved in putting on an event can be excessively high relative to the income generated. Some events require an outlay of 50 to 70 percent of the total gross receipts. For instance, one organization produced a concert and raised $66,000, but its expenses were $60,000—leaving a net return of only $6,000. Although the organization was pleased that the community became more aware of its existence and its cause, the original goal of raising greatly needed money was not realized. Hence, under some circumstances, the actual funds raised may be grossly inadequate in relation to expenses.

Another negative aspect of fund-raising events is that they are highly demanding. They consume inordinate amounts of staff and volunteer time—so much so that the event can detract from other significant efforts of the organization. Volunteers and staff may be diverted from their normal work to make calls, sell tickets, and handle other details. Or, having contributed hours of evening and weekend time, they may be unable to work on a regular basis for a period following the event.

Moreover, the danger always exists that an event can incur a financial loss, and the last thing an organization wants is to lose money. This can have a detrimental effect on the future of the organization, and it can have a demoralizing impact on volunteers and staff.

Finally, income from an event can be erratic. After several years of steady income an event may no longer attract patrons, resulting in the organization's losing money that it has come to depend on. This reduction in income may require a wrenching adjustment by the organization.

In light of these negative aspects, you may want to consider exploring such other approaches as direct solicitation, membership drives, and endowment giving if you feel they have greater payoffs, more efficiency with regard to time and energy expended, and less risk attached.

Positive Aspects

Despite the disadvantages, nonprofit organizations are increasingly considering fund-raising events as a way of augmenting other funding approaches. To be sure, there are clearly some special advantages to conducting events.

Obviously, one major advantage of an event is that it can provide money to the organization that might not otherwise be raised. A corporate contribution to buy a table at a dinner for $500, which then nets $300, is actually a $300 contribution that the corporation might not have made. Moreover, when organization volunteers are reluctant to solicit funds directly, they might be inclined to seek support of an event. For many volunteers fund raising through an event is more palatable than direct solicitation and could serve as a first step toward more ambitious direct solicitation efforts. Then, too, the organization's constituency may not be willing or able to respond to direct solicitations for funding but would participate in a fund-raising event because of the value they perceive for themselves. In addition, events can encourage regular donors to give more and can revive the giving pattern of past donors who have reduced their investment in the organization. So when it is difficult to obtain donations directly, an organization should consider raising monies through events.

Another major advantage is that an event can attract new supporters. By involving people beyond the inner circle of the organization, you open up the possibility of establishing new relationships with people who will eventually want to be part of your ongoing efforts. These are the people who can be solicited in a future direct appeal for funds and who can become part of the organization's constituency. A well-conceived and successfully implemented event will open up the organization to a wider audience who will remember who you are and what you stand for.

An additional advantage of an event is that it can heighten the involvement and participation of members within the organization itself. Through the event you can rekindle the interest of inactive trustees and other members who may thereby become more intensively committed to the work of the organization. A strong organization has active members who are deeply committed and involved and who feel good about their investment in the organization. An event can serve as a tonic for the malaise that almost every organization occasionally experiences.

A final advantage is the event's public relations value. A fund-raising event projects the name of the organization and its cause before the general public. It offers an opportunity to take advantage of a captive audience and a platform from which you can express your message. You can use the event to capture the interest of the media and the general public. Through an event you can also raise the prestige of the organization when, for example, you honor a distinguished person. In some instances, the advantage of public awareness can be of greater value to the organization than the actual money raised. If your desire is to move from a low to a high profile in your community, an event is a route to consider.

CONDUCTING A PRE-EVENT ANALYSIS

Organizations that are considering an event for the first time, adding an event to their existing repertoire, or replacing an event that has run its course must explore two fundamental questions as part of a pre-event analysis.

One question is, "How much money does the organization need to raise from a fund-raising event?" The answer cannot simply be, "All we can raise." Obviously you want to raise as much money as possible, but for the purposes of exploring possibilities, it is desirable to have a financial objective in mind. Prior to a discussion of any particular event you should have determined a budget for the year, including how much you intend to raise from an event. If your budget calls for raising $4,000 from an event, that will suggest one kind of activity; if it calls for $40,000, you will need to consider a different kind of activity. You must therefore determine a money amount to be raised by an event prior to considering the range of possibilities. Then examine the financial returns from a variety of events. For example, if you need to raise $4,000, do not consider a bake sale. If one event will not be sufficient, then you may want to consider several events to achieve your financial objective.

The other question is, "Do you have the people-resources to undertake a fund-raising event?" One of the most essential elements of any event is people who are committed, hardworking, creative, talented, and experienced. Determine if you have the kind of people who are willing to invest in making an event a success, as well as the number of people to carry it through. Also, look inward to your members and constituency groups for special talents and experiences. If you have musicians, then consider a musical event. If you have art patrons, then consider an art show. If you deal with merchants, then consider an event that allows them to donate items and purchase advertising in a program book, such as an auction. And look at your group's connections, such as theater owners, party hall proprietors, owners of mansions or townhouses, or hotel managers. Take time to compile a list of resources within the organization and those to which your members have access.

GATHERING IDEAS FOR AN EVENT

Some organizations have the good fortune of being preeminent in offering the same highly successful event year after year. These organiza-

tions enjoy special places of dominance in the community so that their annual fund-raising events attract a growing audience. Typically, however,
most organizations must develop imaginative ideas for fund-raising
events. For a number of reasons it is important to include creative thinking
as part of the development process, whether you are offering an event for
the first time or repeating a success.

First, you will generally want people to see your event as being something different from the usual. Developing a special niche for your event in
the charitable marketplace is an important way to attract a following.

Second, if you have been offering an event for several years, you know
that people can become tired of repeating the same program in the same
way. Volunteers become stale and the audience becomes bored unless
something new and distinctive is provided. This should not surprise you,
since clothing styles, musical tastes, automobiles, and soap packages are
constantly being revised to appeal to the changing tastes of consumers.
Consider change and innovation as a natural way to prevent your fund-
raising event from winding down.

A third reason is competition. In the long run, whatever initial niche
or special advantage you have for your event, there is a tendency for decline because of competition. If you are successful, you can be certain others will try to copy your idea. You may enjoy the advantage of uniqueness
for a while, but see this as temporary. You need to consider adding innovation to your program or undertaking different, imaginative events to keep
ahead of the competition.

To think creatively you must first develop an attitude geared to imaginative thinking. This will enable you to search for ideas and draw upon
your knowledge and experience. With this open approach you can try various slants. You can function on the premise that nothing is fixed and that
any fund-raising event that you or others have tried is open to challenge.
Even though previous events may have been successful, different circumstances may be operating currently or there may be better and different
ways to continue the event. You must be open to challenging familiar formats. And, if necessary, you have to be willing to fall out of love with a
cherished tradition.

To be creative, you must be willing to take risks. Exploring new ideas
means exposing your organization to the possibility of failure. Later on,
following the exploration of creative ideas, you will want to be critical to reduce the risk of failure. In this initial phase of exploration, you have to be
willing to experience a certain amount of doubt and risk as you move from
the familiar to unchartered territory.

You have to know how to explore and stimulate new ideas through
creative thinking. One of the ways you can do this is by embarking on a series of "What if . . . questions: "What if we held the event at another time
of the year . . . or alternated years . . . or used a different place . . . or added

new features to the event . . . or eliminated certain parts?" By asking "What if . . ." questions you free your group to probe the possible, the impossible, the practical, and the impractical, for ideas. In this exploratory phase, any idea is worth considering.

Another method of opening up your mind to a variety of ideas is to brainstorm. In this process everyone in the group is encouraged to discuss any idea. No negative comments are permitted. Any notion, however trivial or frivolous or expensive, is put on the table. The purpose of the exercise is to bring thoughts—uncensored—out in the open. Hang large sheets of paper around the room and write down all of the brainstorms so everyone can see them.

At the beginning stage you want to be as open as possible. Do not hesitate to welcome free-floating thoughts and to consider many far-out ideas. The impractical concepts may eventually lead to realistic, creative ones. The small inspirations may lead to a major breakthrough.

Once you have exhausted all possibilities, you can modify, critique, and eventually reduce the ideas to a shorter list for more careful scrutiny. By weeding and culling you will develop a manageable list that you can examine more critically regarding the costs, the volunteer requirements, and the logistics.

You must be willing to be open to new ideas at even the oddest times. Often ideas jump from our subconscious when we least expect them—when we are brushing our teeth, when we are listening to a song on the radio, when we are shopping. For example, one event chairperson thought of her idea while driving by an airport hangar. "Why not have our next dance in the hangar?" she asked. This led to an exciting event underwritten by an airline company with decorations including balloons hung as clouds on the ceiling and a raffle for airline tickets. Another chairperson let her mind roam through the possibilities that could be associated with a July Fourth weekend festival, and arranged for prizes to be given to guests dressed in red, white, and blue. A third volunteer, having finished exercising, was dressing in the locker room and thought of using the athletic club, including weight rooms, saunas, and other facilities, for the special event —a sports auction. What all these events have in common is that people were willing to explore new possibilities. They were receptive to many different stimuli. They were escaping from the usual way of doing things.

Take ideas that seem impractical and impossible and use them as stepping-stones. When someone suggests something at a meeting that initially seems wild, do not say, "That's ridiculous." Instead, say, "Let's see if there are other possibilities to build on to that." Suppose, for example, someone suggests a jog-a-thon and you are well aware that the community is saturated with jog-a-thons. But if someone else then suggests combining this with Halloween and having people wear costumes as part of the jog-a-thon, it could become a new, exciting event.

Throughout the creative process, remember that you are not seeking the unique for the sake of just being different. What matters most in this exploratory process is the willingness to look for worthwhile ideas. Before ideas are acted upon you must go through the critical phase of determining whether the new event, or the modification of an existing one, is really worth doing. Every fresh, imaginative proposal needs to be scrutinized from a variety of angles through a feasibility analysis.

Conducting a Feasibility Analysis

After you have generated many event possibilities, you need to ask whether each idea under consideration is feasible. Your goal is to narrow the list down so you can select one event that is right for you. Certainly the possibility always exists that an excellent idea will be dropped. An equal danger, however, is pursuing an event that should have been dropped but was not, due to inadequate screening. It is better to abort early than to continue with an idea that could result in a dud. The value of the screening process is therefore to eliminate all but the most desirable and feasible project ideas. Of course, event ideas that are not pursued can be reconsidered at another time or folded into another event. The following major questions can help you make a selection. The sample "Event Exploration Worksheet" may be helpful as well. Note that your feasibility analysis may include significant considerations in addition to those discussed below.

Is the Event Appropriate for our Organization and Community?

You should be sensitive to the nature of your organization and your community. For example, a neighborhood organization might not want to sponsor a potentially lucrative haunted-house tour at Halloween because of the concern about attracting rowdy teenagers. Similarly, members of a religious charitable organization might find a Monte Carlo night not in keeping with their values.

To be sure, some events flow naturally from the purpose of an organization. A nature center could consider a plant sale or a party in the park, a health association could sponsor a swim-a-thon, a neighborhood center could sponsor a community carnival. In each instance the event has a natural connection to the purposes of the organization.

Will the Event Appeal to our Members?

Since your members will tend to invest themselves in those fund-raising events that are inherently interesting to them, consider what they like to do. Do they like to dance, to gamble, to go to parties? Would they

EVENT EXPLORATION WORKSHEET*

Event Name _____

Estimated Gross Income
(source)   (amount)

_____   _____
_____   _____
_____   _____

Total Estimated Gross Income _____

Estimated Expenses
(source)   (amount)

_____   _____
_____   _____
_____   _____
_____   _____
_____   _____

Total Estimated Expenses _____

Estimated Net Income   _____
(gross income minus expenses)

Estimated Hours
professional staff   _____
support staff   _____
volunteers   _____

Total Hours   _____

Feasibility criteria

	Yes	No
appropriate?	_____	_____
appeal to members?	_____	_____
provide sufficient funds?	_____	_____
achieve nonfinancial objectives?	_____	_____
good track record?	_____	_____
competition?	_____	_____
resource capacity?	_____	_____
meet customer needs?	_____	_____

Additional Considerations: _____

_____

*A worksheet should be developed for each event idea.

find a house tour or a sporting event more appealing? Eliminate those ideas that your members would not look forward to doing. Try to articulate what would be especially appealing about a particular event for your members.

Do We Have the Capacity to Undertake the Event?

Events require both financial and personnel resources. For example, if your organization's treasury is low, you may not want to take the risk of borrowing funds for an event that requires up-front expenses. The potential of the downside risk may be just too great. Consider also whether you have adequate volunteer and staff backup to undertake personnel requirements. It is especially important that the board of trustees and other key members of your organization are prepared to give the proper time and attention to planning and implementing the event.

Will the Event Provide Sufficient Funds to Warrant the Effort?

Time demands in relation to potential income is an important consideration. If estimated income from a potential event will provide only 5 percent of your budget, you will not want 20 percent of the staff and volunteer time devoted to it. Nor will you want to divert time from other essential activities. On the other hand, some events will require minimal time from staff and volunteers, so that tasks can be absorbed along with other organizational activities. For example, if a major part of the event workload is to take phone call reservations, staff and volunteers may be able to handle this requirement along with their regular duties.

Can the Event Accomplish Objectives Beyond Raising Funds?

Reaching out to a new constituency, recognizing important supporters, launching a major fund solicitation campaign, and conducting a major public relations effort are some of the objectives beyond raising funds that an event can accomplish. Analyze your list of potential events to determine which ones most closely meet your organizational objectives.

Does the Event Have a Good Track Record?

Included in your list may be events tried previously by your organization or others. If the results were worthwhile, ask if the conditions leading to the success still exist. If the previous efforts were only partially successful, ask if you now have the ingredients that could make the event a success. Carefully assess various event possibilities on the basis of current circumstances. Also review the experiences of events that have succeeded elsewhere. But be aware that what has worked somewhere else may have had special appeal and resources that might not necessarily fit your own situation. Ask what groups similar to yours have undertaken each event. Determine why it has worked well. Decide if there are elements that you could use, perhaps with some modifications.

Can the Event Compete Successfully?

By examining the events of other organizations, you can avoid planning one that has already saturated the community. For example, if there are presently several auctions in your community, then you certainly should question the appeal of another one.

Truly original fund-raising events, which are free of competition, are rare. These are the exceptions that you may wish you had thought of first so as to preempt the field. Generally, in every moderate-sized community almost all events have been tried at some time or other, thereby providing competition for your event. In fact, some events in your community may be so well-established by other organizations that they cannot be easily challenged. The organizations that sponsor these outstanding events are acknowledged as market leaders. You must determine whether to undertake or avoid these events.

When copying another group's event you may increase your chances of success by selecting a different time period and constituency. Suppose, for example, that an organization in your neighborhood sponsors a popular Monte Carlo night each April, and one of your possible events is a Las Vegas night. Perhaps your event could be held in November. You have to judge whether the distance of time is sufficiently great so that you can enter into the gambling field and appeal to some of the same neighborhood constituents. Or perhaps your Las Vegas night could be held outside the neighborhood to attract a different constituency.

The concern about competition applies not only to events but also to requests for corporate financial support. You should be aware that businesses are bombarded with requests for underwriting, donations, and gifts. Hence, the competition issue may not apply as much to your particular audience as it does to the demands you are making on the business community for support.

MEETING CUSTOMERS' NEEDS

Once you have conducted a feasibility analysis of all of your event ideas, you should be able to narrow the list down to three or four possibilities. To arrive at the best among these good alternatives, you should develop a marketing orientation. This approach differs from what is known as a product orientation.

Through a product orientation, an organization may decide on an event (the product) based entirely on the desires and the strengths of its members. These factors are important considerations. But if the decision-making focuses exclusively on the wishes of the organization members and ignores the interests of the potential audience, then you risk selecting an unappealing event that attracts few outsiders. If, for example, an organization has always had a dinner-dance and attendance is waning, sometimes the tendency is to continue this event because it is what most members feel comfortable with. The traditional product approach focuses on the needs of the organization members without regard to the needs of others.

A marketing orientation focuses not just on the product but on meeting the changing needs and wants of the customers. The business term "customer" is used purposely in this context because an event should be seen as an opportunity to satisfy the needs and wants of those who pay to attend. The primary reason varies for why people pay money to enter a raffle, participate in a golf tournament, attend a banquet, or run in a marathon. Some do it to support the cause, some to satisfy their social needs or to meet obligations, and some because the event itself is inherently appealing. So in making your final selection, ask this question: "What are the needs of our potential customers, and which of these events is most likely to satisfy these needs?"

It is not necessary to conduct a formal marketing survey to gauge the attractiveness of each potential event to the audience you want to reach. Instead, use your members as a barometer, since they will have their own subjective reactions that can influence the selection. For example, find out if your trustees are attracted more to an art auction than to a golf tournament. Determine whether the response to this type of inquiry is typical of the audience you are trying to reach.

If the members of your organization are not the primary audience for your event and you calculate that 90 percent of your potential customers will be drawn from outside the core organization family, then you have to think about who the customers are that you want to attract and which events will appeal to them. For example, if you want to attract businessmen, you might consider planning a golf tournament. Put yourself in the shoes of your potential customers as you calculate which events will likely be most attractive to them while meeting your own objectives.

To gauge the market even more closely, talk to people who are potential customers. Suppose you are thinking of planning a winter holiday festival that would attract parents and young children. Talk to some of the parents in April. Ask if they and their children would enjoy the experience. Determine if they would prefer an ice-cream festival in the summer—or perhaps both events. By obtaining this feedback, you place yourself in a better position to assess the degree to which you will be able to meet your potential customers' needs.

The process of selecting an event is like an accordion. Initially you will want to consider as many ideas as possible. Asking "What if . . ." questions, brainstorming by using your imagination, and uncritically considering diverse suggestions will help to expand the range of possibilities. But then, through a series of feasibility questions and selection criteria, you will need to narrow down the list of ideas into a few selected ones from which you can make your final decision. During this exploratory period set a "go/no go" date to discipline yourself to make a timely decision. Generally you may want to allot about 2 months to the process of selecting an event.

RESOURCES

Ardman, P. & Ardman, H. *Woman's Day book of fund raising*. New York: St. Martin's Press, 1980, pp. 154, 173.

B'nai B'rith Fund Raising Cabinet. *B'nai B'rith fund raising chairman handbook*. Washington, D.C.: B'nai B'rith Leadership Cabinet, p. 42.

Brody, R. *Problem solving: concepts and methods for community organizations*. New York: Human Sciences Press, 1982, pp. 199–207.

Cobb, L. M. Fund raising's revolving door: How it can be stopped. *Fund Raising Management*, March 1985.

Connors, T. D. *The nonprofit organization handbook*. New York: McGraw-Hill, 1980, p. 42.

DeBono, E. *PO: Beyond yes and no*. New York: Penguin, 1983, pp. 3, 61, 94, 97, 121, 140, 142.

Drotning, P. T. *500 ways for small charities to raise money*. Chicago: Contemporary Books, 1979, pp. 15, 20, 73–76.

Flanagan, J. *The grass roots fundraising book*. Chicago: Contemporary Books, Inc., 1982, pp. 8, 142, 279.

Grambs, M. & Miller, P. *Dollars and sense: A community fundraising manual for women's shelters and other non-profit organizations*. San Francisco: Western States Shelter Network, 1982, pp. 9, 48.

Kaiser, L. Fund raising's future lies with creative visionaries. *Fund Raising Management*, March 1985, pp. 34–39.

Kotler, P. *Marketing for nonprofit organizations*. Englewood Cliffs, NJ: Prentice-Hall, 1982, pp. 5, 116.

Mulford, C. *Guide to student fundraising: 129 ways to raise money*. Reston, VA: Future Homemakers of America, 1984, p. 9.

Musselman, V. W. *Money raising activities for community groups*. New York: Association Press, 1969, pp. 3, 22.

Pritchard, J. H. *There's plenty of money for nonprofit groups willing to earn their shares— How to do it successfully*. Phoenix: Cornucopia Publications, 1984, pp. 6–8, 17–18.

Saasta, T. Grass roots fund raising. *The Grantsmanship Center News*, October–December 1977.

Sheerin, M. *How to raise top dollars from special events.* New York: Public Service Materials Center, 1984, pp. 9–10, 13–14, 18, 117–119, 191.

Sweeney, T. & Seltzer, M. Survival planning for the 80's: Fundraising strategies for grassroots organizations. *Community Jobs Reprint*, 1982.

Vapnar, G. S. Fundraising: A common sense approach. *Family Resource Coalition Report*, 1985, pp. 4–5.

Von Oech, R. *A whack on the side of the head.* New York: Warner Books, 1983.

Chapter 2

PLANNING AN EVENT

SETTING OBJECTIVES

Every fund-raising event should have objectives that are relevant, attainable, and measurable. Objectives should pertain to the general mission and goals of the organization. Furthermore, objectives should be capable of being realized within a specified time period, such as 3 months or a year. Also, if at all possible, objectives should be based upon tangible, concrete, and quantifiable results. For most events, financial objectives may be more easily measured than those that are nonfinancial.

Financial Objectives

An event should establish income and expense financial objectives, as illustrated by the following examples:

Income Objectives:
> Sell a minimum of 350 tickets
>
> Raise $15,000 total (gross) income
>
> Obtain underwriting support of $2,000 from 5 corporations
>
> Achieve net income of $12,000

Expense Objectives:
> Keep expenses under $3,000

Secure free floral decorations

Obtain free printing services

Note that each of these is an action-oriented objective that conveys concrete results to be achieved.

In establishing financial objectives, be as realistic as possible. If you strive for too high a net income objective, volunteers will feel unduly pressured. And if the objective is not achieved, they will experience a sense of defeat—even if more money is raised than ever before. On the other hand, too low a financial objective might result in volunteers not stretching themselves. Finding that right balance of stretching people without pushing so far that they experience undue frustration is indeed a challenge. A financial objective that is within reach, reasonable, and achievable, even though it involves tremendous work, gives everyone a sense of positive accomplishment.

Usually net income objectives should be related to a specific cause or project. People generally like to feel that their donations will be going for something concrete. Money raised at a special event should not be lost in the basic operating budget of the organization. Ideally, these funds should be segregated out from the base budget and earmarked for a specific purpose in which volunteers and donors can feel some pride. Examples include a scholarship program, improving day-care facilities, or funding a special teen counseling program.

Nonfinancial Objectives

Establishing nonfinancial objectives for a particular event is an individualized matter. Each organization has to decide what its specific nonfinancial objectives are for the event. Some events, for example, are designed to promote a sense of team spirit, while others may not have that explicit purpose. Unfortunately, organizations rarely take the time to write down their nonfinancial objectives. Prior to the event, however, volunteer leaders and staff should meet to discuss nonfinancial objectives so that after the event they can answer the question, "Were we successful in accomplishing all that we had intended?" In the examples listed below, indicators of success are identified below each nonfinancial objective. Note that in listing objectives two kinds of indicators are included: those that lend themselves to quantifiable measurement, such as the number of volunteers participating, and those that require feedback either in the form of a survey or, more likely, through informal discussion with committee members or participants.

Objective: Increase the quality and quantity of volunteer participation

Indicators of success:

> number of: volunteers participating (compared with last year)
>
> new volunteers
>
> leadership opportunities
>
> committees
>
> total person hours involved (volunteers and staff)
>
> results of a survey regarding volunteers' perceptions of being actively involved

Objective: Increase membership in the organization

Indicators of success:

> number of: people who attended the event and became new members following the event
>
> former members who became re-involved following the event

Objective: Increase visibility of the organization

Indicators of success:

> number of: times the event is mentioned in the media
>
> posters in the community
>
> ticket sellers
>
> people attending the event who are not affiliated with the organization

Objective: Increase goodwill toward the organization from the community

Indicators of success:

> number of neighborhood persons attending
>
> results of informal discussion regarding guests' satisfaction after the event

If the fund-raising event does not achieve its financial objectives, the organization should not be tempted to rationalize the outcome based on nonfinancial objectives that are made up after the event. The reason to spell out the nonfinancial objectives and indicators of success in advance is because these can be of benefit to the organization, independent of financial objectives.

Nonfinancial objectives and indicators of success can provide concrete guidance as to how you will function before, during, and after the event. For example, if you have determined that a major objective is to enlarge your constituency base, then you should gear some of your event activities in this direction. You might ask those attending the event to give their names and addresses for possible follow-up. You might offer a door prize if they complete information on a ticket stub that you can use later for recruitment purposes. You might present a description of your organization at the fund-raising event or distribute materials. You might assign your members to mingle with the audience to discuss the benefits of joining the organization. On the other hand, you probably would not emphasize any of these efforts if increasing your constituency was not a major objective.

By establishing objectives, you sharpen your thinking about events and activities you do not want to undertake, as well as those that you do. For example, if your primary objective is to improve goodwill within your community, you should obviously think twice about sponsoring a booth at another community's festival involving only a few of your volunteers and providing only limited visibility of your organization to those you want to reach.

DETERMINING THE TIMING

The question of when to put on an event—the timing—will depend on a variety of factors, including the following:

Life cycle of the organization.   Organizations that are relatively new in the community are often tempted to undertake a major event to raise money, promote the cause of the fledgling organization, and attract potential new members. These are desirable aims, but unless the organization has established internal strength, it risks putting on an event that is doomed to fail due to a lack of resources. The organization must first build up its internal strength and undertake smaller, manageable events before taking on a major, ambitious one.

Lead time.   Events require a significant amount of time for careful planning and effective promotion. Some events become only borderline successes or even failures because of a late start that resulted in spur-of-the-moment planning and promotion. With many complex details to handle in too little time, pressures build up that may prevent the proper implementing of arrangements and the proper handling of unexpected circumstances. For example, to secure an open date at an auditorium 3 months hence, a group scurried to find a celebrity for the program. Because of time limitations, it was forced to settle on a has-been, which in turn affected ticket sales and resulted in a poor turnout. Had the group secured the date further in advance, it could have been assured of a currently popular star, which would have increased the turnout. As another example, with only 3 months to plan and implement a dinner-dance, an organization did not have sufficient time to obtain corporate underwriting. And the printer made an error in the invitation that was overlooked in the rush to meet their mailing deadline. When everyone is in a panic to meet deadlines, errors and oversights occur that may prove disastrous. Allow sufficient time to plan and implement your event.

Community situation.   Certain characteristics of your community can affect timing. For example, if your community enjoys spaghetti dinners or pancake breakfasts, consider holding them close to election time when politicians are likely to show up. The politicians will draw people to the event as well as bring their own supporters. Or, as another example, consider holding a rummage sale during the first week of the month or whenever most of the people in your community receive their paychecks and are more likely to make purchases. Analyze what may be happening in your community that could effect participation in your event.

Specific times of the year.   Certain times of the year may be particularly bad to hold some events. For example, in locales that have harsh winters, January and February may be poor months since the weather conditions could affect attendance. June may not be good because of weddings and graduations. July and August may also be poor months because of vacations. November and December are questionable months because people want to spend holiday time with their families—at home or away—and because they may not have extra spending money. Holding an event on a holiday weekend (Memorial Day, Father's Day, July Fourth, Labor Day) is taking a calculated risk. Although you have a ready-made holiday theme, people may prefer to spend time with their families or go out of town.

On the other hand, spring does offer certain theme possibilities, such as May Day and apple blossoms. And people may be receptive to an event at the end of the year because of potential tax deductions and because they feel in a charitable and giving mood in keeping with the holiday spirit. Also, they may be particularly receptive to purchasing certain items that some organizations sell, such as calendars, holiday cards, and tree ornaments. Hence, the time of the year needs to be considered very seriously.

Special time in the life of the organization.   An anniversary celebration is a special reason to hold an event. By drawing attention to your milestone year, you dramatize the cause you are working for, your volunteers become excited, and the general public joins in the goodwill generated by celebrating your anniversary.

Clearing the community calendar.   Good timing requires you to be aware of whether other events are going on at the time you intend to hold yours. There is no point in having a house tour or a dinner-dance a few days before or after other groups sponsor similar affairs. Since some months are generally not desirable (midwinter or midsummer), events tend to be concentrated in the periods of April through June and September through November. In light of these limited time periods, set the date for your event as early as possible. Clear it as far in advance as possible with other groups. Check school, church, and civic group calendars. Ideally, your community should have a community calendar provided by the Chamber of Commerce, the central volunteer bureau, or some other organization that acts as a clearinghouse for registering dates at least 6 months to a year in advance. Some communities arrange for volunteers to run the clearing-house and charge small fees for out-of-pocket expenses to participating organizations. Local newspapers and area magazines also print calendars of upcoming events.

Relation to request for donations.   Avoid conducting a direct solicita-tion drive shortly before or after your event. People will resent being asked to give again after having just made a donation. In general, separate re-quests for funds by at least 3 or 4 months.

PAYING ATTENTION TO DETAILS

One of the most important ingredients contributing to the success of a fund-raising event is attention to details. In any one event there are many, many details to master, and the omission of one or several can make the difference between a smoothly run event and a failure. Examine every de-tail; never assume anything. There is an old saying, "When you assume, you make an 'ass' out of 'u' and 'me'!" To your audience the event should appear effortless. But such a smooth running event does not occur by acci-dent; it is made to happen. Comprehensive, detailed planning can prevent cost overruns, volunteer burnout, and other failures; it can greatly contrib-ute to the success of an event. Two tools that will facilitate paying attention to details are an activities list and a timeline chart.

An Activities List

A detailed activities list must be prepared for an event so that you can organize your efforts. Begin by determining the major activities of your event. For example, if you have decided on a dinner-auction event, some of the major activity categories would include the following: pre-event preparation, event structuring, dinner arrangements, auction arrangements, publicity, ticket sales, auction catalog, and follow-up arrangements. Of course, different events will require different major activities. A banquet, for example, would require a program agenda category; a festival would require a booth category.

In developing your list, include tasks under each major activity. Feeding into the major activities, these tasks can range in time from a few days to weeks or sometimes months. Volunteers are generally assigned to carry out these tasks. The spelling out of tasks can sometimes be time-consuming and tedious. But preparing for completion of major activities in this way can more readily ensure that the proper actions will be implemented and problems will be corrected. In distinguishing between activities and tasks you may have to arbitrarily designate one or the other. And you may decide to have sub-tasks, if that level of detail makes sense to you.

Related to each task in the activities list, begin to think about your anticipated time, giving careful consideration to when you will begin and when you will complete the task. Also, indicate after each major activity the chairperson or other responsible person charged with carrying it out.

Two approaches can be considered in specifying tasks: reverse order planning and forward sequence planning. In reverse order planning, the group begins with the final result to be achieved and identifies the tasks that feed into activities by asking the question, "What must we do just before reaching our final result and then what needs to be done before that, and before that, and so forth?" until arriving at the beginning point. In forward sequence planning, the group begins with what it considers to be the appropriate set of tasks and then asks, "What should be done next, and what after that, and so forth?" until the actual event occurs.

In most decision-making situations, a group will combine reverse order and forward sequence planning. That is, typically, members of the group will consider by what date they want to achieve a particular result and then consider all the tasks they need to undertake prior to that deadline. If the major approach is reverse order planning, the group will find it useful to employ forward sequence planning as a double-checking device (and vice versa) to see if any tasks have been omitted.

In reality, no group would compile a complete activities list in its first round of discussions. Whether forward sequence or reverse order planning is used, a review of the list of tasks would reveal the need to omit some tasks because they are unnecessary, reschedule tasks to prevent overload, and add tasks initially omitted. Even when the activities list appears to be in final form, be prepared for further refinements based on new knowledge and circumstances.

In preparing the preliminary list of activities and tasks, consider using large sheets of paper with a major activity heading on each one and the tasks listed underneath. Or use large sheets and attach stick-on notes that have the tasks written on them. The stick-ons can easily be moved from one activity category to another and then put in proper sequence.

A Timeline Chart

After you have prepared an activities list, you may want to display the tasks and activities on a timeline chart, as illustrated, to check your progress visually. The advantage of a timeline chart is that it is comprehensive and comprehensible, easy to prepare, and simple to revise. The lines related to each task graphically show beginning and ending points. By reading the chart from top to bottom, it is possible to determine which activities and tasks are expected to occur within a particular time period. A review of the sample timeline chart shows, for example, that during the sixth month you will have to prepare the mailing lists, send out save-the-date postcards, select the invitations and the printer, prepare contracts and solicit ads for the catalog, and recruit members for the ticket sales committee. People will therefore need to be available during this busy month to carry out their assignments. The timeline chart can also be used to monitor whether the tasks are being accomplished on schedule.

ANALYZING POTENTIAL CUSTOMERS

In many instances, an event will involve reaching beyond your own organization, since most memberships are too small to support most events. Certainly, you want your own members to contribute to and participate, but their greater value lies in their ability to mobilize and encourage outsiders to participate. By reaching beyond your core membership, you avoid "going to the same well too often." You also spread the base of your commitment. Analyzing your market of potential customers to involve more people is a major component of the planning process. In doing so you will normally reach beyond the boundaries of your organization's constituency to identify those parts of the community that are likely to attend your event. This involves two processes. The first is market segmentation —the breakdown and analysis of the total market into submarkets or customers who must receive special marketing efforts. The second is target marketing—the act of concentrating on those market segments that the organization can most effectively reach.

Market Segmentation

As you plan your event, ask this important question: "To whom is this event likely to appeal?" One major way of analyzing potential custom-

MONTH:

ACTIVITIES/TASKS	ONE	TWO	THREE	FOUR	FIVE	SIX	SEVEN	EIGHT	NINE
Pre-event preparation (Shipman)									
Review (or establish) organizational mission, goals, and nonfinancial objectives									
Establish general financial objectives									
Review event possibilities									
Obtain board approval									
Event structuring (Shipman)									
Select event chairperson									
Select activity chairpeople									
Prepare job descriptions/committee objectives									
Recruit committee members									
Determine general event plans (budget, date, location)									
Dinner Arrangements (Olson)									
Select caterer									
Select menu									
Determine theme									
Prepare decorations									
Develop registration procedures									
Mail out tickets									
Arrange seating									
Prepare presentations									
Arrange parking, coatroom, security									
Oversee cleanup									

ONE TWO THREE FOUR FIVE SIX SEVEN EIGHT NINE

Auction Arrangements (Pasqual)

Prepare guidelines for donating items
Orient volunteer solicitors
Solicit items
Arrange for pickup and warehousing
Prepare visual aids
Obtain sound system
Develop oral auction procedures
Develop silent auction procedures
Obtain volunteer auction workers
Arrange for money handling
Arrange for bidding paddles, etc.

Publicity (Harris)

Develop or update mailing lists
Send out pre-invitation
"Save the Date" postcards
Arrange for TV and radio PSA spots
Arrange for newspaper coverage
Prepare invitations
Select design
Select printer
Proofread invitation
Mail out invitations

39

ONE TWO THREE FOUR FIVE SIX SEVEN EIGHT NINE

Ticket Sales (Fein)

   Recruit committee
   Print tickets
   Prepare sales packet
   Prepare orientation
   Conduct sales campaign

Auction Catalog (Wallace)

   Develop mock-up
   Select printer
   Solicit ads
     Prepare ad contracts
   Prepare volunteer
     sales force
   Prepare catalogs for oral
     and silent auctions

Follow-up Arrangements (Clemo)

   Send thank-you notes
   Box up unsold merchandise
   Request summary reports
     from each chairperson
   Select new auction chairperson
   Prepare financial statement

ers is to divide them into constituencies based on how they are related to the organization. These can include a core institency, an incidental constituency, and a general community constituency.

Your core constituency consists of those persons who are closest to the organization or who are affected by it directly. These include the board of trustees, active members, and clients of the organization. They care most about the organization's achieving its financial and nonfinancial objectives. Obviously, the larger your membership and the greater the sense of identity with your organization, the larger the pool from which you can draw your core constituency.

Your incidental constituency includes former members, inactive members, active members' families, friends, and business associates, and vendors who sell goods and services to the organization. They may participate because of some incidental relationship to the organization and its core constituents.

Your general community constituency consists of people who have little involvement with your organization directly but have potential for participating in your event because they believe in your cause, feel an affinity to your organization because they live in the area, or find a particular event to be of interest to them.

Thus, the distinguishing features of the three constituencies are these: Core constituents will attend regardless of the event—they are so totally committed to the organization that they will come no matter what the event is; incidental constituents will attend because of special relationships

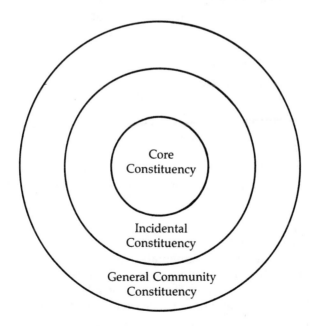

with the organization and its members; and general community constituents will attend because the organization is of general interest to them or
the event is inherently appealing to them.

The best way to reach the general community constituency is to break
it down into subpopulations or segments. Then analyze these divisions to
arrive at profiles of your potential customers. Among the variables to consider are these:

> geographic segmentation:
>> west side, east side, south side, or north
>> side
>> suburban or urban
>> affluent, middle-income, or low-income
>> areas
>> ethnic areas
> demographic segmentation:
>> age: young adult, middle-aged, retirees,
>> teenagers, young children
>> sex: male, female
>> nationality: ethnic affiliation
>> income: low, middle, high
>> religious affiliation
> life-style or special personality segmentation:
>> gamblers
>> social climbers
>> bargain hunters
>> upwardly mobile professionals
>> culturally oriented groups
>> politically involved people

The value of market segmentation is that you can identify a set of relevant
characteristics or distinguishing features about your potential audience or
customers.

Target Marketing

Having gone through a segmentation review, you are now in a position to undertake target marketing, especially in relation to the general
community constituency. Broad strategies for relating to the markets include undifferentiated marketing, concentrated marketing, and differentiated marketing.

With undifferentiated marketing you decide to sponsor an event that appeals to the entire community in an attempt to attract as many customers or as large an audience as possible. Frequently organizations that do not conduct a market segmentation analysis inadvertently undertake an undifferentiated, shotgun marketing approach. When asked who they are trying to reach, the answer is, "Everyone." Over time, however, they may more precisely pinpoint their submarkets. Organizations that have an inherent broad appeal and a large membership pool may purposely use this strategy, particularly with such events as festivals and popular performances. Undifferentiated marketing, though, can reflect fuzzy thinking. By appealing to everyone you may run the risk of attracting a limited audience if only a few people consider the event especially related to them.

With concentrated marketing you seek out one narrow market segment and develop an event that directly appeals to this group. If you identify a fairly homogeneous group that will naturally respond or if competition is fairly intense in all but a few segments of the market, you may want to concentrate on a particular segment. A mixed doubles tennis tournament or a bowl-a-thon are examples of concentrated marketing because they appeal to a narrow subpopulation of the community. Through concentrated marketing you can achieve a special following and standing with a particular subgroup. You also have the benefit of operating more effectively and efficiently by being more focused in your efforts. Here are some additional examples of concentrated marketing:

> Suppose you are a free clinic offering services to older teenagers and young adults. To attract your clientele and their friends, you determine that a rock concert at a farm outside of the city would be appealing.

> Suppose you are a health organization planning to sponsor a golf tournament for businessmen. You would most likely try to obtain mailing lists from country clubs and public golf courses so that you can build attendance for the event.

> Suppose you are a family planning association organizing a boutique that has special appeal to young single adults. To reach this population, you would probably promote the event among singles clubs and young adult groups attached to religious and other organizations.

With differentiated marketing, you concentrate on several specific marketing segments, tailoring an effective activity for each of them. For instance, you may decide to have one event with several components that would appeal to different market segments. Or, in the course of a year, you could purposefully decide to hold several different events, each appealing to different market segments. By offering event variations, you can hope to achieve higher attendance and income—although expenses may also increase. For example, an organization that has a black-tie dinner for $300 per couple followed by a dance later in the year that couples can attend for $50 is, in effect, appealing to differentiated customers. Here are some further illustrations:

> Suppose you are a neighborhood organization in an Italian community. How might you attract suburbanites with Italian heritage as one major segment of your audience to attend a gala dinner and purchase tickets to a raffle with a grand prize of a trip to Italy? You could obtain lists from those in the neighborhood who have friends and relatives living outside that community. You could also try to obtain mailing lists from churches with large numbers of Italian families.

> Suppose you are sponsoring a dance to benefit a local hospital. What would be the likely marketing segments? Your profile of those who might be involved in the dance could include doctors, nurses, hospital vendors, trustees, and community party-goers.

> Suppose the zoo, located on the west side of town, is planning an opening celebration of the tiger compound. Based on past events, over 90 percent of the celebrants are likely to be from the east side. How might you increase the number of west siders? Special efforts might be made to increase west side representation on the board of trustees and other committees of the zoo in anticipation of a different geographic distribution.

Regardless of the kind of event you are planning, it is important to give serious attention to the particular market to which your event is geared.

CONSIDERING THE IMPORTANCE OF THE CAUSE

The importance of the cause in attracting people to an event varies. To some people the cause can be quite important—especially to those members who volunteer significant amounts of their time and invest a great deal of energy in your organization. They need a driving force that compels their commitment and allows them to tolerate the frustration and aggravation that sometimes accompanies putting on events. Obviously, the more committed that the board of trustees and volunteers are to the work of the organization, the more inclined they will be to contribute their own efforts to an event and work to convince their friends to participate.

When the cause is a special item or program, such as a van to transport retarded children, increased funds for diabetic research, food for the hungry, the preservation of an endangered species, or a group home for mentally ill people, it plays an important role since it provides tangible evidence that the contributions will be going to something specific. Organization volunteers, and to some extent the general public, want to believe in the worthwhileness of their contributions. Earmarking funds can also have an attractive appeal for obtaining corporate support.

But while it is important to have a cause as a general rallying point or for focused appeal, it usually is not sufficient by itself to attract your general audience. The drawing point is often the event itself. Many people attend an event because of its inherent interest. They ask first, "What is in it for me?" and second, "How can I benefit the cause?" The cause provides an added inducement, but it is not the primary reason most persons outside the organization will attend the event. The one exception to emphasizing the event over the cause is that rare and unprecedented urgent situation that rallies the community. An example might be the result of a devastating hurricane, a surge in the welfare rolls, or great media concern about the homeless or the hungry. But if a crisis provides the primary motivation, be aware that the emphasis on the critical situation cannot be repeated, since most people will only tolerate limited numbers of crises as an inducement to attending events.

RESOURCES

Brody, R. *Problem solving: Concepts and methods for community organizations.* New York: Human Sciences Press, 1982, p. 2.

Colwell, P. T. The use of charts: A tool for management. *Fund Raising Management,* August 1984, p. 52.

Drotning, P. T. *500 ways for small charities to raise money.* Chicago: Contemporary Books, Inc., 1979, p. 22.

Flanagan, J. *The grass roots fundraising book.* Chicago: Contemporary Books, 1982, pp. 141–147.

Gaby, P. V. & Gaby, D. M. *Nonprofit organization handbook.* Englewood Cliffs, NJ: Prentice-Hall, Inc., 1979, p. 76.

Kotler, P. *Marketing for nonprofit organizations.* Englewood Cliffs, NJ: Prentice-Hall, 1982, pp. 20, 23, 82, 93–106, 182, 195–201, 206, 224–231.

Leibert, E. R. & Sheldon, B. E. *Handbook of special events for nonprofit organizations.* New York: Association Press, 1972, p. 26.

Lord, J. G. The marketplace perspective: A new approach to the development of institutions. *Philanthropy and Marketing.* Cleveland, OH: Third Sector Press, pp. 4, 15, 55.

Lovelock, C. H. & Weinberg, C. B. *Marketing for Public and Nonprofit Managers*. New York: John Wiley & Sons, 1984, p. 111.

Loykovich, J. Special events in the 80's: A case for marketing approach. *Fund Raising Management*, January 1985, pp. 28, 30.

Mulford, C. *Guide to student fundraising: 129 ways to raise money*. Reston, VA: Future Homemakers of America, 1984, p. 7.

Pritchard, J. H. *There's plenty of money for nonprofit groups willing to earn their shares —How to do it successfully*. Phoenix: Cornucopia Publications, 1984, pp. 16, 21, 23, 24, 68, 74, 75.

United Way of America. Guidelines for organizing special events. *Community Magazine*, July 1985.

Chapter 3

DEALING WITH SPECIAL SITUATIONS

ORGANIZING A FIRST-TIME EVENT

If you are embarking on an event for the first time, consider the following questions:

> *Why do we want to have the event?* As discussed in Chapter 2, you must be clear about your purpose. Is it primarily to raise money, attract new members, or increase the publicity about the organization? Your objectives will influence the kind and style of your event.
>
> *Do we have the kind of leadership and members to make a first-time event successful?* Make sure that you have the organizational resources to make the event work. For example, depending on the type of event, ask whether there are enough members to sell tickets or whether you have the leadership capability to attract underwriting.
>
> *Do we have an entrepreneurial, risk-taking attitude—especially if an innovative event is being considered?* An aggressive, enthusiastic, committed group spirit is especially important when embarking on a new event. People should be willing to risk venturing into the unknown.
>
> *How can we reduce risks?* Use careful planning. Talk with people who have been involved in a similar event. Determine the difficulties they have encountered. To re-

duce risks, mentally walk through planning and carrying out the event.

*Do we see the new event as something that will grow and expand
over time?* Develop a long-term plan in which you see the
first year or two as a dry run toward bigger and better
annual events. Start small with the idea that you will be
expanding, based on the experience you gain. For example, you may decide to rent out 100 seats rather than
500 for a theater party. Or you may buy $1,000 worth of
flowers instead of $2,000 worth the first time you do a
plant sale. As you improve in your sense of the market
and strengthen your organizational command, your
event can grow bigger. Obviously you are involved in a
trade-off: by thinking small you lose potential for bigger
profits, but you gain peace of mind as you reduce the
downside risks of taking on an ambitious project that
may not succeed. On the other hand, some organizations that have extraordinary talents and leadership may
launch a first-time event on a more ambitious scale. Usually volunteers for such organizations have had experience elsewhere, or the organization is large enough and
the event is of such magnitude that a consultant can be
hired.

Can we take advantage of special opportunities? The arrival of a
celebrity in town to perform in a show or an organization's anniversary are examples of opportunities that are
conducive to holding first-time events.

Is there a type of event that is already popular but could be varied?
For example, cocktail parties might be popular, but a
wine-tasting affair could be seen as being unusual and
might be especially appealing.

Is there an event that has not been tried in our community? People are often attracted to novelty, to something unique.
Any event that is a "first" is usually a money-maker. Of
course, after the event has been carried out once, it loses
its uniqueness, although it could continue to be popular.
Look through this book to identify events that you do
not think have been tried in your community, and consider them as possibilities.

OFFERING A RECURRING EVENT

You may want to consider holding one or more events on a regular or
recurrent basis. Every time you repeat an event you become more profi-

cient, you streamline your procedures, and you develop a following. In some instances it may take 2 or 3 years for an event to hit its stride, but eventually the name of your organization and the event will become synonymous. The activity will become identified as a tradition in your community. And each year, as it improves and more people attend, you will likely raise more money. Conversely, if you sponsor a different event each year, you may spend a considerable amount of time learning, and you may not operate at your highest efficiency level.

Because your volunteers and other supporters have limited time and energy to invest in your organization, you should make the most of the expenditure of their resources. This means you will want to achieve fewer but more successful recurring events. Two or three major affairs will probably be less wearing on your members than a dozen smaller ones.

The Life Cycle of Recurring Events

If your event is an annual one, you will want to keep it from stagnating. Any event can become stale over time if an organization becomes too self-satisfied, complacent, and overconfident.

Assume you have sponsored an event for the past 5 years. You have watched its profits grow from $5,000 the first year to $20,000 by the fourth year. In the fifth year, though, you raise $18,000 and speculate that you have reached your peak. In fact, interest may even be waning. You have, in effect, gone from an introductory phase (years 1 and 2) to a growth phase (years 3 and 4). You anticipate that you are in a maturity phase because you think you have reached all of the customers you are likely to reach. You have become aware that other organizations are beginning to sponsor similar events. You fear that you have reached a plateau or perhaps even the beginning of a decline. The following strategies should be considered for maturing or declining recurring events:

> *Dropping the event*: You could consider discontinuing an event when you experience a decline in profits, when volunteers express a sense of being tired of the repetition, or when competition is drawing people away.
>
> *Holding the event on alternate years*: Alternating one event with another or with none has the advantage of allowing volunteers to become invigorated and then feel as if they are returning to an old friend. If your event requires people to spend a tremendous amount of time and energy to begin planning for next year's event almost as soon as the previous one is completed, then your volunteers may need a respite. Just as farmers rotate crops to give the soil new vigor, so the framers of events may want to

rotate them so people can approach events two years later with renewed energy.

Recycling the event: Sometimes an event that was previously tried for several years and then dropped is ready to be surfaced again. For example, a progressive international dinner party that was successfully tried 5 years ago may be ready to be tried again with people who have fond memories of the past and new people who want to experience a novel event.

Modifying the event: Through creative thinking you can add features, arrange different combinations of activities, select a novel setting, change the attire, or alter the theme of an event. For instance, you may make a dinner event a "happening," an event to be remembered, by giving out attractive door prizes, inviting celebrities, choosing an outstanding speaker, or by providing a musical ensemble as people arrive. Any of these features can make the event dramatic and memorable. And you establish a tradition of doing something original and exciting that will make people want to attend next year's event.

Recreating the planning committee: Sometimes it is not the event that is stale. Rather, the volunteers working on it lose their enthusiasm after going through the same motions year after year. New people bring a sense of invigoration. While you may want to retain some of the experienced people who can provide continuity, at the same time you may want to rotate certain members off the event committee and replace them with new volunteers. To keep their feelings from being hurt, you might establish ground rules that each committee is to rotate volunteers every 2 or 3 years.

Seeking new markets: Assume there will be a number of dedicated people who will attend the event every year. But in addition you may want to reach segments of the community that have not been involved previously. For example, you may want to hold a semiannual rummage sale in two different areas of the community in an attempt to reach numerous different constituencies and new customers.

Other Life-Cycle Patterns

As noted earlier in this chapter, the normal life-cycle pattern of many recurring events includes an introductory phase, a growth phase, a maturity phase, and a decline phase. Here are some variations of the life-cycle pattern:

> *Growth spurt pattern*: During its maturity phase, net profits of an event can break into a new surge of growth because of changes in the way the event is presented or because of changing tastes of constituents. For example, a jog-a-thon that finds participation declining after 7 years may bring in twice as much income during its eighth year because prizes are offered to the runners who obtain the most money from sponsors.

> *Cyclical pattern*: Some events go through a cyclical pattern, often reflecting changes in the economy and the availability of discretionary income in the community. For example, if the community experiences high unemployment or temporary lay-offs, this could affect attendance at an event during a certain time period. On the basis of an anticipated upturn in the economy, you might maintain your event even though it experienced a down year.

> *Fad*: Sometimes an event attracts enthusiastic support for a few years and then declines rapidly. For example, a trivia game competition may last only as long as the fad is fueled by the media. Be prepared to move out of the fad event when interest subsides.

PUTTING SIZZLE AND ZEST INTO AN EVENT

An event should have an aura of excitement and be so fascinating that it compels people to attend. The planning process must therefore build sizzle and zest into an event, particularly one that has been tried before. These are several approaches that invite imaginative thinking:

> *Give an old idea a new twist*. Ask, "How can we take a conventional event and reshape it?" For example, instead of holding an annual jog-a-thon, plan a triathalon involving swimming, bicycling, and jogging.

> *Hold the event in an out-of-the-ordinary place*. For example, hold a cocktail party at an aquarium or on a boat, or hold a dinner-dance at a train station or in a designer showroom or professional studio. The character of the location should draw people who might not otherwise attend.

Add excitement by providing pre-events before the big event. For
example, the week before a benefit dinner-dance to be
held at a racetrack, schedule a 10K race that will begin
and end at the racetrack. The race may not be intended
as a major money-maker itself, but it will add excitement
and publicity building up to the main event.

Select an unusual theme. This, in turn, may generate a whole
series of new ideas. For example, turn the usual summer
festival into a medieval fair with costumes and jousting
and Renaissance music. Or hold a dance and call it a
prom, replicating a school prom of the 1950s. Note that
these affairs are basic festivals and dances, but the
themes add flair and panache and engage people's
imaginations.

Hold multifaceted events. Instead of planning a single-dimen-
sional event, consider several subevents, each contributing to the overall effect. This synergy, in which the
whole is greater than the sum of its parts, can occur
when several events take place at the same time or in
rapid succession. The events have far more impact in
raising money together than if each were held separately
since synergy gets people excited. For example, a woman's organization could sponsor a week of activities, including a wearable art show at an art store, a class on
auto mechanics at a car dealership, a picnic at a university featuring women politicians, a luncheon honoring
women judges, a wine-and-cheese party at a bookstore
for a prominent woman author, a brown-bag lunch focusing on the future of the organization, a cocktail party
at an art gallery saluting women in art, a fitness and nu-
trition panel presentation, a wardrobe clinic at a shopping mall, a women's tennis tournament, and a concert
with women performers. As another example, a group
of peace organizations could cosponsor a peace week
that includes week-long events, such as a theatrical production, an art exhibit, poetry readings, and concerts,
with separate admissions or a reduced subscription rate
to the entire series.

Take advantage of unusual circumstances. Ask yourself, "What
is occurring in the community that we might take advantage of in planning our event?" For example, invite a celebrity appearing in town to attend your organization's
dinner party.

Piggyback on another exciting happening. Plan an event that can be combined with another happening in your community. For instance, purchase a block of tickets to the opening night of a touring Broadway show that has arrived in your community.

ENGAGING IN CONTINGENCY PLANNING

Contingency planning is practiced when an organization attempts to determine in advance what it will do if certain situations take place. The purpose of such planning is to provide a timely response to a range of possible occurrences. Contingency planning is a useful way of dealing with "What if . . ." situations: "What if there is a severe snowstorm on the night of our winter holiday dance? What if our luncheon's out-of-town speaker experiences a delayed flight? What if 10 days before the dinner honoring our community leaders only half of the tickets are sold?" Questions like these can trigger a sense of panic and turn you into a walking ulcer. Probably 90 percent of the time the "What if . . ." exercise results in unnecessary worry. The evening of the dance turns out to be pleasant, the speaker's plane lands on time, the dinner is sold out a week in advance. But it is better to be prepared with a contingency plan, for things can and do go wrong.

For example, if an event has been held outdoors successfully for several years, you know that sooner or later you will experience a rainstorm. If you are concerned about rain, consider holding the event near a pavilion, under a tent, or near a gymnasium. Think about taking out rain insurance. Or indicate on your tickets that no refunds will be made in the event of rain and establish an alternative rain date. Decide which course of action you will take if the worst-case scenario comes true. And plan more than a general notion of what you will do—work out specific details. For instance, decide how you would decorate the gym in the event of rain, whether you would hire a custodian, and how you would keep the room cool if the night is sweltering. Ask each committee chairperson to submit a contingency plan if the event is not to be held outdoors.

Sometimes if every contingency is fully thrashed out, volunteers and staff might be reluctant to take on the event in the first place. For example, you might be reluctant to develop a contingency plan based on a situation where only 50 percent of your tickets are sold one week before an event. If that situation actually occurs, such a plan would require a burst of energy far beyond anyone's expectations to turn the situation around. Friends at various corporations might need to be contacted at the last minute to fulfill promises of IOUs. Volunteers might have to buy tickets that they were unable to sell. Staff and volunteers might have to spend hours on the phone

soliciting ticket sales, thereby diverting their time from other important duties. These extraordinary efforts might spell the difference between the failure and success of your event, but they come with costs. So anticipate as
best you can "What if . . ." questions without unduly frightening your volunteers. And be prepared to develop plans at the last minute to deal with
unforeseen circumstances.

HANDLING COMPETITION

Competition is inherent in many fund-raising events. This is because
most of the people you are trying to attract will have many demands for
their limited discretionary dollars. Also, any good fund-raising event is
bound to be copied by other organizations for their own use. Keep in mind
three kinds of competition as you plan your event:

Generic competition.   Occurs when your target market is attracted to another event in your community. For example, your progressive dinner may
compete with a jazz concert the same night. Or your neighborhood festival
could conflict with a performance by the local school choir. Furthermore,
competition can be experienced when your event is held at the same time
as college graduations or high school reunions. Scrutinize the calendar and
try to avoid potential conflicts of events that will compete for your audience.

Head-on competition.   Occurs when you and another organization
want to offer the same event. If you decide to plan your event despite the
competition, consider the following strategies:
Price discount strategy.   Offer the event at a lower price. For example, if
dinner dances in your community typically cost $100 per couple, consider
offering yours for $80. You may be able to attract more people and develop
a following.
Prestige strategy.   In contrast to the price discount strategy, launch a
high quality event at higher prices. For example, hire a larger band and
offer better food than your competitors and reflect these features in your
ticket price.
Product proliferation strategy.   Provide more variety to your event. For
example, provide entertainment, conduct an auction, or feature a raffle at
your dinner-dance.
Distribution-innovation strategy.   Expand your potential market by
holding an event in an unusual place or in a different part of town. For
example, hold a dinner-dance at a new corporate headquarters.
Mutual pact strategy.   Work with another organization. Although organizations naturally tend to be wary of each other—especially if they are

vying for the same constituency—under some circumstances two or more organizations might benefit from joining forces and working together rather than competing with each other. This is especially true if an organization considers a new event that is too big for its limited membership, if it needs up-front funding that its own treasury cannot handle, or if it lacks the appropriate constituency to pay for a big-ticket event. The organization could then take the initiative to request a partnership arrangement in which each group shares in the workload, the costs, the volunteer investment, and eventually in the proceeds. But be cautious about combining forces. Because of the added complexities involved in a joint effort, it is important to have a formal agreement drawn up.

Internal competition. Occurs when two different parts of the organization seek funding from the same source for the same event. For example, the table solicitation committee might ask for a corporate contribution while the promotions committee seeks the same corporate sponsorship of a program book's printing costs.

If, in addition to fund-raising events, you have direct solicitation efforts underway, then be watchful about this type of internal competition. For example, you may not want to be in the position of seeking corporate underwriting of an event and then, 2 months later, seek a direct donation from the same corporation. An exception to this rule is if you are able to determine that a corporation has two different funding streams—one for donations and one for event underwriting—and it is willing to separate the two decisions. Most organizations will find it advisable not to compete internally during the same quarter or half year.

In general, it is desirable to avoid direct competition with another organization in your community. Although you might succeed in competing, if the other organization feels diminished by your efforts, the ensuing ill will may prove more costly in the long run than the extra dollars raised. Therefore, try to plan events that are not viewed as competitive. In most communities there exists an unwritten rule not to steal another organization's event—especially if you are appealing to the same customers.

CONSIDERING TAX IMPLICATIONS

To receive donations, your organization must have certification as a tax-exempt organization under Section 501(c)(3) of the Internal Revenue Code. If your organization does not already have 501(c)(3) status, then ask an attorney on your board or a tax attorney from a local law firm to provide services to obtain certification. Documents are also available from the Superintendent of Documents, US Government Printing Office, Washington, D.C. 20402, which provides information on preparing an application for tax-exempt status. Ask for Publication 557, *Tax Exempt Status for Your Organization*, published by the Internal Revenue Service.

Assuming you have a 501(c)(3) status and can receive donations, you now need to know how to determine what types of charitable deductions can be claimed by your donors. To avoid making this sort of determination, some organizations simply state that a donation is deductible to the full extent of the law. Unfortunately, this statement does not provide much guidance to most taxpayers. For accurate guidelines you may want to write to the Superintendent of Documents for Publication 526, *Charitable Contributions*. Or look in the telephone book under US Government/Internal Revenue Service for the number to call to obtain information on tax deductions. Some of the major points regarding tax deductions are summarized below, but be sure to check with your attorney and the IRS for up-to-date laws and regulations.

Benefits Received

Your contributors may deduct a contribution only if the value of the contribution is more than the value of any benefit or privilege they may receive. If a contributor pays more than the fair market value to a qualified organization for merchandise, goods, or services, only the amount paid that is more than the value of the item may be a charitable contribution.

Example: Assume that a contributor pays $20 for a box lunch at a church picnic and that the lunch plus any entertainment or other services provided has a fair market value of $5.50. The excess paid of $14.50 is a tax-deductible contribution to the church as long as all the proceeds of the picnic go to the church.

Benefit Performances

If a contributor pays more than the fair market value to a qualified organization for a charity ball, banquet, show, or sporting event, the contributor may deduct only the amount that is more than the value of the privileges or other benefits received. If there is an established charge for the event, that charge will fix the value of your event. If there is no set charge for the event, only that part of the payment that is more than the reasonable value of the event is a gift. Even if the entire amount is underwritten by a corporation or individuals, a donor can only deduct the amount that exceeds the fair market value of the event. Whether or not the tickets are used has no effect on the amount that may be deducted. If, however, the donor wants to make a cash donation and refuses the ticket (i.e., rejects the right to admission), then the entire amount of the donation is a tax deduction.

Example: Consider a charity that plans a theater party consisting of admission to a movie premiere and an after-the-theater buffet at a price of $15 per ticket. The charity advertises that $5 of the total is the admission charge and $10 is a deductible contribution to the charity. Even if $5 is the established admission charge for movie premieres in the community, the specified $10 "contribution" does not qualify as a deductible gift because the charity failed to take into account the fair market value of the buffet dinner.

Example: Consider an organization that sponsors a symphony concert and agrees to pay an amount that is calculated to reimburse the symphony for the hall rental, musicians' fees, advertising costs, and printing expenses. Under the agreement, the organization is entitled to all receipts from ticket sales. The organization charges $20 for balcony seats and $25 for dress circle seats. These prices approximate the established admission charges for concert performances by the orchestra. The tickets to the concert and the materials promoting the event emphasize that the concert is sponsored by and for the benefit of the organization. Notwithstanding the fact that taxpayers who acquire tickets to the concert may think they are making a charitable contribution for the benefit of the organization, no part of the payment made is deductible as a charitable contribution for tax purposes. Since the amount paid approximates the established admission charged for similar events, there is no gift. The situation would be the same even if the materials promoting the event stated that the amount paid for tickets was "tax deductible" and people purchased their tickets in good faith.

Example: Assume a contributor pays $20 to see a special showing of a movie for the benefit of a charitable organization. Printed on the ticket is the following: "Contribution—$20." But if the regular price for the movie is $5, then the person has actually made a contribution of only $15. To avoid ambiguity, the invitation should specify how much of the ticket is tax deductible. The fact that the amount shown on a ticket or other evidence of payment is a "contribution" does not mean a person may deduct the entire amount. If the ticket shows the price of admission and the amount of the gift, only the gift amount can be deducted.

Fair Market Value

Fair market value is the price at which property changes hands between a willing buyer and a willing seller when neither is required to buy or sell and both have reasonable knowledge of all the necessary facts.

Example: Consider a charity that sponsors a bazaar and offers articles for sale that have been contributed by persons desiring to support the charity's programs. The prices for the articles sold are set by a committee with the intent to charge the full fair market value of the articles. Anyone who purchases items at the bazaar is not entitled to a charitable contribution deduction for any portion of the amount paid for the purchases since the items are being sold at fair market value. This is true even though the items sold at the bazaar are acquired and sold without cost to the charity and the total proceeds from the sale are used by the charity exclusively for charitable purposes.

Example: Assume the members of a charity sell Christmas cards to raise funds for the organization's activities. The cards are purchased at wholesale prices and are resold at prices comparable to the prices at which similar cards are sold by regular retail outlets. On the receipts furnished to customers, the difference between the amount received from the customer and the wholesale cost of the cards to the organization is designated by the organization as a tax-deductible charitable contribution. But the organization is in error in designating this difference as a tax-deductible charitable contribution. The amount paid by customers in excess of the wholesale cost of the cards to the organization is not a gift to the organization. Instead, it is part of the purchase price or the fair market value of the cards at their retail level.

Gambling Tickets

A contributor may not deduct as a charitable contribution amounts paid to buy raffle tickets or to play bingo or other games of chance. These are gambling losses, and they may be deducted only to the extent of gambling gains.

Example: Assume that a person pays $50 for a raffle ticket for a chance to win a new car. Although the raffle is conducted to raise funds for a charity, no part of the payment for the ticket is deductible as a charitable donation, even if the charity states that it is. Only the person who wins the car and reports the value of the car as income can offset the cost of the raffle ticket against that income.

Donated Items

Individual donations of tangible items to an organization are tax deductible up to the amount of their fair market value. Business donations of goods from inventory are tax deductible up to the amount of their actual costs. Restrictions for other types of donations vary, so be sure to check the law. Although some organizations may indicate in writing the value of a donation, many organizations leave it up to the donor to determine the amount that will be listed on their tax returns as deductible.

Example: Assume that a dinner at a well-known food critic's home is donated as an item to be auctioned. The host can deduct the cost of the food and the expenses of a caterer. But if the host does the cooking, the value of that time cannot be deducted since a price tag cannot be placed on volunteer time. As another option, the organization could work out a procedure in which the host would submit verification of all expenses to the organization, which pays the bill. The host would then write a check for the same amount to the organization as a charitable contribution.

Note that the IRS requires any donated art valued in excess of $5,000 to be appraised by a qualified appraiser. So be prepared to have the IRS challenge expensive donated art. From the Superintendent of Documents you can order Publication 561, *Determining the Value of Donated Property*, which explains how to determine the taxable value of donations of merchandise and gifts other than cash.

RESOURCES

Ardman, P. & Ardman, H. *Woman's Day book of fund raising.* New York: St. Martin's Press, 1980, pp. 9, 23, 161–166, 228.

Council of Better Business Bureaus, Inc.—Philanthropic Advisory Service. Special events and charitable contribution deductions. *In-Sight*, March 1979.

Drotning, P. T. *500 ways for small charities to raise money.* Chicago: Contemporary Books, 1979, pp. 12, 20, 21, 44, 53.

Flanagan, J. *The grass roots fundraising book.* Chicago: Contemporary Books, 1982, pp. 4, 7, 8, 145, 163, 164.

Gaby, V. & Gaby, M. *Nonprofit organization handbook.* Englewood Cliffs, NJ: Prentice-Hall, Inc., 1979, p. 75.

Hay, J. T. *534 ways to raise money.* New York: Simon & Schuster, 1983, p. 17.

Kotler, P. *Marketing management—Analysis, planning, and control.* Englewood Cliffs, NJ: Prentice-Hall, Inc., 1980, pp. 14, 85, 207, 273, 282, 296, 365.

Leibert, E. R. & Sheldon, B. E. *Handbook of special events for nonprofit organizations.* New York: Association Press, 1972, p. 22.

Lovelock, C. H. & Weinberg, C. B. *Marketing for public and nonprofit managers.* New York: John Wiley & Sons, 1984, p. 193.

Mulford, C. *Guide to student fundraising: 129 ways to raise money.* Reston, VA: Future Homemakers of America, 1984, p. 11.

Musselman, V. W. *Money raising activities for community groups.* New York: Association Press, 1969, pp. 22, 28.

Pritchard, J. H. *There's plenty of money for nonprofit groups willing to earn their shares— How to do it successfully.* Phoenix: Cornucopia Publications, 1984, pp. 9, 12, 67, 75.

Sheerin, M. *How to raise top dollars from special events.* New York: Public Service Materials Center, 1984, pp. 30, 44, 49.

Chapter 4

MANAGING THE FINANCES

BUDGETING FOR AN EVENT

Budgeting for an event is not a single effort but an ongoing process that requires estimating both income and expenses on a continuing basis. Often you will be dealing with projections of unknown figures or "guesstimates" that will be revised as you obtain more information. This new information should be plugged into your modified budget. Generally, the budgeting process may be divided into four phases, one blending into the other.

In the first phase, when the organization is considering an event, an initial budget is prepared of income and expenses to assess whether the event has the potential for sufficient profit. In this phase, be conservative: Estimate expenses on the high side and income on the low side. Add 10–20 percent for unforeseen expenses. Then determine whether you want to proceed with the event, abandon the project, or consider other possibilities. Phase 2 occurs once you have made a decision to proceed with the event. This phase involves the preparation of a detailed budget. Phase 3 involves continuous monitoring of income and expenses and comparing actual with budgeted amounts. Phase 4 occurs after the event and involves an evaluation of how well you anticipated income and expenses. Phase 4 also involves consideration of what revisions you would make in preparing next year's budget for the event.

SETTING FISCAL OBJECTIVES

Prior to establishing fiscal objectives, you should become familiar with certain key terms. The following financial terms and calculations should be understood:

Gross profit is the amount needed to cover all costs as well as your net profit or financial goal. To calculate gross profit, add expected costs and the desired financial goal:

Example:

$$costs = \$1,200$$
$$financial\ goal = \underline{\quad 3,000}$$
$$gross\ profit = \$4,200$$

Net profit or financial goal is the amount left over after all costs are paid. To calculate net profit, subtract costs from gross profit:

Example:

$$gross\ profit = \$4,200$$
$$costs = \underline{\quad 1,200}$$
$$net\ profit = \$3,000$$

Fixed costs are those that occur no matter how many people come to the event. For example, whether 200 or 300 attend a dinner dance, you will have the fixed costs of the band, hall rental, and promotion materials.

Variable costs are related to per-person units. For instance, the cost of a luncheon will vary according to the number of people attending. Similarly, the cost of souvenirs for a swim-a-thon will vary with the number of entrants.

Break-even point is the number of sales you have to make in order to meet your expenses. After that point, all sales are net profit. If your costs are primarily fixed, then you can simply divide the total cost of the event by the cost of each ticket to determine your break-even point. For example, if your costs are $2,200 and you charge $10 per ticket, you will need to sell 220 tickets to cover the costs and break even. Any ticket sales above 220 are profit.

If, in addition to fixed costs, you have to consider variable costs, then these must be subtracted from the projected per-ticket income before dividing by the cost per ticket. For example, assume that the fixed costs of a dinner dance (band, hall rental, promotion) equal $2,200, that each meal has a variable cost of $15, and that you think $50 would be an appropriate price for each ticket. To calculate the break even point, use this formula:

$$\frac{\text{fixed costs}}{\text{ticket price} - \text{variable costs}} = \text{break-even point}$$

$$\frac{\$\ 2,200}{\$50 - \$15 = \$35} = 63 \text{ tickets}$$

In this example, you would have to sell 63 tickets to break even.

Percentage of profit reflects an event's cost-effectiveness by relating the profits to the costs. Sometimes this is referred to as the profit margin. Determine what percent of your gross profit is net profit so that you can see how efficient the event is and make comparisons of one event with other events you have conducted, or plan to conduct. For example, assume that you expect a gross profit of $25,000 from your dinner-dance, expect your costs to be $11,000, and expect your net profit to be $14,000. Calculate your percentage of profit as follows:

$$\frac{\text{Net profit (gross profit} - \text{costs)}}{\text{gross profit}} = \text{profit percentage}$$

$$\frac{\$14,000\ (\$25,000 - \$11,000)}{\$25,000} = 56\%$$

You can now compare the profit percentage of this event with, for example, an art auction where you expect to raise $10,200 gross profit and have expenses of $2,000 for a net profit of $8,200. The net profit of $8,200 divided by $10,200 equals a percent profit of 80 percent. Clearly, the auction is more cost-effective than the dinner-dance. Of course, you may want to override the cost efficiency consideration if you determine that the net amount raised is your primary objective. You may decide to undertake the dinner-dance because it is likely to produce a higher net profit, even though it is less cost-efficient than the auction.

Once you are familiar with key financial terms, you can prepare your budget. In setting up a budget, you should determine two fiscal objectives.

First, establish a net profit goal that is achievable. For example, it is better to set a $1,500 goal for a raffle and raise as much as $1,800 than to establish a $2,500 goal and raise only $1,800. If you do not reach your goal, you risk having your volunteers become discouraged and unwilling to repeat an event that is identified as a partial failure. You may eventually hope to achieve $2,500 for this annual event as your ultimate financial objective, but expect to raise less than your optimum goal the first year of an event. Consider it a "dry-run" as you work to establish a structure, procedures, and training for your volunteers. In subsequent years, expect to exceed your first year's performance, but be mindful that events do plateau and even decline (refer to Chapter 3 on life cycles of events). If you are uncertain about establishing a specific net profit objective, consider a range (e.g., $2,000–$2,500). Another reason for establishing a net profit objective is that later you will want to evaluate your event by asking these questions: "Did we achieve our profit goal? If not, why? Were expenses higher than expected? Was the income lower than expected?"

Second, determine your percentage of profit (or profit margin). In the example given previously, the estimated profit margin of a dinner-dance was 56 percent. Suppose you determine that this figure is too low. To increase your profit margin, you would strive to reduce expenses or increase income. As a general rule, any anticipated profit margin less than 65–75 percent should be seriously assessed. For profit margins less than 50 percent, you should reconsider whether to hold the event. For example, if you expect to raise $120,000 through a concert with anticipated expenses of $80,000 for a profit margin of 33 percent, you may still consider the $40,000 net profit worth the effort, despite the extremely low profit margin. In other words, under some special circumstances you may accept a low margin of profit if this is the price you have to pay to achieve your financial or nonfinancial objectives.

KEEPING ACCURATE RECORDS

It is an absolute must to establish a good accounting system for your event. If possible, recruit a volunteer accountant to head your finance committee and to set up an accurate accounting system that includes, for example, not only expenditures directly related to the event, but also some apportioning of expenses that might ordinarily be blurred with the general expenditures of the organization (e.g., apportioning postage and telephone costs that are attributable to the event).

Good accounting procedures require that the event income should be reported separately from other sources of the organization's revenue. The event income should be reported after subtracting (netting out) the direct costs of the benefits of the event provided to the participants. These direct costs of the benefits received by the participants (e.g., the cost of the meal, music, decorations) are not considered fund-raising costs. They are subtracted from the gross proceeds of the event. All other expenses of planning, promoting, and conducting the event, including staff time, advertising, and mailings, must be reported as fund-raising costs. Check with your state attorney general's office regarding additional record-keeping and reporting requirements.

CALCULATING EXPENSES

The key to preparing the expense side of the budget is to be as specific and as accurate as possible. This requires one or more persons to do a considerable amount of homework and checking of information. Suppose, for example, you are renting a facility for your event. Check out what is covered in the rental fee: Are lights, sound system, tables, chairs, and coffee makers included? Is there an extra labor charge after a certain time? If a piano must be moved, is there an extra fee? Do not assume anything.

If this is the first time for the event, assign a researcher to determine what items might have to be purchased and what might be borrowed or donated. For example, by calling other groups, you might be able to borrow serving pieces or a truck for unloading equipment. Try to find someone who has worked on a similar event to help determine your potential expenditures and to review your calculations.

If you are repeating an event, recheck every cost. Determine whether and to what extent costs have risen for each item. Inquire, too, if you will be receiving the same special discount this year from a supplier. Or try to find a new supplier who will donate items. All this information requires special research time to make cost comparisons in a methodical way. No expense is too little or unimportant to be listed. After you list all your items, remember to add 10–20 percent for unforeseen expenses.

Certain costs are highly specialized. For example, you may want to take out liability insurance on an event to protect your organization from unavoidable accidents. Other costs often are not normally considered, but should be. For example, rarely will an organization identify costs of regular employees' time. If a salaried staff person devotes half time for a 3-month period in planning an event, it is the unusual organization that earmarks this portion of the staff person's salary as an expense of the event. If this were done more frequently to reflect actual costs, many organizations probably would not undertake fund-raising events, because costs would appear to be excessive. The rationale that is usually given for not including staff time is that staff squeeze in the event responsibilities along with other demands on their time. Still, if employees are spending time on the event, at least note the costs of these hours as an in-kind contribution. The value of this calculation is that it will assist the financial manager and volunteer leaders of the organization in determining whether staff investment is worth the outcome of the event. Of course, there may be benefits other than profit involved (e.g., improved community relations) that will justify providing staff time.

ANTICIPATING INCOME

You should be as precise about anticipating income as you are about projecting expenses. Identify each source of income. Suppose you are planning a dinner-dance with a raffle and cash bar. You expect a total of 500 persons, including 100 patrons paying a premium price of $100 each, 350 regular diners paying $75 each, and 50 latecomers paying $25 each just for dessert. You also expect to sell 250 raffle tickets at $5 each and 300 drinks at $2 each. Your calculations would be as follows:

$$
\begin{aligned}
100 \text{ patrons} \times \$100 &= \$10,000 \\
350 \text{ diners} \times \$\ 75 &= \$26,250 \\
50 \text{ latecomers} \times \$\ 25 &= \$\ 1,250 \\
250 \text{ raffle tickets} \times \$\ \ 5 &= \$\ 1,250 \\
300 \text{ drinks} \times \$\ \ 2 &= \$\ \ \ 600 \\
\hline
\text{Total income} \quad\quad\quad & \quad \$39,350
\end{aligned}
$$

Estimate each of these items as specifically as possible to arrive at your total projected income, but be conservative in your projections. The second time you do the event you will have greater accuracy in predicting income.

CONSIDERING CASH FLOW

After you determine your income and expenditures, you must anticipate when the payment for each item will be due. Most bills should be paid within 30 days after you receive the invoice. Many creditors will accept payment after the event, some will expect that you pay them as soon as the expense is incurred, and others may require a deposit in advance. Information about due dates is important, because it will help you determine the timing of your payments and possibly the need for up-front money. To avoid being caught cash-short, you may have to consider a loan, or borrowing from the organization's budget. To aid the cash-flow situation, some organizations set aside money raised from the previous year's event for the following year's up-front, seed money. You do not want to lose credibility with your creditors who, for example, are expecting to be paid in August, but cannot be since your cash is not available until after your event in November.

Here is an example of a cash-flow chart for a November first event:

Cash-Flow Chart

Item	Total Cost	First Payment Date	Amount Due	Balance Due by November 30th
Advertisement	$1,300	August 15th	$1,300	Previously paid in full
Hall Rental	1,500	September 1st	500	$1,000
Graphic Designer	500	September 1st	200	300
Printing	1,800	September 1st	800	1,000
Postage	100	October 1st	100	Previously paid in full

Note that cash-flow problems should be distinguished from income problems. A cash-flow problem is a timing problem involving the receipt of cash. An income problem occurs when money that has been projected to be received is not coming in, for one reason or another.

MAKING THE PRICING DECISION

Your decision on how to price tickets to your event should be based upon your expectations about profits, the prevailing rates and competition in your community, and how people are likely to perceive the value of your event.

Pricing Based on Profit Expectations

If your quest for maximizing profits is the primary consideration in determining the price of tickets, then you should consider various price options to arrive at a figure that would produce your highest income in relation to expenditures. But be prepared for the likelihood that, as you raise ticket prices, you potentially diminish the size of your audience.

Suppose you decide to sponsor a community concert in an auditorium that seats 1,300 people. You calculate that your fixed costs are $3,000 for equipment rental, publicity, facility rental, transportation, and professional fees. Below is a Pricing Worksheet (A) that is based on tickets costing $10, $15, or $20. Also indicated in the worksheet are hypothetical estimated quantities of the number of persons likely to attend at each of these prices.

Pricing Worksheet (A)
(Fixed Costs)

Ticket Option	Price	Estimated Quantity	Total Revenue	Fixed Costs	Net Profit
A	$10	1,000	$10,000	$3,000	$7,000
B	15	600 (700)	9,000 (10,500)	3,000	6,000 (7,500)
C	20	300	6,000	3,000	3,000

According to these calculations, you would select Option A and sell $10 tickets to 1,000 people. There are, of course, assumptions reflected in the projected numbers that may not hold true. For example, in reality you may not have the capability to sell 1,000 tickets—in which case you might choose Option B and the $15 ticket. If, however, you have established $6,500 as your minimum net profit objective, then you may decide to push for attracting the larger attendance at $10 per ticket. Of course, if you assume 700 (rather than 600) people will attend under Option B, resulting in a net of $7,500, you might go with the $15 ticket option after all. These alternative assumptions about projected attendance underscore how speculative this process is. The value of the pricing worksheet is that you can consider various possibilities to arrive at your target profit.

Suppose, in addition to fixed costs, you think that by including variable costs of dessert and coffee you can increase attendance by 20 percent. Assume the variable costs amount to $4 per person. The Pricing Worksheet (B) reflects increases in the price of tickets, increases in attendance, and the addition of the variable costs:

Pricing Worksheet (B)
(Variable Costs)

1 Ticket Option	2 Price	3 Estimated Quantity	(2 × 3) 4 Total Revenue	5 Fixed Costs	6 Variable Costs	(5 + 6) 7 Total Costs	(4 − 7) 8 Net Profit
A	$12	1,200	$14,400	$3,000	$4,800	$7,800	$6,600
B	18	720	12,960	3,000	2,880	5,880	7,080
C	24	360	8,640	3,000	1,440	4,400	4,200

In this example, Option B tickets selling at $18 each would produce the most profit, although Option A would also achieve your target net profit of $6,500. This chart also shows that adding the variable costs (and increasing the costs of tickets) would not produce much more profit than if you had excluded them (refer back to Pricing Worksheet A).

If you do not think it is necessary to explore ticket price options, and you have determined a specific net profit target, then calculate the number of people likely to attend your event in order to figure out your break-even point. For example, if you expect 250 couples to attend a dinner-dance and you want to achieve a net profit of $5,000, then you need to charge $20 per couple—exclusive of costs. If fixed and variable costs for 250 couples total $7,500, then $30 has to be added to the cost of each ticket. If, in addition to these costs, you are concerned that you may underestimate either expenses or the number of people attending, you may want to add a 20–25 percent override to the ticket price ($10). Your pricing would be as follows:

> Estimated profit per couple = $20
> Costs of dinner dance   = 30
> Override   = <u>10</u>
> $60 ticket price

Of course, even with the override built in, you are gambling that you can sell the number of tickets needed to achieve your target profit.

Pricing Based upon Prevailing Rates and Competition

"How much are people likely to pay for this event?" is a question that should be asked as you consider pricing options. But it is also a question that is difficult to answer with any certainty. When considering prevailing rates and competition, profit is of secondary importance. Instead, you decide on a ticket price according to what you think the market will bear. In other words, you concentrate on market demand rather than the level of costs and anticipated profits in setting and determining the price. You determine how much value your potential consumers see in your event and then price it accordingly.

For example, if last year tickets to your event sold out, you might be influenced this year to charge more because obviously the event is popular. If you desire to increase attendance at an event that did not sell out last year, you might consider a price reduction. If you are offering an event for the first time, you might decide the price on the low side of a range to ensure maximum attendance. The problem, of course, is that it is difficult to predict whether and to what extent changes in price will affect demand.

The way potential customers respond to price changes is called price elasticity of demand. If an increase or decrease in price is likely to cause a fluctuation in the volume of tickets, then demand is considered elastic. On the other hand, if demand is not greatly influenced by price (i.e., the same number of people attend even if you raise the price by 20 percent), then demand is inelastic. In practice, elasticity of demand is extremely difficult to measure. If the change in price is small (e.g., 5 or 10 percent), then elasticity of demand may be negligible. If the change in price is substantial (e.g., 20–25 percent), then elasticity of demand is likely to be affected. This change in prices may be more influential at lower price levels (e.g., $10) than higher price levels, because presumably people paying higher prices have more discretionary income and therefore may be better able to afford the increase. Because the elasticity of demand is so speculative, one of the best things you can do is to survey friends, family, and acquaintances who might be attracted to the event. And discuss prices with persons who have organized similar events in your community or in communities comparable to yours to obtain their sense of pricing alternatives. Keep in mind that, based on prevailing rates, pricing may differ greatly among various communities. The going rate for a dinner-dance in a large city with a large pool of wealthy contributors may be $300–$500 per couple; a similar dinner dance in a smaller community might be able to command only $50–$100 per couple.

Frequently you will be influenced by what others are charging in your community for similar events. In situations where both costs and the response of consumers are difficult to measure, the going price probably represents the collective wisdom of the nonprofit organizations in your community. Consider the going rate carefully, because if people are used to paying a certain rate, they will be reluctant to pay a higher price.

You may purposely decide to charge less than the going rate of your competitors to attract a larger part of the market or to discourage possible new competition. By charging less you strive to corner the market. Sometimes you can think of the price of admission to an event as a "loss leader" and set the price purposefully low or not charge for admission at all to attract a large or special crowd. For example, at a casino night the price of admission might be low to attract a large group of gamblers who then spend their money on the gambling activities.

Under some special circumstances your organization may be able to charge an unusually high price for admission. These circumstances include little competition because of the uniqueness of the event, a product with special value, and enough potential buyers from which you can draw your clientele.

Pricing Based on Perceived Value

Just as prevailing rates can influence the price, the perceived value of an event can also be highly influential. For example, the prevailing rate for a luncheon in your community might be a maximum $25. But by obtaining an outstanding celebrity speaker you could raise the price to $35. Adding a fashion show to a luncheon may allow you to raise the cost by another $10. With these added features, people perceive that they are obtaining increased value for their money.

To increase income, you may want to offer differential value for different priced tickets to the same event. Before charging two or more prices, you should be clear about your different market segments. For example, you might ask, "What is the profile of those paying $50 and how does it differ from that of those paying $100?" But do not limit your thinking to a differential profile of your audience; determine, in addition, what you will be offering to your consumers at the different price levels.

You should offer something special to those paying the higher price, such as a reception before or after the event, valet parking, or better seating. People paying the higher price must feel they are special. If this sounds elitist, it is. After all, you are appealing to a certain market segment to spend more than they ordinarily would. On the other hand, sometimes an organization purposely decides not to have price distinctions because it wants to reduce its elitist image in the community. All tickets are priced the same. You have to decide whether the possibility of additional income is worth overriding in favor of the kind of image you want to project.

Some groups are sensitive to persons of moderate incomes in their market segment when they determine their pricing. In these instances, most of the people attending the event pay one price, but a reduced price is charged for those who participate in only part of the event. For example, if you charge people $50 for a gourmet dinner, you can charge $15 for those who want only dessert at the end of the evening. The reason for the price stratification is to attract a larger crowd, and, particularly, younger adults who might be future members and supporters of your organization.

In summary, charge differential rates only when you can provide different values for the different price levels. If there is nothing to distinguish between your lower and higher prices, you will probably find that most of your consumers will choose the lower-priced tickets.

RESOURCES

Ardman, P. & Ardman, H. *Woman's Day book of fund raising*. New York: St. Martin's Press, 1980, pp. 120–122.

Berson, G. *Making a show of it: A guide to concert production*. Ukiah, CA: Redwood Records, 1980, pp. 26, 32, 33.

Drotning, P. T. *500 ways for small charities to raise money*. Chicago: Contemporary Books, Inc., 1979, pp. 12, 48, 49, 50, 74.

Flanagan, J. *The grass roots fundraising book*. Chicago: Contemporary Books, Inc., 1982, pp. 48, 49, 51, 52, 53, 105, 148, 149, 151, 153, 154, 155, 157, 158.

Fox, H. W. Astute pricing for nonprofits. *The Nonprofit World Report*, May–June 1985, p. 12.

Honig, L. Fundraising events, Part three: Budgeting. *Grassroots Fundraising Journal*, August 1982.

Kotler, P. *Marketing management—Analysis, planning, and control*. Englewood Cliffs, NJ: Prentice-Hall, Inc., 1980, pp. 290–291, 309–314, 387–396, 399.

Lovelock, C. H. & Weinberg, C. B. *Marketing for public and nonprofit managers*. New York: John Wiley & Sons, 1984, pp. 363, 366–368.

Sheerin, M. *How to raise top dollars from special events*. New York: Public Service Materials Center, 1984, pp. 18, 46.

Stevens, S. K. A reflective budget means you'll never have to say you're sorry. *Fund Raising Management*, December 1984, p. 24.

Chapter 5

MAXIMIZING PROFITS

USING MARKETING STRATEGIES

It is important always to be on the lookout for ways to maximize profits from fund-raising events, whether they are new, successful, at a plateau, or declining. To do so you need to develop marketing strategies.

Marketing strategies designed to enhance income can be divided into four major approaches: 1) market penetration, which involves taking an existing event and penetrating deeper into your existing customer base; 2) market development, which involves taking your current event and attracting new customers; 3) event expansion/development, which involves expanding your current event or providing a new event to your existing customer base; and 4) diversification, which involves both developing new events and seeking new customers. The chart below displays these four marketing strategies:

MARKETING APPROACHES

	Existing Events	Expanded or New Events
Existing Markets	Market penetration	Event expansion/ development
Expanded or New Markets	Market development	Diversification

Penetrate the Market

Market penetration consists of enhancing income through the increased sale of your existing event. The event remains essentially the same, but you present it to your customers in more attractive ways or you more aggressively promote your efforts. You would use a market penetration approach to increase the number of people attending your dinner-dance, for example, by exploring the questions listed below, which could be adapted to other events:

> Should we increase the frequency of the event by offering more than one dinner-dance each year?
>
> Should we lower the price from $75 to $50 to make the event appealing to more of our members?
>
> Can we improve our promotion efforts through more publicity and advertising to attract more people?
>
> Can we make the dinner-dance more attractive by altering the location or the time? For example, should we change from a Friday night at a local gym to a Saturday night at a hotel?
>
> Can we make the event more accessible by arranging for transportation for people who are reluctant to drive?
>
> Can we heighten the attractiveness of the event by using a more exciting theme or decorations?
>
> Can we schedule pre-events to build up excitement for the event and attract more people to the actual event (e.g., dance lessons before the event)?

The purpose of these questions is to examine ways to make the current event more attractive to your anticipated audience while still preserving the inherent character of the event itself.

Develop the Market

Market development consists of seeking increased sales by attracting new market segments to the event. Listed below are the kinds of questions to be explored regarding the same dinner-dance example:

> Can we expand to additional geographic markets by holding the dance on the north side instead of the customary south side of town?
>
> Can we appeal to different market segments, such as younger and less affluent groups, by offering a "night

owl" arrangement (e.g., dessert and dancing) at a reduced cost?

Can we attract a special segment of the community by honoring a community leader who has many personal and
business associates who will want to attend?

Can we add to our current potential attendance by expanding our mailing list of invitations from 1,000 to 4,000?

These questions reflect a way of thinking about seeking changes in your
customer base.

Expand or Develop the Event

Event expansion or development consists of seeking increased attendance by significantly improving the event for current market segments.
These are the kinds of questions to be explored:

Can we alter the program by adding, rearranging, or combining features? Some examples of these include the
following:

adding special entertainment,

including additional money raisers (e.g., a
raffle, a cash bar, charging for
photographs),

cutting down the length of the speeches,

combining two major events, such as a
dinner-dance and an auction.

Can we change the basic character of the event? For example, you might make the dinner-dance more formal
(black-tie) or less formal (square dance).

Considering questions such as these encourages thinking about ways to
improve your event.

Diversify

Diversification consists of developing a new event for a new market.
This strategy makes sense when the organization thinks that its present
event is waning or if other opportunities appear to offer a superior financial
return. Of course, this does not mean taking up just any opportunity that
comes along; it means focusing on areas where members have skills and interests. Here are some questions that might be asked:

> Can we change the event from a dinner-dance to an entirely different event—such as a decorators' showcase tour—which in turn could attract a different market?

> Should we continue to hold a dinner-dance but shift some of our energy and time from the dinner-dance to another event, such as a rummage sale? The result may be a slight decline in the dinner-dance, but the rummage sale should bring in new attendance and more than enough money to offset the decline in the income from the dinner-dance.

The value of examining these four strategies is that they force you to think purposefully about current and potential events in relation to current and potential markets.

INCREASING INCOME

Obviously, every organization needs to consider seriously ways to increase income. Depending on your event, you might consider offering a patron ticket category, increasing the price of tickets, planning an inexpensive event, adding special features, participating in a promotional event, and seeking donations.

Offer a Patron Ticket Category

A major way to increase income is to establish a separate category of premium-priced patron tickets. Frequently patrons are persons who are close to the organization, such as current trustees and their friends, past officers, and others who are motivated to contribute generously. In exchange for their generosity, certain privileges are accorded to patrons, such as valet parking, cocktails before dinner, a private party with the guest of honor, their names in the program, or special seating. Some organizations begin recruiting special contributors long before the event by carefully selecting these potential patrons to work on the event or other activities of the organization. Additionally, trustees or other key members may write personal notes or make personal contacts to encourage their friends to become patrons. In turn, patron solicitors of your organization may then be asked to support the charities of those persons they have recruited as patrons. In other words, a considerable measure of "quid pro quo" exists in the charity business in which people keep track of favors owed.

Increase the Price of Tickets

Another way of increasing income is to increase the price of tickets. If you think the market will bear an increase and you are prepared to aggressively sell tickets at the higher price, then consider this option. Chapter 4 provides a detailed discussion on making the pricing decision.

Plan an Inexpensive Event

If your organization does not have money to cover any up-front costs, consider an event that requires little in the way of expenses. You could, for example, plan a rummage sale, knowing that you will be able to acquire the sale items for free. Or, if you can obtain donations of appealing prizes, you might want to consider a raffle.

Add Special Features

By adding special features to your main event you might encourage customers to spend more than they would otherwise, or you might attract new customers. For instance, a raffle for a trip to Paris that is added to your dinner-dance may attract more people. Or you may produce more income from a golf tournament by featuring side bets on the longest drive, or a grand prize for the winner of a hole-in-one contest. These special attractions add to the excitement and allure of the main event.

Participate in a Promotional Event

You may agree to permit the use of your organization's name for a promotional event (e.g., a tennis tournament, horse race, or car race). This arrangement allows the promoter to use your charity's name to enhance its event's image. The promoter can also attract corporate purchases of expensive seats to the event or pre-event, such as a dinner-dance the night before a tennis tournament, since the corporations can use their purchases as tax deductions to your charitable cause. The promoter, in turn, gives at least a portion of the profit to the charity. The advantage to the organization is that the promoter shares in the handling of the details and covers all the up-front costs, which can be considerable. Often the nonprofit organization is left with little to worry about—including the weather. Sometimes all the organization has to do is lend its name and volunteers—and receive a donation.

But there are some cautions to bear in mind about what, on the surface, appears to be an easy way to enhance income. Be certain to delineate responsibilities, which at times may be numerous, and put your agreement in writing so that there will not be any misunderstandings later. Be aware that when the promoter approaches corporate support in the name of your charity, this could later reduce your chances of obtaining funds from the same corporation on your own. Also, be sure to consider the compatibility of the event with your organization and the availability of your volunteers to help out. Finally, remember that because this is a one-time windfall, you will have to work extra hard the following year to compensate for the absence of this revenue.

Seek Donations

Contact businesses for donations that will increase the appeal, attendance, and income of your event. Local merchants and businesses are ideal donors to community organizations. Travel agents and airlines can provide free trips. Grocery stores, jewelry shops, and department stores can provide goods and gift certificates. Bowling alleys, amusement parks, movie theaters, arcades, health clubs, and miniature golf courses can provide free passes. It never hurts to ask for donations. The worst someone can do is say "no," and often you will be fortunate enough to obtain a donation. If you ask for a donation and the prospective donor turns you down, do not take the response personally and do not be resentful. The donor may be able to help you the next time.

For an annual fee, an organization can join a national clearinghouse that searches for free product donations from corporations. Called the National Association for the Exchange of Industrial Resources (NAEIR), it provides nonprofit organizations access to office supplies, audiovisual equipment, and building materials. You pay for shipping and a small handling charge for the free merchandise. Contact NAEIR, 560 McClure Street, Galesburg, Illinois 61402, (309)343-0704.

REDUCING EXPENSES

There are a number of ways to reduce the expenses of an event, thereby maximizing its profit. These approaches include designating a shopper, buying large quantities, bartering, asking volunteers to absorb certain costs, reducing staff costs by increasing volunteer time, arranging an exchange, negotiating for price reductions, and obtaining free goods and services.

Designate a Shopper

To reduce expenses, identify at least one volunteer whose assignment is to obtain everything for the event at the lowest possible price. This shopper or scrounger should seek out items in person or on the phone and keep meticulous records. The shopper should have the attitude that the items must be obtained inexpensively—or free—and therefore must be persistent. The shopper cannot be afraid to ask for a special deal. The attitude should be that your organization is doing important work in the community and that any expense reduced is income gained. To spend as little as possible, the shopper should start off by asking for a donation. If this is not possible, then the shopper should ask for a discount. When a number of items are involved, the shopper should act as a dispatcher, sending out other volunteers to pick up the items. It helps to remind the merchants you are soliciting that your members patronize their businesses. Acknowledge their contributions to the event and send them copies of the program book that lists their names.

To keep costs down, the shopper should:

> Identify items that the group already has (e.g., cash box, glasses, tablecloths).
>
> Ask members to donate or lend items.
>
> Consider renting rather than buying.
>
> Buy on consignment and return unused portions for refunds.
>
> Only purchase items that are likely to be used for subsequent events (e.g., a coffeemaker).
>
> Obtain competitive bids on items over a predetermined amount (e.g., $300).
>
> Purchase items at a discount price either from a discount store or from the central purchasing organization of a large nonprofit agency. Note that in many communities around the country the Catholic diocese has established a Central Purchasing Office (CPO) which, through its mass purchasing arrangements, can buy thousands of items at below market costs. Such items include videocassette recorders, microwave ovens, office supplies, and even automobiles. You do not have to be a Catholic organization to take advantage of this resource.

A "Shopper's Guide" chart, as illustrated, may be used to assist the person responsible for obtaining the various items for your event.

Buy Large Quantities

Think about buying supplies and prizes in large enough quantities so that you can obtain them at a discount. If you expect to run the same event for several years, buy items and store them. Consider joint purchasing with another local organization. Or, if you belong to a national group, you may be able to make purchases centrally.

Barter

Bartering is the process of exchanging goods and services; money is not involved. For instance, if you are sponsoring a concert, you could offer free admission tickets to a printing business in exchange for providing your promotional materials. The company could use this as a tax deduction, and the exchange would actually cost you very little.

Ask Volunteers to Absorb Certain Costs

Volunteers involved with your organization may be willing to incur some of the event's expenses and then list these expenses as tax-deductible donations. In a progressive dinner, for example, each home sponsor could buy the food and cook the meal or pay for a caterer.

Reduce Staff Costs by Increasing Volunteer Time

You may want to make extra-special efforts to find volunteers with talents that can reduce staff costs. Computer programmers, typists, accountants, graphic designers, and public-relations specialists are examples of people who can volunteer their time and expertise, thereby allowing you to reduce the staffing costs of your event.

Arrange an Exchange

In an exchange arrangement, both the organization and other involved parties benefit by working together on an event. The organization benefits by obtaining some special service, gift, or financial donation. In return, it offers something of value to the other parties. For example, a free clinic might sponsor an evening of dancing at a suburban mall. A local radio station might provide the disc jockey and equipment for free in exchange for considerable publicity. The mall could provide the setting and refreshments in exchange for the opportunity of attracting a large crowd to its facilities. The station, the mall, and the free clinic would all benefit from this exchange arrangement.

Negotiate for Price Reductions

If you are determined to spend as little as possible, then you inevitably will be engaged in negotiating. Do not accept the first price offered as final. For example, in dealing with an entertainer's agent, inquire whether the performer might be willing to do the show for no fee. If a free performance is not possible, ask for a reduced fee or a charitable contribution. Or offer to pay only for the entertainer's transportation and lodging. Explore a variety of options.

As another example, in discussing meal prices with a hotel, negotiate to reduce the price by 10 percent if you can guarantee the hotel the rental of several rooms. Or in setting up a cash bar, offer a guaranteed minimum to-

Shopper's Guide Chart

Item	Group Has	Purchase	Price	Donation	Borrow	Responsible Person	Considerations
Tickets		ABC Vending	$ 50			R. Bucy	
Room				St. Mary's Church		R. Alexander	Provide gift to church
Door prize				Alpine Travel		M. Camargo	
Sound system	Available					J. Hillman	
Desserts				Obtain from local bakeries		A. Vargo G. Jarrett	
Records				Members		V. Chapman V. Benford	Agree to reimburse for breakage
Tables				Obtain from 10 families		A. Ice	
Chairs				Obtain from 10 families		M. Callender	
Coffee maker		AAA Discount	$ 60			L. Duncan	Retain for other events
Decorations		XYZ Store	$ 50			A. Gaines R. Black	
Program		Amigo Printing	$150			B. Hampton	Reviewed bids of 4 printers

tal amount and then negotiate the cost of individual drinks. Work to develop a package deal in which you offer something to the hotel in exchange for price reduction or added profit. Negotiate from your strengths, such as the number of people who will be attending the event. Do not automatically accept the first price you are given.

Note that often you stand a better chance of negotiating if you involve an intermediary—someone who has an established relationship with the person with whom you are negotiating. The intermediary can get you in the door and also convey support for your request.

Obtain Free Goods and Services

Obtaining free goods and services can take different forms: An advertising firm can design advertisements at no cost, a law firm can provide pro bono services, a printing firm can print tickets for free, an accounting firm can provide a free audit, a grocery store can contribute food items, a business or hotel can provide the free use of its facility, local companies can supply complimentary consultation and staff assistance, and labor unions can provide free labor.

The best way to obtain free goods and services is through established relationships. Since vendors are frequently asked to make donations, many develop a preference list. At the top of the list are those with whom they do business. Find the most appropriate person, such as a good customer of the vendor, to do your asking. You have a special advantage if a favor is owed.

If you do obtain a commitment for free goods and services, put your mutual understanding in writing by sending a letter of acknowledgement. For even greater protection, arrange to have your attorney draw up a contract and convey to the donor that the contract is to protect both the donor and you. Link the contract to your being able to put a dollar value on the goods or services offered for later use in calculating tax deductions. The contract may not stop the donor from reneging entirely, but it may make the donor pause before deciding not to follow through.

Overall, to increase income and reduce costs, you have to be obsessed with the idea of a "zero budget" where you pay out as little as possible. But do not be penny-wise and pound-foolish. Be prepared to incur necessary and essential expenses that will reduce an extraordinary burden on volunteers and potentially generate increased income. You may need to hire secretarial service to send out letters, pay for advertisements to reach a target audience, or pay for the costs of printing invitations. The point is this: Try to reduce expenses as much as possible, but be willing to pay if you are convinced the event will be better as a result of the expenses incurred.

OBTAINING CORPORATE UNDERWRITING AND SPONSORSHIP

Underwriting and sponsorship are often used interchangeably when referring to the provision of corporate financial support of an event. The major distinction between the two terms is that sponsorship often involves greater visibility of the corporation's contribution to the event. Another distinction between underwriting and sponsorship is that under a sponsorship arrangement, the costs are likely to come out of the company's public-relations budget rather than out of the civic-affairs budget, which usually provides underwriting for tables and other components of an event. Be aware that some local companies are not inclined to sponsor an event—they would rather spread their limited dollars around to many different organizations in the community.

Determine Why Corporations Become Involved

The reasons corporations might consider underwriting or sponsoring an event will vary, but essentially they fall into one of these categories:

The business believes in your organization and its cause. Some corporations develop a set of priorities of the kind of organizations and causes they will support. Some, for example, will be supportive of neighborhood organizations. Some will want to finance events whose proceeds provide scholarships. Some will find the cultural arts of special appeal. Determine if the businesses you want to approach have in the past supported causes that resemble yours.

The business sees the event as a means of providing benefits to its employees. By supporting such events as golf or tennis tournaments, high-priced dinner-dances, and jog-a-thons, a business can give its employees who participate or attend a perquisite ("perk"), or extra benefit, while helping a charity. Also, if the business sees that the services of the organization benefit its employees or customers (e.g., a health care organization), the business may want to be identified with the organization's event.

The business receives high visibility throughout the community and at the event for its contribution. Printed materials publicizing the event and materials distributed at the event itself (e.g., a program book) provide high visibility for the corporate dollar.

The business leadership wants to respond to a request from a high official or special customer. The motivation for corporate support is in response not so much to the organization or the event, but to the person who is requesting the donation.

The business sees competitors as contributors. If a business is considering a contribution, it may be positively influenced by learning that similar businesses or competitors have also contributed.

Decide Who to Approach

When considering potential underwriters or sponsors, select those companies that have a natural relationship to your organization. For example, if you are fortunate enough to have the head of a corporation as the chairperson or the honoree of your event, consider asking that company to be an underwriter or sponsor. Otherwise, look at companies that are appropriate for your event. For instance, an organization that is planning a children's event might appeal to a toy company, an organization that is planning a chili cook-off might appeal to a spice company, or an organization that is planning a walk-a-thon might appeal to a soft drink company. Because the association of the name of your organization with a product implies a tacit endorsement of that product, you should carefully consider whether you want to be identified with certain products, such as cigarettes or liquor.

In deciding who to approach, consider each corporation's policies and procedures. Smaller companies that are not able to make major contributions may be willing to participate to a lesser degree. For example, they might not be able to purchase entire tables for $500, but they might be willing to purchase half tables for $250. Sometimes a company may be willing to purchase tickets for those who otherwise would be unable to attend. For example, a concert organized to benefit poor people could have tickets donated by a corporation to welfare recipients or to the unemployed.

Some corporations decline participating in any events. They prefer making a direct donation instead of, for example, buying expensive tickets to a dinner. If you learn of this preference, be certain that the staff or volunteers responsible for soliciting contributions are made aware of this.

Present Your Case

Keep in mind that for most corporations if the request is under $500, then it may not have to go up the corporate hierarchy for approval. Regardless of the amount of your request, you must present the corporation with a good rationale for supporting your event. Some companies receive over 100 requests a year and may only be able to fund 10 or 20 of them.

When you approach potential underwriters or sponsors, provide them with evidence that the event is well-planned and has strong potential for succeeding. If the event has been held previously, you should include newspaper clippings and materials that give evidence of its previous success. You might provide a brochure and a mock-up of the invitation. Information about the target audience and the expected attendance is also important. In addition, your case statement should describe how your event will contribute constructively to the well-being of people in your community. You should provide a budget to show how you are keeping event expenses down and how you intend to spend the money from the event.

Most companies do not want a computerized or photocopied form letter. Take the time to have the letters individually typed. Keep your presentation to under three pages. You may want to consider a two-phased approach in your contribution letter. The first phase would be directed to those companies most likely to support you. They are the pacesetters. Then upon securing their commitment, you can indicate in your second batch of letters where you have already received underwriting. This may help generate additional support.

Decide Who Should Contact the Corporation

Give careful consideration to who should write to the company. Ideally, your board of trustees will have on it people who are connected with various companies in the community. These trustees could include company managers and officers or their spouses. Having on your board of trustees an "up-and-comer"—someone who is likely to move up in the hierarchy of the company—is another important consideration. If appropriate, your letter should convey the relationship between the writer and the company. For example, if you have in your constituency a valued customer of the company, this would be of high importance.

Although a relationship with the potential underwriter or sponsor can certainly influence decisions, do not be inhibited in asking for underwriting support even if you have no connections with the company. Sometimes you may have to find an indirect relationship to a company. For example, a group wanting a reduced airfare to Paris as a raffle prize went to the French consulate, who supported their request to the airline. This worked for them. If you cannot find an indirect relationship with a corporation, remember that corporations give to organizations that fit into their priority categories. Thus, if your request is not excessive and your budget makes sense, even if you are not well-known by the company, you have a chance of receiving support.

Make the Request

Before sending your letter, call the company to determine who normally receives requests, such as a vice president, the public relations officer, or the civic affairs officer. Then indicate the proper person's name in your salutation. If a standard letter is being sent out by your chairperson and someone in your group knows the recipient of the letter or the president of the company, ask that person to add a personal note, such as "I hope you can support this request." Normally you would want to transmit your request on your agency letterhead, but if a valued customer of the potential underwriter's company is willing, ask that person to write the request on the customer's stationery.

The timing of your request is important. Most corporations budget on a calendar year. They have some general idea, based on their previous year's requests, of what to expect and how much funding will be available in a given year. If you are a new entrant to the process, consider starting small—but be sure to start early—to get into the process. You may wish to send a letter 6 or 7 months in advance of your event to alert businesses that your formal request will be forthcoming. If possible, contact underwriters and sponsors before they establish their budgets for the year so that your event can be planned into their budgetary allocations.

After the letters are transmitted, it is extremely important to follow up with phone calls if you do not receive a response. Sometimes companies are initially passive in making decisions. In other words, the person in charge feels neither strongly for nor strongly against the request, and so it is placed in a pile for later decision making. A phone call can activate your request out of the "passive pile." If you feel that it is appropriate, you may want to stress in your call that others in the community are supporting your event, implying that the company might not want to be left out.

Keep in Mind Special Considerations

While corporate underwriting and sponsorship can be tremendously beneficial, consider these caveats:

Do not expect the support to go on indefinitely. A day of reckoning may occur when corporations want to spend their money differently or when they want you to broaden your base of support. Be wary of becoming too dependent on any one source of funds.

Corporations are becoming increasingly concerned about the high ratio of expenses to net income of events. They want to see more of their charity dollar actually being used directly to support a cause rather than just provide a good time for people. Thus, be prepared to show the value of their contributions to the cause you are promoting. Determine whether this trend of direct corporate contributions in preference to underwriting is beginning to occur in your community. If so, you may want to rethink holding an event that requires significant corporate support.

Corporations may be prohibited by their local United Way from making contributions during the "freeze period" of the United Way corporate campaign. This often will occur in the late spring or summer months and extend into the early fall. If you are a United Way organization, check with your local United Way about the freeze period and the guidelines governing your solicitation of corporations. Check also with your local chamber of commerce and state attorney general's office to see if they place any restrictions on solicitations of underwriting funds.

Be careful not to make excessive demands for corporate support. Corporate funders are often annoyed by frequent requests for support from the same organization. Generally, once a year is sufficient, although if you have a special relationship, you may consider a maximum of twice a year. Avoid the situation of asking for a major underwriting gift and then a month later requesting a direct contribution. For instance, you may decide not to request underwriting of $500 in anticipation of a direct donation later in the year of $5,000. The only exception to this is if you have an unusually strong relationship with the company and if you are aware that two different budgets are involved (e.g., the civic affairs unit and the corporate charitable foundation).

Be mindful that the type, place, and timing of the event may influence corporate decisions. A luncheon in the downtown area in the fall may be more attractive for corporate underwriting than a dinner held in a distant suburb on a summer evening, because the luncheon may be more accessible to the corporate representatives who are expected to attend the event.

For larger gifts, the president of the company or a committee of officers is likely to be involved in making the decision. So your case has to be strong.

Remember to thank in writing all companies making special contributions. Be sure that the letter is not perfunctory but comments on the specific contribution and how it was used. Your genuine appreciation can be a prime (but not the only) factor in their motivation to contribute the next year. Some companies receive so few thank-you letters that when they do receive them, these are transmitted directly to the president.

Corporate underwriting and sponsorship have become extremely popular ways of gaining substantial support for events. Unfortunately, every good idea, when carried to excess, creates the possibility of its own demise. Corporations are becoming so inundated with requests to support expensive events that some are now having strong negative reactions to being asked. Expect in the future that corporate support will be increasingly difficult to obtain.

SELLING THE EVENT

"Selling is what you think about first." This is how most successful event chairpersons proceed. They know that to raise money for their events they must wage a tremendous selling campaign.

A few events may be fortunate enough not to have to undertake a major selling campaign. If the event is popular enough, all that may be necessary is to send out invitations and wait for the reservations to come in. Either the event is inherently attractive or the cause is so appealing that the main task is not selling but taking reservations. For some events, publicity, invitations, and word-of-mouth may be sufficient. But, generally, these approaches do not bring people to an event. People bring people to an event. You must build a sales force of people to reach out aggressively to convince others to attend. PEOPLE SELL TO PEOPLE.

Sell Tickets

Some organizations make the selling of tickets mandatory. The leadership decides how many tickets must be sold and distributes that number to their board of trustees or other members with the admonition, "Return the money—not unsold tickets." Tickets not sold are, in effect, purchased by the members. Of course, the organization requires a high degree of loyalty, affluence, and commitment to enforce this kind of expectation.

Most organizations do not mandate this sell-or-purchase approach; they rely on the voluntary participation of their sales force. It is important to recognize, however, that almost everyone would prefer to do anything else for a fund-raising event than to sell tickets. Even people who are natural persuaders and who are gregarious by nature sometimes have to pump themselves up to sell. Here are some suggestions for developing a cadre of strong salespeople:

In considering the overall structure of the event, give foremost consideration to putting your sales force together. Form a special ticket-selling committee consisting of people who have the ability to contact large numbers of friends and acquaintances. The selection of people for your other committees should be done with an expectation that they will be selling tickets as well. People should not just be selected because of their planning experience, interest in decorations, or expertise in promotions but because they have a network of friends to whom they can enthusiastically sell tickets. The larger the event, the greater the number of volunteers needed to sell tickets.

Focus on group sales. Depending on the nature of the event, many organizations try to sell tables, since it is easier to ask ticket sellers to try to put together a certain number of tables than to give them an open-ended assignment. In selling table tickets, they can use the added incentive of seating friends together. Identify table hosts and hostesses who commit themselves to selling tables and are listed on the invitation and in the program book. Some groups are so effective with this approach of preselling an event that 80 percent of the tickets are sold in advance of the invitation going out to the public.

Prepare a selling kit for the sellers, since they need concrete information. The kit should include details about the event (where, when, cost, etc.), about who will be benefiting from the profits, and about the work and cause of the organization. The sales force will also need written procedures for handling the return of money or unsold tickets and other details.

If you can afford it, hold a kick-off party for your ticket sellers. You will generate enthusiasm, and they will appreciate your support for them.

Take the time to convey the importance of the cause and the inherent fun of the event to your ticket sellers. If there is one important ingredient that makes a good salesperson, it is enthusiasm for the product. And enthusiasm occurs when people believe in what they are doing. They can then convince others that the event is a special opportunity that should not be missed.

If you sense people are uneasy about their sales role, try role-playing. One person can pretend to be a potential buyer and the other the seller. Make sure that the role-playing deals with how to handle buyer resistance.

Keep in continuous contact with your sales force, preferably in person or by phone. You need to know how many tickets have been sold so you can determine whether to step up selling activities. Consider brief memos saying how many tickets have been sold and reminding people of deadlines. But do not let written communication substitute for personal contacts with your sellers.

Ask your volunteers to plan an approach to the people they will be soliciting. For example, ask them to make a list of those they think they can reach personally. Then ask them to consider where they will be in the next few weeks and project how many tickets they can sell at each place. Get them in the frame of mind that sales can occur in a variety of settings. Remind your sellers that many of the friends they will be approaching are already inundated with ticket requests. Some potential buyers may be receiving four or five requests each week. But the single most important reason they will purchase a ticket is because a friend or a business acquaintance asks them. PEOPLE BUY FROM THEIR FRIENDS.

Encourage ticket sellers to "work the crowd" at other social events — to talk about the event, make mental notes of interest and commitments, and follow up with invitations, letters, and phone calls.

If at all possible, make sure that solicitors are at the same economic level as potential buyers. For example, if you want someone to buy a $250 patron ticket, be sure that the person asking is capable of purchasing a ticket of that price. Better still, arrange to have sellers ask people who have previously asked them to buy tickets to events. In certain circles a considerable amount of exchange occurs.

If it is appropriate for your organization, consider offering premiums to persons who sell the most tickets. This approach works especially well for such events as carnivals or raffles. The ticket sellers have a powerful incentive to win a prize or to be eligible for a drawing because they are among the top sellers.

For a large event with broad appeal, consider "geometric networking." Rather than selling 200 tickets directly, through geometric networking a volunteer could identify 20 friends who would each sell 10 tickets. The network of ticket sellers should purchase the tickets from the original ticket seller so that this delegator does not have to chase after the sellers.

Select individuals not directly connected with the organization to participate as ticket agents. For example, if you are having an event honoring a well-known sports figure, contact booster clubs and ask them to sell tickets to their members. For certain events (e.g., professional concerts) you might consider using a professional ticket-selling agency, such as Ticketron.

Convey to your sellers that personal contact and continuous follow-up are what sells tickets. Ask your sellers to see as many prospects as they can in person and to use the phone only when a personal visit is impossible. Follow up personal visits with a phone call or, as a last resort, with a letter. Emphasize that it is hardest to tell a ticket seller "no" face to face.

Maintain Ticket Control

Ticket control is an absolute must. A running total should be kept of tickets sold and not sold. This will help track those sellers who are doing well and those who are not achieving projected quotas. If some ticket sellers are doing poorly, arrange to have them return their tickets in sufficient time so that someone else can sell the tickets. One person should be responsible for the accounting of tickets and for arranging that funds be turned over on a continuous basis. Volunteers should know in advance that if they do not return unsold tickets by a certain deadline, they are responsible for payment.

RESOURCES

Ardman, P. & Ardman, H. *Woman's Day book of fund raising.* New York: St. Martin's Press, 1980, p. 22.

B'nai B'rith Fund Raising Cabinet, *B'nai B'rith fund raising chairman handbook.* Washington, D.C.: B'nai B'rith Leadership Cabinet, p. 50.

Flanagan, J. *The grass roots fundraising book.* Chicago: Contemporary Books,Inc., 1982, pp. 41, 45–46, 79–81, 151, 164–165.

Gaby, P. V. & Gaby, D. M. *Nonprofit organization handbook.* Englewood Cliffs, NJ: Prentice-Hall, Inc., 1979, p. 78.

Groman, J. E. Growing through donor acquisition. *The Nonprofit World Report,* May–June 1985.

Hay, J. T. *534 ways to raise money.* New York: Simon & Schuster, 1983, pp. 153–155.

Jaffe, L. Gifts-in-kind organization gives something for nothing. *Fund Raising Management,* January 1985, pp. 50–51.

Kotler, P. *Marketing management—Analysis, planning, and control.* Englewood Cliffs, NJ: Prentice-Hall, Inc., 1980, pp. 341, 352, 557.

Leibert, E. R. & Sheldon, B. E. *Handbook of special events for nonprofit organizations.* New York: Association Press, 1972, p. 29.

Lord, J. G. Marketing nonprofits. *The Grantsmanship Center Reprint Series on Management,* 1981.

Shakely, J. Exploring the elusive world of corporate giving. *The Grantsmanship Center News,* July–September 1977.

Sheerin, M. *How to raise top dollars from special events.* New York: Public Service Materials Center, 1984, pp. 21, 23.

United Way of America. Guidelines for organizing special events. *Community Magazine,* July 1985.

Chapter 6

PROMOTING AN EVENT

DEFINING THE MESSAGE AND THE MEDIA

The event's message is the broad idea or image that describes the event and is injected into every event communication. The success of an event depends on developing the right message and communicating that message through the media to your intended audience. Begin to develop and sharpen your message early in the planning process and then use the media to send your message to a very large number of people, either by seeking free news/public affairs coverage or by paying for advertising. Communication can also be achieved with printed materials, as discussed in Chapter 7. Since you cannot expect to meet personally every possible supporter of your organization, you must depend on news/public affairs coverage, advertising, and printed materials to make contact. An organization that does an impressive job of communicating its message through the media and printed materials will enhance the success of an event.

SELECTING A COMMUNICATIONS COORDINATOR

Select an experienced communications coordinator to be responsible for all news/public affairs coverage and advertising arrangements. This person might be a public relations practitioner, a journalism teacher, an advertising student, or a retired reporter.

The communications coordinator should be able to meet these qualifications: commitment to your organization and the event, writing skills, good judgment, knowledge of both the electronic and the print media, familiarity with the local media, the ability to act quickly and decisively, the ability to meet deadlines, skill in handling representatives of the media, and the ability to create news opportunities. The communications coordinator should work with staff and volunteers on developing a communications plan for the event.

DEVELOPING A COMMUNICATIONS PLAN

Before you seek news/public affairs coverage or pay for advertising, the communications plan—a very important part of the overall event plan—must be developed. In creating the communications plan, consider your audience and your budget.

Research is necessary to identify your intended audience. This type of research is known as targeting, and it involves collecting and analyzing data about your potential audience and then directing your promotional efforts where the analysis indicates those efforts will be most productive. The goal of targeting is to concentrate your promotional resources where they will do the most good.

Your event budget will greatly influence the content and extent of your communications effort. For instance, with ample funding in a large urban community, you might consider using limited advertising as well as news/public affairs coverage. If, however, your budget is small, you will have to rely on news/public affairs coverage only. In general an event should concentrate on getting news/public affairs coverage, since it is free. Any promotional funds that the event has in its budget should be spent on the printed materials that are crucial to the success of the event (e.g., fliers, posters, invitations, and program books) and, if possible, limited advertising.

CONDUCTING A MEDIA SURVEY

To use the media effectively, you must know as much as possible about the news/public affairs and advertising sources in the community. Many larger communities have their own media guides that can serve as a shortcut to doing a media survey. The expenditure for such a resource will be well worth the amount of survey time that is saved.

In smaller communities, where media guides are not compiled, it is necessary to conduct some sort of media survey. The first step in this effort is to obtain information through observation. Read the local newspapers, listen to the radio stations, and watch the television stations. Notice what they are doing and gain a sense of what they think is happening in the community. This insight will enhance the answers you obtain to such media survey questions as these:

What are all the radio and television stations, daily and weekly newspapers, and other publications in the area? Place the name, address, and phone number of each media outlet on a separate card (in a file box) or page (in a loose-leaf notebook). Other valuable information can be added to each entry as the survey progresses.

What is the circulation/audience rating? Find out the circulation of the newspapers by calling them. To determine the audience ratings of radio stations and local television newscasts, look for newspaper articles on the ratings or check with an advertising agency that subscribes to a rating service and has this information.

What are the audience profiles? You can get this kind of information from the *Editor and Publisher Yearbook* (newspapers), *Standard Rate and Data* (radio and television), or the *Broadcasting and Cable Yearbook* (radio and television). These publications may be available in the public library or a nearby university journalism department. If you cannot find them, ask a newspaper, broadcast outlet, or advertising agency for help.

Who should be contacted? Call the various media to find out the names of the editors of the newspapers and the names of the station managers, public affairs directors, and news directors of the radio and television stations.

What are the news deadlines? When calling the media also find out when a news release must get to the newspapers, radio stations, or television stations to make the next print edition or newscast.

What is the policy on covering events? If any of the newspapers, radio stations, or television stations are not going to cover events, it is better to know this before going to the trouble of sending them information.

Will the newspapers accept your photographs? If a newspaper accepts photographs, find out what size or quality requirements must be met, what kind of written information must be provided with the photograph, and what the photo deadlines are (they are usually earlier than news deadlines).

When all of this information is collected in a card file or notebook, it should be placed in a central location for easy access.

OBTAINING NEWS/PUBLIC AFFAIRS COVERAGE

Types of news/public affairs coverage include the noncommercial use of television, radio, and newspapers. It is important to remember these factors about all news/public affairs coverage:

> *It is not automatically available.* The existence of an event does not guarantee that it will ever be noticed by a newspaper, radio station, or television station. An event must be seen as being newsworthy to get coverage from the media.

> *It is difficult to control.* An event has virtually no power over what is actually said by the news media.

Communicating your message in an attempt to obtain news/public affairs coverage through television, radio, or newspapers involves preparing and distributing a media kit, learning to work with reporters, issuing news releases, using community calendars, seeking feature stories or interviews, and seeking coverage of the actual event. For radio and television, you can issue public service announcements and arrange to get on public affairs programs. If possible, you should also seek coverage from organizational newsletters. And, just as importantly, you should make every effort to promote your organization year-round.

Prepare and Distribute a Media Kit

The purpose of a media kit is to provide basic information about the event in a compact format that will be easy for reporters to use. The media kit, which should be hand-delivered or mailed to each newspaper, radio station, and television station, should include the following: the news release announcing the event and any other event literature; the identification of the communications coordinator, organization location, and a telephone number for obtaining additional materials; a description of the sponsoring organization and the cause that will benefit from the proceeds of the event; information about how much money the event hopes to raise, how many volunteers are involved, and other interesting facts; a list of prominent individuals involved in the event; and a list of ideas for media coverage. The media kit can be assembled in an inexpensive folder with side pockets.

Learn to Work with Reporters

The way you work with the media can be as important as what you have to say to the media. If you want to increase your chances of making news, you need to know how to work with reporters. These suggestions should be kept in mind:

> Always learn the deadlines and policies, and conform to them.
>
> Always keep appointments.
>
> Always provide information.
>
> Always give direct answers to questions.
>
> Always thank the people you work with—in writing. Not only is it good public relations on your part, but they need to be able to show that they are serving the public.
>
> Never try using pressure or influence to get media coverage or favorable treatment. It usually will not work.

Columnists and social editors can be particularly important to an event. Daily or weekly columns in local newspapers and weekly or monthly columns in area magazines that are devoted to items about residents and activities are a great place to seek mention of people and information pertaining to your event. Make every effort to obtain their coverage during the early planning stages of the event, just as the invitations to the event are being mailed (to spark the interest of potential supporters), and at the actual event.

Issue News Releases

A major activity in obtaining news/public affairs coverage is writing and distributing news releases. The general purposes of news releases are to announce an event and then to keep the media informed of interesting developments regarding the event. These basic rules should be followed when writing news releases:

> Type the release on 8½ × 11 inch paper, double-spaced, with wide margins so that the editor has room to write on it.
>
> Identify the organization and the contact person at the top of the page, and provide a telephone number to call for more information. If you can afford it, have this information imprinted on the news release sheets. Otherwise, type it single-spaced.

Include release instructions, typed in all capital letters, such as FOR IMMEDIATE RELEASE or FOR RELEASE: (date). Normally you should not delay the release date more than a few days after you issue the release, since reporters may lose track of it in the flurry of other stories. Also, a newspaper or station may break the release date and run the story too early.

One-third from the top of the page put the heading of the release, centered and typed in all capital letters. It should briefly and accurately summarize the content of the release. The empty space above the heading can be used by the editor to insert a headline or to make notes.

Include the most important information in the lead (first) paragraph with the remaining information included in descending order of importance. Since a copy editor may cut the release to fit the available space, your most important information should be at the top where it is least likely to be cut. The lead paragraph should answer these questions: who, what, when, where, why, and how. The other paragraphs can add interesting information about the event, list the names of the volunteer leaders, explain the beneficiary of the event, and highlight some of the sponsors of the event.

Be sure that facts, figures, and quotes are absolutely correct.

Use active rather than passive verbs, make sure that spelling and grammar are correct, and do not abbreviate anything in the first reference.

Keep the release brief and factual with short sentences and paragraphs. The release should not be longer than one page. However, if the release does run longer, at the bottom of the first page, type "more" in parentheses and all capital letters: (MORE). At the top of the second page, type either "Page 2" or "Page 2 of 2" or "Add 1."

A page should not end in the middle of a paragraph. If an entire paragraph will not fit at the end of a page, start the paragraph at the top of a new page.

At the end of the release, type "- 30 -" or "###." Either of these devices will tell the reader that the release has concluded.

Editors will, of course, edit and rewrite copy. But the less work they have to do on your material, the better the chance that it will be used.

Hand deliver the release, if that is the recommended approach in your community. Otherwise, mail it addressed to these people: the city desk of daily newspapers, the editor of a certain section, if this specialized newspaper coverage is desired, the editor of weekly newspapers and special-interest publications, the news director of radio stations, the news assignment desk of television stations, and the public affairs director of radio and television stations that have such programs. Do not send copies of the same release to two places within the same medium without clearly indicating the duplication. Otherwise you will only cause confusion and irritation; you will not increase the chances for coverage of a story.

When submitting news releases, remember that the media operate according to very strict deadlines. No rules are more rigid or necessary. So you must know what the media deadlines are, and structure your activities to conform to those demands. Deadlines usually follow these guidelines:

> Daily newspapers that appear in the morning must have materials by late in the afternoon on the day before they go to press. Daily newspapers that are published in the evening must have their information by noon of the day of publication. Since many pages of a daily newspaper are put together much earlier than the official, last-minute deadlines, the news available at that time is used to fill the space. You will have a better chance of getting into print if you get your news releases in well before the deadlines.

> Weekly newspapers require releases at least 2 days before publication.

> Foreign newspapers usually have very early deadlines since they need time to translate the material.

> Radio and television have much shorter deadlines because they do not involve the same time-consuming production of newspapers. Radio, in particular, has very flexible deadlines, since many stations broadcast news every hour and a few broadcast news continuously, day and night. The latter can accept and move news on the air within minutes.

If your media survey has determined that certain newspapers will accept photographs with releases, provide them. After all, a picture has great power to be noticed and remembered. When submitting photographs, keep these points in mind:

Almost all newspapers prefer 8″ × 10″ black-and-white glossy prints. Photos that are 4″ × 6″ or 5″ × 7″ are also acceptable, but it is easier to reduce a print than enlarge it.

Action photos are more likely to be used than still portraits.

The fewer the people in the picture, the better the picture and the better each person will look.

If possible, offer the photo editor a contact sheet with a variety of shots to choose from.

Always attach a typed one- or two-sentence caption to the bottom or back of the photo to identify the people, the place, and the action. Do not actually write on the back of the photo since your writing could show through when the photo is printed.

If possible, do not deliver identical photographs to different newspapers.

If you want your pictures returned, indicate where they should be sent.

With or without photographs, remember that the news release is the basic means the organization has of communicating with the media.

Use Community Calendars

Nearly every local magazine and newspaper includes a listing of events and activities of interest to its readers for the next several days or weeks to come. Most radio stations and television stations provide a similar service to listeners and viewers in the communities they serve. By getting on community calendars beginning about a month before your event and then each week thereafter until the week of your event, you will be able to have your event listed several weeks in a row on a variety of calendars.

Every magazine, newspaper, radio station, and television station that has a community calendar also has a policy for how it must be notified of events to be listed. Although a few media outlets may accept information over the telephone, most insist that the information be provided in writing to prevent errors. To learn the community calendar policies of the media serving your area, call them. Most will want the information considerably before it will be passed on to the public. Usually information for community calendar listings will be the same as the first paragraph of your news release. This should briefly tell everything that can be put into a short calendar announcement.

Seek Feature Stories or Interviews

Newspapers, radio stations, and television stations are all open to ideas for interesting feature stories or interviews that will appeal to large segments of their audiences. A newspaper feature story or interview will usually appear in the "Living" section of the paper, since readers are used to turning to that section to read articles with human-interest elements. A radio station is likely to include a brief feature story or interview as part of the regular newscast. A television station may incorporate a feature story or interview into its morning, noontime, early evening, or late evening news show.

Sometimes an event is so unique and fascinating that it will justify becoming a feature story or the subject for an interview. Because most events are not that unusual, however, to get exposure of this nature it is necessary to find other reasons for this type of coverage, and then include the event in the presentation.

Before seeking feature-story or interview coverage, first evaluate the types of features and interviews that appear frequently in your area's newspapers and on local radio or television. Are they mostly human-interest stories? Do they deal with interesting people? Do they try to present the "unusual"? Do they highlight humorous happenings? Are they educational? Once you become aware of what type of feature and interview items are most frequently presented in your area, you can decide what sort of ideas to submit.

Well-known celebrities can be good subjects for a feature story or interview. If your organization has celebrity members, or if your event includes a celebrity, bring this to the media's attention. When you lack celebrities for feature stories and interviews, look at the other aspects of your event. Ask if any of them are new enough, unusual enough, or exciting enough to justify exposure to the public through this type of coverage. For example, the cause that will benefit by the proceeds from your event is another possible feature story or interview topic. If you suggest that cause as an idea and the idea is accepted, be certain to mention in the story your upcoming event to earn money for the cause.

Also look to the members of your organization as the subject or contact person for a feature story or interview. If you can get coverage for one of your members, they can almost always mention their involvement in your organization and the upcoming event. In addition, an excellent way to present feature-story or interview ideas may be through members who personally know local editors, columnists, radio and television station producers, or broadcasters. Otherwise, feature-story and interview ideas must be submitted in writing. The letter should serve as an inquiry and as a sales tool. It should be brief but enticing. Do not offer the exact same idea to more than one newspaper, radio station, or television station at the same time. Feature stories and interviews are not like news releases—they must be exclusive to one media outlet at a time.

Seek Coverage of the Actual Event

News/public affairs coverage of an actual event is possible when the event is particularly newsworthy and fairly easy for reporters to cover and for camera crews to set up. In seeking coverage, write a news release to announce the upcoming event and deliver it to media assignment editors at least 2 or 3 days before the activity actually occurs. This will give the assignment editors the opportunity to plan ahead.

If you feel it is appropriate, then provide a courteous follow-up phone call the day before a morning event or the morning of a late afternoon or evening event. When telephoning a reminder, deliver the message quickly and succinctly. Do not insist that a reporter be assigned to cover your event, since such an approach rarely works.

For those reporters who do show up, make sure that they have complimentary tickets (if needed) and a media kit about the event. If you anticipate that a photographer will be present to cover the event, have good picture suggestions in mind. And make sure that all of the necessary people and props are ready.

Consider videotaping or filming the event yourself, should television reporters and camera crews not show up. Even if a station does not attend, it may use your film (if it is of acceptable quality) along with a script for the reporter.

If you would like columnists or social editors to attend your event, try to establish ongoing relationships with them before the event by consistently feeding them items of interest throughout the planning process. When they do agree to attend your event, request that they be accompanied by a photographer if possible. When providing information to several columnists or social editors working for different newspapers or stations, try to give each a different exclusive piece of information pertaining to their particular interest.

Issue Public Service Announcements

A public service announcement (PSA) is a short message (10, 20, 30, or 60 seconds) that is broadcast by a radio or television station at no charge for a nonprofit organization. The supply of PSAs far exceeds the demand, and stations are bombarded with these messages every day. So do not be too disappointed if yours is not selected to be aired.

PSAs for radio stations can be read live by the station announcer or prerecorded. If prerecorded, you can send a tape to the station or the station can record the message for you. No matter how the message is communicated, you must begin by writing copy. When writing copy, a good rule of thumb is to allow about two and a half words to each second: 10 seconds = 25 words, 20 seconds = 50 words, 30 seconds = 75 words, and 60 seconds = 150 words. Count extra seconds if your copy has a lot of long words. Also, count each digit in a phone number as a word so that a phone number is seven words (e.g., five-five-five-two-nine-four-four). Test the length of the copy by reading it out loud.

PSAs for television stations can be live announcements using slides and written copy that is read by the station announcer, or they can be filmed or videotaped announcements. The copy for television PSAs should be prepared in the same manner as radio announcement copy. In addition, be sure to give special attention to relating the words to the pictures. The audio portion of the PSA should be timed to run about 2 seconds shorter than the visual portion—8, 18, 28, or 58 seconds. If you are working with 35mm slides and copy, you will need one or two slides every 10 seconds. Keep the presentation simple, direct, and not too detailed (e.g., type should be large and bold). Do not put too much information on one slide, or it will not be read by the viewers.

To produce an effective, compelling audio-visual communication in 10 to 60 seconds takes skill and work. This is your responsibility. The station will help, but do not expect it to give you the time plus pay for your art-work, photography, and filming. Instead, consider seeking professional assistance from an advertising agency. More and more agencies are creat-ing free PSAs since they may profit in the long run. They are also adding PSAs to commercials that are paid for by local businesses.

In preparing PSAs for radio or television, consider these guidelines:

> Know in advance what a station's policies and formats al-low (e.g., a television station may only accept 10-second PSAs for its news program). Shorter PSAs generally have a better chance of being used. Consider writing the same message in different lengths so the station has a choice.

> Communicate only one idea in a PSA and be sure the idea is of interest to a wide range of listeners or viewers. Do not confuse the audience by trying to say too much in a short message. Give an address or phone number for more information.

> Type only one PSA to a page.

> Separate the lines of copy according to what can easily be read in one breath. If you establish natural breaks, the announcer will be able to read more smoothly. For tele-vision PSAs, present the text so that it is clear which slides accompany which portions of the message.

Provide "pronouncers"—assistance in saying any unusual names or words.

Include the length of the PSA (e.g., 10 seconds) and the dates for which the announcement is good (e.g., October 1–14). Note that you cannot indicate what time your PSA should be aired. If your announcement is accepted, that decision will be made by the station's public affairs director. Usually PSAs are broadcast in a rotation.

Send your PSA to the station's public affairs director as far in advance as possible.

Include a cover letter that explains the purpose of the announcement and any other pertinent information. Consider writing a fact sheet about the event discussed in the PSA. When listeners or viewers do not remember the specifics of an announcement, they often call the station. With a fact sheet, the station operator should be able to handle most calls.

Arrange to Get on Public Affairs Programs

There are many regularly scheduled public affairs programs on radio and television. These shows range in length from a few minutes to an hour, and are heard and seen at all times of the day and night. Monitor the programs in your community to determine their format and style. If you feel that something about your organization or event would fit into one of these programs, present the idea as specifically as possible to the station's public affairs director or to the program producer (refer to the section on feature stories and interviews for suggestions on how to obtain coverage). Planning ahead is important, since many programs are recorded weeks in advance of air dates. Also, if you cannot arrange something with one station, there will still be time to try another.

In addition to their regularly scheduled programs, most stations welcome good ideas, such as the cause that your organization's event will benefit, for special public affairs programs. These must be of general, areawide interest and significance. Although the station will provide technical staff and equipment, you will have to do extensive background research and other preparations. If you are not able to appear on a program, take advantage of any call-in opportunities to communicate your message.

Seek Newsletter Coverage

If you have an opportunity to do more than cover just the general media (television, radio, and newspapers), then approach the vast network of organizational newsletters and bulletins that reach the membership of special-interest groups. Although the circulation of these publications varies, the readership is quite interested in the subject matter.

To reach the special-interest groups in your area, find a resource that covers the organizations you are interested in. For example, many communities publish directories of local organizations that provide current names, addresses, and phone numbers. Also use the Yellow Pages: Under "Newspapers" and "News Publications" you will find all of the major special interest newspapers. Under "Clubs and Associations" you will probably find just about every professional, trade union, religious, veteran, fraternal, ethnic, and political organization in town. It is a simple matter, with this list in hand, to call and find out if a group puts out a publication and if the publication wants to receive news from your organization.

Be sure to use your own organization's newsletter. It can provide an excellent means for telling your members and other readers about an upcoming event, as well as the event's development. Your newsletter can feature progress reports from the chairperson, an update on ticket sales, samples of promotional pieces to be used, and accounts of amusing incidents. The newsletter should keep readers excited about the event until it actually takes place.

Promote Your Organization Year-round

Promoting an organization should begin long before a specific event is selected and continue long after the event is held. Promotion means keeping your organization's name and its activities in front of your community all year long through every newsworthy opportunity. It also means keeping your public constantly aware of the project or the cause that will benefit from your organization's endeavors and fund-raising efforts.

If you can keep the name of your organization and its good work in the news all year long, it will be much easier to get additional exposure when your event is announced, being planned, being implemented, and underway. It is easier to get coverage when your community knows your organization and what it stands for, when people know about the purpose or cause you support, and when members of the media know your communications coordinator due to previous contact.

PURCHASING ADVERTISING

Advertising involves paying money to the media to communicate your message, which can be carried through television, radio, newspapers, and outdoor displays. The greatest advantage of advertising is control. Because you are paying, you can decide exactly what to say, how to say it, in what form to say it, where to say it, and when to say it. Pictures and words can create precisely the impression you wish to make. The major drawback to advertising is cost, since it can mean a large expenditure of limited dollars. Another drawback is that once you pay for advertising, the media may be unwilling to give you free news/public affairs coverage. However, the advantage of advertising outweighs the drawbacks when advertising can help an event achieve two very important objectives: making people aware of the organization and its event, and persuading people to support the organization and attend the event. If you feel that advertising is appropriate for your organization, you should carefully choose an advertising agency to work with, set up an advertising calendar, and select the type of advertising.

Choose an Advertising Agency

Too much money is invested in advertising for an organization to depend solely on volunteers' advice—unless, of course, the volunteers are advertising professionals—and to risk not communicating its message as effectively as possible. If it is financially possible, your organization should consider obtaining the services of an advertising agency to assist in all advertising efforts.

In determining whether your organization can afford an advertising agency, note that advertising agencies obtain most of their income through commissions they receive from the media for the ads they place. This means that ad space will cost you the same whether or not you place it through an agency. The other costs are creative costs for staff time, which may be a one-time fee, and costs for materials, which are usually billed at agency cost plus a commission (such as 15 percent) on the total. This may not sound too expensive, but it can add up fast in an organization with a small or medium event budget.

If you do decide to hire a professional advertiser, be sure to shop around. Obtain the names of local agencies from people involved in your organization, such as people in the advertising business themselves, or people in other businesses who retain advertising agency services. Or check the Yellow Pages under "Advertising Agencies and Counselors." Also check the *Standard Directory of Advertising Agencies* in your local library. For additional help, write or call the American Association of Advertising Agencies, Inc., at 666 Third Avenue, 13th Floor, New York, New York, 10017, (212) 682-2500.

Once you have put together a list of potential advertising agencies, make some phone calls to determine which agencies have had experience in special events and which might be willing to work within your estimated advertising budget. Be sure to tell the agencies right away how much you are thinking of spending. Then meet with those agencies that interest you most. Look at samples of previous work, especially other events the agency has handled, and get honest estimates of what the advertising expenditures are likely to be.

The agency you do select should be involved in the communications planning process from the start. This will allow you to secure desirable broadcast time and printed advertisement space early. Also, the more time an agency has to work on your plan and get the materials ready, the better your advertising campaign will be. Compared to the usual advertising timetable for business clients, an event offers a relatively short time to prepare and conduct an advertising effort. In addition, the more time there is for you and the agency to get to know each other, the better you will probably work together.

You can expect the advertising agency to do the following: contribute to the creation of the event's message, organize your advertising plan, serve as a source of ideas and as an objective sounding board, help finalize your advertising budget, reserve newspaper and outdoor display space and radio and television time, prepare and place ads and commercials, supervise printing and broadcasting, and consolidate and check all media bills. The agency cannot be expected to guarantee success. It can only help assure that your message is properly conveyed and your advertising funds are effectively spent.

Your responsibilities in working with an advertising agency should be these:

Keep the lines of communication open. The agency should be included in all planning and strategy sessions that are in any way relevant to the advertising and promotional aspects of the event.

Hold regularly scheduled meetings with the agency. If a meeting must be called off, see that it is only postponed, not cancelled.

Designate the communications coordinator or somebody else in your organization as the final authority on matters relating to advertising. Be sure that this person is available at all times—day or night—for consultations, discussions, and decisions.

Do not expect the agency to solicit donations of space, time, materials, or cash. The advertising agency is not your fund-raiser—the event is.

Establish an advertising budget at the beginning of the planning process. The agency will understand that it may not be possible to decide at the outset exactly how much will be spent, but at least you can work out a preliminary cash-flow system.

Keep firm control on the budget for advertising materials and services. The most effective procedure is one in which all materials and services ordered by the advertising agency are on a pay-as-you-go basis or are covered by a written purchase order signed by a designated official of your organization.

Do not expect the agency to yield automatically to your wishes on advertising content. Carefully consider the agency's ideas and candid opinions.

Have it clearly understood from the beginning that, where there are differences of opinion, the final authority will rest with your organization.

It is advisable to have a written agreement between your organization and the agency so that there are no misunderstandings. The following items should be covered:

Compensation—Spell out the handling of media commissions and the charges and commissions on staff time and materials.

Terms of payment—Arrange when and how the agency will be paid.

Cash discounts—Sometimes the print media will allow a cash discount for prompt payment. It is expected that the agency will pass these cash discounts to you if you agree to pay the agency in advance.

Termination—Keep these thoughts in mind regarding an organization's decision to terminate the agency's services:

If the agency has made an uncancellable contract with a medium on your authorization, the agency may need to carry the contract to completion.

If the agency has started production on any materials or has ordered any services on your authorization, it is expected that you will pay for any costs incurred or committed.

The agency should agree to transfer to you or your representative all contracts or reservations with advertising media (with the possible exception of uncan-

cellable contracts), all property and materials that you have paid for, and all
information regarding the advertising.

Unused plans or ideas that have not yet
been published or broadcast ordinarily
remain the agency's property.

Set up an Advertising Calendar

Set up a calendar to plan and budget your advertising. The calendar
can help your organization avoid these common mistakes: overspending
too early, forgetting an important medium, missing an advertising deadline, and failing to have enough money on hand to pay for advertising.

The advertising calendar should list the weeks across the top and the
media along the side. In the media listing along the side, write down the
following data under each medium: name, address, and phone number of
the medium; name of the advertising contact; cost per unit of time and
space; and any special production instructions. When the page is divided
into a grid, you can then fill in key information, such as the date of the
deadline, the date the ad is to be printed or broadcast, the size or duration
of the ad, and the total cost of the ad. This type of calendar can also be
adapted to news/public affairs coverage.

Select the Type of Advertising

Before deciding what type of advertising to use, it is critical to determine your particular advertising objectives and to understand your audience. Then you can select the best possible medium for the available
money. The choices, again, are television, radio, newspapers, and outdoor
displays. Since your financial resources will be limited, money should be
concentrated on the medium that will best reach your intended audience at
the lowest cost.

For each medium in your area, you should determine the following:
how much of the area is covered, how many people and/or households are
covered, how much it will cost to reach the area, who to contact to buy time
or space, what the deadlines are for reserving time and space and for deliv-
ering materials, and what special requirements exist for production materials.

Consider Television Commercials

Television commercials most effectively reach an audience's senses
and emotions, since people can both see and hear the message. Television

is an excellent medium for persuasion purposes, but it is extremely expensive. Most organizations cannot use television because the costs are simply prohibitive. One 30-second spot can cost thousands of dollars, depending on the time slot and the city. For television advertising to be effective, it must be repetitive, and at extremely high prices not many organizations can afford to be repetitive. In addition, for all the money that is spent on television, you cannot avoid sending the message to people who are not part of your intended audience. That is not the most cost-effective way to spend advertising dollars.

Still, if yours is the rare organization that does decide to use television, your television commercial should craft a message that is right for your audience and that is within your financial resources. The production of a television commercial is directly connected to the creative concept of the commercial. High-quality, expensive production will not be able to save a poorly created concept. But professional-level production can give a good concept the sparkle and impact to persuade people to attend an event.

Be careful not to spend so much money on production that the expense cuts into funds that could be better spent on buying time. About 15 to 20 percent of the total television budget should go into production costs. For example, if there is $10,000 to spend on television, about $1,500 to $2,000 should be spent on production, with $8,000 to $8,500 left to buy time. If there is only $3,000 budgeted for television, the money would probably be better spent elsewhere, because there will be only about $2,400 to spend for the actual purchase of time to run the spots. That amount of money does not buy very much repetitive contact.

It is possible, of course, to produce television spots with limited funds. For instance, the commercials can be made in the television studio with the station employees as production crew. Or a college television facility can be used to produce the commercials. If you decide to take either of these routes, it is imperative to know what you are doing. Seek professional advice to make the most of these options.

Commercial rates for television depend on the classification (time of day or size of audience). Most stations have two rate structures—one for national advertisers and one for local advertisers. The local rate is always lower. In addition, nearly all stations have volume discounts built into their rate structure. This allows a customer to receive a discount on the purchase of a block of spots, significantly reducing the cost per spot. Such rates are not always published on the stations rate cards, and you may have to ask for them.

If you have a reason to question the rates offered by a station, you can request to see its contracts with other advertisers. Under law, the station is required to show them, if asked. Also inquire about special rates for nonprofit organizations.

When advertising agencies buy broadcast time for clients, they earn a

15 percent commission from the price listed on the rate card (the rate card prices include the 15 percent commission). If a representative of your organization buys that time directly from the station without using a recognized ad agency, you may be able to get that discount and thus pay only 85 percent of the lowest local rate. This will not happen automatically. You must ask for it.

The timing of television commercials is based on the principle of using television when it will do the most good. Regardless of the number of spots you can afford, to make a strong impression your spots must be concentrated. A sprinkling of spots over a wide range of time will probably be a waste of money. The most important thing to remember about timing is that you must buy television time early. As soon as it has been determined that television will be an integral part of the media plan, purchase the time to run paid spots. Before you buy any time, find out the following information from the station manager, station advertising manager, or your advertising agency:

> What are the station and program ratings?
>
> What prime time and other spots are open to local advertisers?
>
> How much does the time cost?
>
> What is the station policy on length of material?
>
> What special opportunities are available for advertising (e.g., sports or entertainment events that will draw larger-than-usual audiences)?

It is possible to air commercials during certain times of the day or adjacent to specific programs that primarily attract the audience you are trying to reach.

If you have paid for advertising, you are entitled to have your commercial shown at the time and in the manner stipulated in your contract. Monitor all of your commercials to make sure the stations follow the contract. If your commercial is not aired at the correct time or is only partially shown, call the station and seek restitution. Most stations will schedule your commercial for another showing.

Consider Radio Commercials

Radio advertising is often within the financial and production reach of many organizations. Radio commercials help achieve event identification, reinforce the message, and build momentum.

The content of a radio message should be simple and repetitive. Only one idea should be worked into a 30- or 60-second spot. Few listeners give their full attention to what they hear on the radio, since they are usually also driving, reading, or working. Listening to the radio is almost always incidental to other activities. An impression—or a key phrase—is about all a radio commercial can transmit from the organization to the listener.

Music is an important consideration in a radio commercial. Because most radio listeners are music-oriented, the right kind of music in a radio commercial can help convey the right kind of impression to them. Use music—or special sound effects—to get the listeners' attention. But be wary of musical jingles or songs that sound amateurish. If the spot calls for something other than original music, check the copyright situation and make sure you have permission to use familiar or popular musical tunes.

The production of a radio commercial, which should be relatively simple, generally requires a timed script, an announcer, other talent (if it is called for), music (if it is to be used), and a recording studio. The cost for commercial recording studio time is normally charged by the hour. At least 1 or 2 hours of studio time will be needed for each spot. You will also have to pay for tapes ("dubs") to supply to each station. Rates for announcers and musical talent will vary from city to city. Costs can be kept down if the announcer's time, musical talent, or studio time are donated.

When buying radio time, remember to consider the size of your audience. Note that radio audiences are largest in the morning. More people listen to the radio from 6.30 a.m. to 9.30 a.m. than any other time of the day. Your first priority radio buys should be during this "early morning drive time." The next largest radio audience occurs during "evening drive time"—from 4 p.m. to 6.30 p.m. This time period should be used for second priority radio buys. Audience size decreases during other times of the day or night. Third priority radio buys should be based on audience rating information, which can tell approximately what age and economic groups are listening to each time slot during the day and evening. This type of information should be available through an advertising agency or the station's marketing director. Remember that, as with television, if you cannot afford to repeat your radio message, then you cannot afford to use the medium.

Radio commercials can be targeted in communities that have many radio stations specializing in a variety of musical and/or news programming. Because certain listeners tune in to a particular radio station for the programming it offers, it is possible to be selective in using radio and to send your message to just those audiences that you need to reach. To obtain this type of information, consult with an advertising agency or the station's marketing director.

Consider Newspaper Ads

Newspaper advertising should promote and reinforce your message. It can be used to get across more information about an event, since the reader can take the time to read the copy, which is not limited to the 30- or 60-second time frame of television and radio advertising. Newspaper advertising can also provide a good place to communicate event endorsements. Ads that feature group endorsements can be impressive; people will look for and be influenced by the endorsement of someone they personally know and respect.

A newspaper ad should be designed based on the premise that, to be read, your advertisement must be distinguishable from the usual clutter of other ads. To insure the kind of visual quality that will draw the readers' attention, consider hiring a graphic artist to lay out the ads. If your organization cannot afford to do this, at least seek professional advice—it is a must for print advertising. The ad should have the same graphic layout as your other printed materials, for purposes of continuity and recognition. You can, of course, present variations on the major style.

A newspaper ad must be large enough or frequent enough to attract attention. However, this can mean significant costs, particularly in comparison to radio advertising. Before deciding to invest funds in newspaper advertising, determine your priorities, assess your resources, and target your audience.

It is easier to target a specific audience with a weekly suburban newspaper than with a major daily metropolitan newspaper. In many metropolitan areas, the suburban weeklies reach thousands of readers, and they focus news on community events that never reach the major daily papers. If your community has suburban weeklies with high readership, it might be worthwhile to place advertising there.

Special interest newspapers (e.g., labor union, religious, social, and ethnic group newspapers) are aimed at specific audiences. If such groups are included among your targeted audience, investigate those advertising possibilities.

Consider Outdoor Displays

Outdoor displays—billboards and transit posters—can be used to make people aware of the event. The content of an outdoor display should be simple since people's attention will only be focused on it for a few seconds. The design should be bold, big, and bright, so that it can be seen from a long distance.

The cost of billboards is determined by the size of the audience. Billboards are sold on a monthly contract with the price of each determined by the location: the more traffic passing the board, the greater the cost. Illuminated billboards are more expensive than billboards that are not illuminated. To cut costs, consider using junior billboards, which are about half the size of the standard large outdoor advertising boards. Also, do not hesitate to ask for free billboard space. Many companies are quite willing to provide this public service to nonprofit organizations.

The number of billboards bought in a single market is based on a "#100 Showing." This means that the purchase of a certain number of boards within a given area guarantees that almost 100 percent of the driving population will have an opportunity to see at least one of the purchased boards within the month. If you decide to pay for a #100 Showing, make sure most of the billboard locations are in or adjacent to your community. It is also possible to buy boards with a #50 Showing or even a #10 Showing. This, of course, costs less, because fewer drivers will pass the purchased locations. It may be a worthwhile expenditure, however, if the locations are right. Billboard companies have detailed data on how many people go by their billboards, and the companies can give you a good idea of what you will get for your money.

Targeting billboards is not difficult, since it is possible to limit placement to areas where targeted groups of people live or travel. Be sure to check your selected locations personally. A billboard that looks great on a map can actually be blocked by trees or lost in a group of surrounding billboards.

Transit advertising rates vary with the particular bus, rail, and taxi company. Exterior transit advertising (e.g., on the outside of a bus) is generally a good buy, because the people using the vehicle, other motorists, and pedestrians can see the ads.

Targeting transit posters—both inside and outside buses, trains, and taxis and in stations and terminals—can be precise. It is possible to place the posters on a certain mass transit line or in a certain station according to the travel routes of the people you want to reach.

Billboards and transit poster space should be reserved early. For billboards, check the Yellow Pages under "Advertising—Outdoor." For transit poster space, contact the transit company.

Other types of outdoor displays, such as billboard parades (using decorated cars and vans) and human billboards (volunteers wearing signs and passing out literature), can also be considered.

RESOURCES

Alberti, C. E., Macko, G. S., & Whitcomb, N. B. *Money-makers: A systematic approach to special events fund raising.* Ambler, PA: Whitcomb Associates, 1983, pp. 1.7–1.9.

Ardman, P., & Ardman, H. *Woman's Day book of fund raising.* New York: St. Martin's Press, 1980, pp. 125–150.

Berson, G. *Making a show of it: A guide to concert production.* Ukiah, CA: Redwood Records, 1980, pp. 70–75, 79–83.

Brody, R., Goodman, M., & Ferrante, J. *The legislative process: An action handbook for Ohio citizens groups.* Cleveland, OH: Federation for Community Planning, 1985, pp. 83–89.

Brody, R., Goodman, M., & Josephs, S. *Tax levies and other ballot issues: A campaign handbook.* Cleveland, OH: Federation for Community Planning, 1984, pp. 43–44, 57–67, 69–90, 96–97.

Connors, T. D. *The nonprofit organization handbook.* New York: McGraw-Hill, 1980, pp. 5.3–5.66.

Contact Center, Inc., *Getting yours: A publicity and funding primer for nonprofit and voluntary organizations.* Lincoln, NE: Contact Publications, pp. 7–21.

DeSoto, C. *For fun and funds: Creative fund-raising ideas for your organization.* West Nyack, NY: Parker Publishing Co., 1983, pp. 155–159.

Federation for Community Planning, *Publicity Guide.* Cleveland, OH: Federation for Community Planning, 1987.

Flanagan, T. *The grass roots fundraising book.* Chicago: Contemporary Books, Inc., 1982, pp. 257–267.

Gaby, P. V. & Gaby, D. M. *Nonprofit organization handbook.* Englewood Cliffs, NJ: Prentice-Hall, Inc., 1979, pp. 197–206, 215–235.

Grambs, M. & Miller, P. *Dollars and sense: A community fundraising manual for women's shelters and other non-profit organizations.* San Francisco: Western States Shelter Network, 1982, pp. 24–30.

Kotler, P. *Marketing management—Analysis, planning, and control.* Englewood Cliffs, NJ: Prentice-Hall, Inc., 1975, pp. 200–213.

Martinez, B. F. & Weiner, R. Guide to public relations for nonprofit organizations and public agencies. *The Grantsmanship Center Reprint Series on Management,* 1979, pp. 1–15.

Miller, A. & Williams, E. Peddling a social cause. *Newsweek,* September 1, 1986, pp. 58–59.

Mulford, C. *Guide to student fundraising.* Reston, VA: Future Homemakers of America, 1984, pp. 17–20.

Pritchard, J. H. *There's plenty of money for nonprofit groups willing to earn their shares—How to do it successfully.* Phoenix: Cornucopia Publications, 1984, pp. 77–121.

Sheerin, M. *How to raise top dollars from special events.* New York: Public Service Materials Center, 1984, pp. 109–115.

Chapter 7

USING PRINTED MATERIAL

DEVELOPING PRINTED MATERIAL

Printed material tells people the facts about your event. It can provide either general or very detailed information. Printed material for publicizing an event can consist of brochures, fliers, posters and signs, table tents, banners, and specialties and novelties. Printed material for implementing an event can consist of invitations, tickets, and program books.

Good content and design are essential ingredients in the development of all effective printed material, since they help set the mood and quality of your event, as well as enhance people's respect and interest. The content should be understandable to the average reader. It should emphasize the most important information that you want to share and then feature any additional information. The design should be consistent with your organization's image, appropriate for your event, clear, and simple. If the design has a keen sense of proportion, space, and contrast or balance, it will help communicate your message. But if it is complicated, cluttered, or vague, with poor graphics, messy type, or bad photographs, it will obscure the message. When developing printed material, keep these suggestions in mind:

> *Be consistent in graphics and copy style.* Each piece of printed material should be part of a cumulative impression. Be sure that colors, typeface, and writing style are consistent from one piece to the others. This repetition will reinforce the event's image, help achieve greater recogni-

tion, and add to the effectiveness of printed materials wherever they appear.

Design and order for economy. Before making a final decision on the dimensions of a piece of printed material, consider standard paper stock and envelope sizes. Try to avoid waste. Also, carefully estimate the number of pieces you will need so that you do not have to reorder or throw away any printed material. And, keeping in mind that the type of paper is a major variable in the cost of printing, do not order an unnecessarily expensive quality of paper. Obtain a number of competitive price quotes before placing any order.

Allow enough time to get printed material properly prepared and printed. Do not rush the preparation and printing because the quality and accuracy of the finished work can suffer and costs at the print shop can go up if there is a rush job. Allow about a month for writing, design, proofreading, and production, and another 2 to 3 weeks for printing, depending on quantity. Additional time should be set aside if the material has to be broken up into smaller lots for distribution after printing. Be prepared to pay the printer up front if required.

If you do not have volunteers with graphics experience, and your organization can afford it, consider hiring a design studio to do the job. The cost will depend on the company you hire, the number of people on the job, the hourly rates, and the price of the materials that are needed. Once you decide to hire a design company, before making a final selection you should look at samples of finished work of the companies you are considering. Then call some of the clients of the companies, and check on their level of satisfaction. Make sure that a designer is not known for missed deadlines, broken promises, and budget overruns. Always obtain a written estimate from each company, as well as a written projection of the total amount of time required, and how much time each of the project steps will take. Select the company that can best meet your needs at the lowest cost.

If you can neither recruit a volunteer graphics expert nor afford to hire a professional, then rely on a local printer to help you. Ask for an estimate of the cost of doing a job, based on the product's quantity, size, number of ink colors, type of paper, and amount of copy. When approaching more than one printer for comparative price quotes, make sure that you provide each printer with the exact same information as the basis for their estimates. Prices can vary greatly among printers, depending on their materials on hand, current workloads, costs of operation, labor capabilities, and pricing policies.

DISTRIBUTING PRINTED MATERIAL

Generally, printed material is distributed through the mail. Effective distribution of printed material is essential to the success of an event. Therefore, carefully consider your mailing lists and your mailing procedures.

An extremely important factor in a successful mailing program is a targeted mailing list. The better the mailing list, the better the results. Unless you are mailing only to your own members and current supporters, you will be interested in obtaining additional mailing lists from other organizations or professional mail services.

To determine the kinds of lists you may want to use, brainstorm about the types of people you would like to reach. Then decide how to obtain the mailing lists directed to your intended audience. You may seek lists from your own members (e.g., their Christmas lists, Rotary Club lists, or country club lists), your previous events and other fund-raising efforts, other organizations, business and professional directories, or a professional mailing service.

If you decide to approach other organizations, ask for their lists on computer printout labels to make your mailing procedures easier. Request that they be in zip code order and brought up to date. Note that it can take as long as a month to get the lists you want. Many organizations will ask for a copy of what you intend to send out to the people on their lists, so be prepared to meet that request. You might want to offer an exchange—your organization's mailing list for another organization's list.

Note that the United States Postal Service will help organizations clean up their small computerized mailing lists (350 to 50,000 entries) at no charge. They will accept floppy disks in popular formats and then validate five-digit zip codes, update the lists to nine-digit zip codes, and standardize spellings and abbreviations. For more information, contact your local customer service representative, or write to the United States Postal Service's Address Information Center, 6060 Primacy Parkway, Memphis, Tennessee 38188-0001.

If you determine that you can afford to purchase mailing lists from a professional mailing service, first seek their advice on the most appropriate lists for your event. The mailing service may present ideas that never would have occurred to you. For example, if your intentions are to seek a young, urban, professional audience for an event, the mail service might suggest purchasing the subscription list of a trendy local magazine or the mailing lists of the largest foreign car dealerships in the area. Note that charges for mailing lists are generally based on the complete list or per thousand names. Some specialized or hard-to-get lists may cost more than other lists.

It is generally a good idea to evaluate the effectiveness of the lists that you use, especially if you will be using them again. A professional mailing service can help you do this through various coding methods. Or you can use your own coding system for each different mailing list. Reservation cards and registration forms can be easily coded.

When sending mail first class, be sure to check your mailing (the envelope and contents) for weight and dimensions. You do not want to spend more than necessary on the postage, and you do not want to risk having a piece of mail get to the recipient marked "Postage Due."

Since postage is such a large expense, you may opt to send your mailing for the lowest possible cost—bulk rate. Substantial savings can be made by applying for and purchasing a third-class bulk rate permit through your main post office. Remember to allow extra days for local delivery when using bulk rate. Also, keep in mind that bulk mail must be presorted and bundled by zip code, and a minimum of 200 identical pieces of mail must be sent at one time. To obtain more information on bulk mailings, ask your local post office for a copy of the United States Postal Service Publication, *First-Class, Third-Class, and Fourth-Class Bulk Mailings—Permits, Preparations, and Regulations.* Another United States Postal Service publication, *Mailers Guide,* contains abridged information on a variety of topics that are basic to organizations' mailing needs. In addition, all post offices maintain copies of the *Postal Service Manual* and the *Postal Bulletin,* which are primary sources for current rates and postal regulations. If you plan on doing more than one bulk mailing, consider having copies made of your mailing labels. That way you will not have to retype the same labels.

Regardless of how you decide to mail your pieces, be certain that you recruit enough volunteers to get the mailing out. And allow them enough time to get the job done. Generally, you can assume that one person can address about 30 envelopes per hour or stuff 100 envelopes per hour.

Make sure that you schedule the mailing realistically. Working backward from the desired date of arrival, allow 3 days for the delivery of first-class mail (if you are using bulk rate, check with your local postmaster for an accurate estimate of delivery time). Once you have your delivery date, determine how much time you will need to prepare the mailing lists, print the material, stuff and address the envelopes, and deliver the mail to the post office. In every mailing include a piece of mail addressed to yourself so that you will know when everyone else included in the mailing receives the mail. Note that a professional mailing service will handle the actual mailing process for you if you can afford the expenditure.

Sometimes, to save money on postage, literature drops or distributions can be used to deliver printed materials to each house in the area. Since it is illegal to put literature in mailboxes, the materials are usually left in screen doors or are designed so they can hang from door knobs. Literature drops are most feasible when the intent is to distribute generalized materials to the entire area or specialized materials to a particular area.

SELECTING THE TYPES OF PRINTED MATERIAL

The types of printed materials that your organization selects for publicizing or implementing an event will depend on the purpose of the particular piece. Different types of printed materials have different uses.

Brochures

A well planned, well designed brochure can be the basic document of an event. It can be handed out, mailed, and used for a variety of purposes—from an information piece for potential underwriters, to an invitation, to a registration form. A brochure's style and substance can help establish a vital connection between the event and key elements of the intended audience, including the media.

The brochure should describe the event in simple, clear terms. It should also provide people with a reason to support and attend the event. If desirable, the brochure can include photographs. With any piece of printed material, besides reading the headlines, people are most likely to look at the pictures and read the captions. Make sure that the photographs are good quality. Get the assistance of a professional, or at least an experienced, photographer.

Fliers

Fliers are an excellent source of early promotion to a wide audience. They need only to provide basic information about the event and instructions on how to obtain additional details. Fliers can be included in any mailings that your organization sends, or they can serve as mail pieces themselves. They can also be left in piles at key locations in your community. And they are easy to hand out in person.

Fliers should be produced as inexpensively as possible and in large quantities. They should be made to look different from the mail that people get every day through the use of unusual colors or an appealing design.

Fliers can be distributed in the following ways:

Every member of your organization should be supplied with a quantity of fliers to hand out personally.

Some stores will permit you to place small stacks of fliers in areas they have for that purpose. Try to replenish the supply as it becomes depleted.

If members of your organization have professional offices with waiting rooms, small supplies of your fliers should be placed in those waiting rooms.

Door-to-door distribution of your fliers by members will allow your information to reach every residence in your community.

Place fliers on windshields of parked cars—under the windshield-wiper blades so they will not drift away. But first make sure that it is legal to do this in your community. Also, check with the owners of large private parking areas, such as shopping centers or parking lots and garages, before placing fliers on cars parked in those places.

Fliers can be used in place of posters or signs in locations where they will be viewed up close. Check your list of poster and sign locations to see where less expensive fliers can replace the posters or signs.

Mail fliers to targeted populations in your area.

Posters and Signs

Posters and signs that are displayed in public places serve as an excellent way to increase people's awareness of your event. Eye-catching posters and signs easily attract attention.

Before deciding on the size of your posters or signs, look around at storefronts and on bulletin boards and see if there is a common or maximum size. For instance, 11" × 14" may be popular, or you may be able to produce something larger. But be careful to avoid a poster or sign that is too large, since it will be ineffective if there are not many places to hang it.

Before any posters or signs go up, members of your organization should help prepare a comprehensive list of good places to put them. Such a list not only indicates where to put your posters or signs but also lets you know how many to produce. This list should include—but certainly not be limited to—businesses and stores that will allow your posters or signs to be displayed on their premises, other organizations in your community that will agree to help publicize your event, any public buildings that will permit your posters or signs to be displayed on their bulletin boards (e.g., community centers, churches, clubs, city hall, libraries, and schools), bulletin boards in multi-unit dwelling complexes (often in their laundry rooms), utility poles (check the legality of this, however, and be sure to remove them after the event is over), and any place where people gather or wait and will see your posters and signs. Posters and signs should be put up 2 to 4 weeks before the event. One week before the event try to return to all poster and sign locations to replace those that have been removed, destroyed, or defaced.

Table Tents

Table tents make excellent advertising pieces if you have access to enough good locations to display them. Most often seen on tables in restaurants, table tents include messages printed on pieces of cardboard that are folded like a tent so that they can be read from either side. If members of your organization can get local restaurants to keep your tents displayed on their tables for a few weeks before your event, then having them printed may be worthwhile. After all, people dining are likely to read these tiny billboards several times during the course of a meal.

Banners

Banners are effective, though expensive, ways of communicating a brief message to a large number of people. Since the message on a banner is necessarily short (because the print size is so large), a banner should only be used along with many other types of promotion. A banner serves only as a reminder about an event.

A local sign company can make or obtain banners to be hung temporarily across busy streets in your community. When your activity is an annual event, these banners can be used year after year.

At certain times of the year, when there are huge outdoor gatherings of people (e.g., for fairs, ball games, or parades), you might consider using an aerial banner attached to an airplane as a further way to promote your event. Like a street banner, an aerial banner serves only as a reminder. This type of banner is expensive, but it can be very effective. To learn about the costs in your area, contact your airport and ask about the service.

Specialties and Novelties

Specialty and novelty items can be used as publicity for an event (e.g., bumper stickers and buttons), as souvenirs at an event (e.g., key rings and pens), and as a way to build interest for the following year's event (e.g., T-shirts and hats). You can purchase all sorts of specialty and novelty items that can be uniquely imprinted for your event. These items are costly unless you order huge quantities—and even then the total price can be high because of the number.

Take great care in selecting an item that relates to your event. Possibilities include the following items: aerial pennants, balloons, books of matches, bumper stickers, buttons, coloring books, combs, emery boards, hats, key rings, litter bags, napkins, pencils, pens, potholders, rain bonnets, sewing kits, shopping bags, and T-shirts. These items can be purchased from local suppliers as listed in the Yellow Pages under "Advertising Specialties." Prices and delivery schedules may vary, so shop around.

If you decide to use such giveaways, be sure to determine how many items you can afford to order and reasonably distribute so that you do not overorder. Then order them early and get them distributed. During the selection process keep in mind that, like all printed material, specialties or novelties should be colorful, creative, simple, and consistent with other event graphics.

Invitations

An invitation can be an extremely important tool for selling a well-planned event. An invitation can be in the form of a brochure, a flier, a letter, or a specially printed piece. Whatever form an invitation takes, it can only be prepared after all of the elements of the event are in place (e.g., the name of the event, date, time, place, price, type of attire, use of proceeds, list of volunteer leaders, and list of supporters) so that this important information can be included in the invitation. A considerable amount of time is needed to design an invitation, have it printed, prepare it for mailing, and actually mail it far enough in advance of the event. Generally, at least 2 to 3 months are required. Note that some organizations send "save-the-date" postcards months in advance to the people who will eventually be receiving the actual invitation.

The appearance of a good invitation will vary from event to event and from market to market. For instance, a formal dinner-dance might require an elaborate, expensive invitation; a pancake breakfast might rely on only a colorful flier. In general, however, any invitation must be on quality paper stock, have an appropriate typeface, have excellent design, and be in an appealing color. All components of the invitation's appearance must be well coordinated.

Because invitations are expensive to produce, unless they are underwritten, they probably should not be too elaborate. After all, the purpose of an event is to raise money, and an organization may come across better if people feel that its expenses are being carefully watched. Also, the personal ticket-selling process is much more effective than fancy invitations for attracting guests.

Due to the overwhelming number of special event fund raisers that are characteristic of many communities, invitations are often unopened and thrown away. To prevent your invitation from being tossed, make sure that its appearance is too enticing to overlook. Also, consider hand-addressing instead of using labels, using colorful commemorative stamps, and putting only a return address—not the name of the organization—on the back of the mailing envelope so that the recipient must actually open the invitation to see who it is from.

An event that requires advance registration, such as a dinner-dance, should include a response card and envelope along with the invitation. The front of the response card should list the various ticket price options and note to whom the check should be made payable. The back of the response card can be used for people to list the names of other guests they would like to be seated with. Since the response card is part of an invitation to an event, do not use it to ask the potential supporter to do a variety of other activities for your organization. If presented with additional options, the person can easily avoid purchasing a ticket or making a contribution. By asking for the person's telephone number, you can follow up later with requests for additional involvement.

Use a self-addressed return envelope for the reply card and check. If your organization can afford it, pay for the return postage. Although this is more costly, it saves the supporters the time and effort of having to look for a stamp. If you cannot afford to pay for the return postage, remember that most people who send a contribution are willing to donate a stamp. As a sort of compromise, you might use business reply envelopes, for which the organization pays the postage, but suggest that the donor save the organization this cost by putting a stamp on the envelope. To use business reply envelopes, you will need to apply for and purchase a business reply permit through your main post office.

Obtain from printers competitive bids and timetables on invitation production. When ordering your invitations from the printer you select, request that the return envelopes, with your organization's return address printed on them, be delivered as soon as possible so that volunteers can address them. Insist on proofreading the invitation, response card, and envelopes before they are printed.

Personal invitations to events that rely on the advance purchase of high-priced tickets should be followed up with handwritten notes or phone calls, particularly from committee members who are friends of the people invited. Personal calls are particularly important and effective since it is difficult to refuse a friend who talks to you directly.

Tickets

Tickets that are purchased in advance of the event, such as dinner-dance, raffle, or concert tickets, should include the date, time, and place of the event so that they can serve as a reminder of these important facts. The ticket design should be consistent with the other printed materials associated with the event. Obtain competitive bids and timetables from printers on ticket production.

Program Books

Although they cannot be used to publicize an event, printed program books are an important feature of many events. They provide information and they raise funds. A program book can include an agenda of the event, information about your organization, a list of volunteers, a list of financial supporters, additional information particular to the event (e.g., a catalog of items at an auction or a biography of the honoree at a luncheon), and paid advertisements. Depending on the type of event, some organizations sell advertisements and produce printed materials other than program books. For example, at its annual pancake breakfast, one community group had placemats printed with advertisements. Another group produced memo pads to distribute as souvenirs at their luncheon. Numerous companies paid money to have their logos included on the sheets.

Fees from advertisements often pay for the production of a program book and even result in a profit for the organization. Ads can be solicited from businesses, retail stores, hotels, restaurants, vendors, suppliers, members, friends, and others. Because the circulation of a program book is limited to the guests attending the event, the commercial value of an ad is minimal. Advertisers mainly buy space as an act of goodwill toward your organization and the community.

Some organizations choose to solicit ads only from individuals or groups that pertain to the event. For example, one organization held an art auction and included in its exclusive program book ads only from galleries, auction houses, art dealers, museums, and art schools. No one wanted to be left out of this prestigious program book. Another organization featured ads only from clothing stores, boutiques, jewelry stores, cosmetic firms, and hair salons in its fashion-show program book.

Rather than ads, some program books include messages. People purchase space in the program book and communicate their messages in a manner appropriate for the event. For instance, a dignified, tasteful salute would go to the recipient of an award, while a congenial, witty salute would go to a person being roasted. These program books are especially enjoyable to read.

A special committee of volunteers who have good connections in the community should be formed to sell ads. They should make their contacts through the mail, over the telephone, or, preferably, in person. Consider giving each volunteer a goal and providing an incentive—such as a free ticket to the event—for reaching that goal.

The prices for ads depend on the size of the ad, (e.g., full page, half page, or quarter page), its location (e.g., ads on the inside covers or the back cover of a program book are generally more expensive than ads on inside pages since they offer the greatest exposure), what your printing costs will be, the type of event, and the going rate in your community. A contract should be given to all potential advertisers that includes the size and price of the ad, copy and artwork requirements, and the deadline for submission. All contracts should be signed and dated by the advertisers. Always send a copy of the ad and a thank-you note to all advertisers following the event.

Try not to solicit ads or messages from potential ticket buyers. After all, if the same person is approached to buy a table of tickets and an ad, that person is likely to take the ad, since the ad will probably be less expensive than the table.

It is expensive to design and print a program book. If you are not selling advertisements, then try to have the costs underwritten. Or at least seek expert volunteer assistance in putting the book together, and shop around for a printer who can do the best job at the lowest cost.

RESOURCES

Alberti, C. E., Macko, G. S., & Whitcomb, N. B. *Money-makers: A systematic approach to special events fund raising.* Ambler, PA: Whitcomb Associates, 1983, Supplement 2, pp. 1–18.

Ardman, P. & Ardman, H. *Woman's Day book of fund raising.* New York: St. Martin's Press, 1980, pp. 216–219.

Beatty, B. & Kirkpatrick, L. *The auction book.* Denver: Auction Press, 1984, pp. 78–83.

Berson, G. *Making a show of it: A guide to concert production.* Ukiah, CA: Redwood Records, 1980, pp. 65–69, 76–78.

Connors, T. D. *The nonprofit organization handbook.* New York: McGraw-Hill, 1980, pp. 5.80–5.85.

DeSoto, C. *For fun and funds: Creative fund-raising ideas for your organization.* West Nyack, NY: Parker Publishing Co., 1983, pp. 160–165.

Flanagan, J. *The grass roots fundraising book.* Chicago: Contemporary Books, Inc., 1982, pp. 242–244.

Gaby, P. V. & Gaby, D. M. *Nonprofit organization handbook.* Englewood Cliffs, NJ: Prentice-Hall, Inc., 1979, pp. 207–212.

Loykovich, J. Special events in the '80s: A case for marketing approach. *Fund Raising Management,* January 1985, pp. 32, 34.

National Council of Jewish Women, Inc., *The raiser's edge.* New York: National Council of Jewish Women, Inc., pp. 6–8.

Sheerin, M. *How to raise top dollars from special events.* New York: Public Service Materials Center, 1984, pp. 57–59, 98–105.

Chapter 8

IMPLEMENTING THE EVENT

IDENTIFYING KEYS TO SUCCESS

Planning is a crucial element of a fund-raising event, but unless ideas are properly carried out, you run the risk of limiting your success. Paying attention to details, taking corrective actions, making extraordinary efforts, maintaining cash control, and using a computer are all important keys to successfully implementing an event.

Pay Attention to Details

In implementing an event, as in planning one, attention to detail is crucial. The more that can be thought through in advance and the more problems that can be anticipated, the easier will be the implementation process. Keeping track of details can be done in different ways. For example, those responsible for major activities might want to keep special calendars and jot down names of people to call, letters to write, deadlines to meet, and future activities requiring follow-up. One of the best ways of scheduling your priorities is to make daily lists on your calendar in three columns: one is a must-do column, two is a desirable to do but could wait column, and three is a column of minor items. Often the minor items can take care of themselves. Occasionally, however, if they are not handled in time, the minor items can later become crises.

Another way of keeping track of details is with a timeline chart. The value of a timeline chart, as discussed in Chapter 2, is that it provides a

guide for what you need to do and when you need to do it. As time progresses, you will want to update and revise the chart.

Some events require a myriad of details to be aware of, especially on
the day of the event itself. A detailed checklist is essential in ensuring an
event's success; the more detailed, the better. One way of determining
these details is mentally to walk through the event. Pretend, for example,
that you are arriving at a dinner event. Consider what you would be exper-
iencing at the start of the evening, including these possibilities: parking the
car (valet parking); walking to the entrance (red carpet); hanging up coats
(coatroom); walking to the sign-in table; signing in; sitting at the table (table favors, room decoration, souvenirs), and viewing the speakers' table
(electrical outlets, working microphone, lectern adjustable to different
heights). Your mental picture will provide some guidance. People who
have previously worked on the event or on similar events will also be able
to provide the details necessary to make the actual evening go smoothly.
For added assurance, conduct a rehearsal the day before the event to see
that everything is working properly.

Take Corrective Action

In addition to paying attention to details, you must be able to take corrective action throughout the implementation phase. Despite the best planning efforts, some unpredictable implementation problems may arise. In
new ventures, especially, you cannot anticipate all occurrences or contin-
gencies. You have to be prepared to handle the unexpected. Two ingredients are essential in taking corrective action.

First, you need a good review and monitoring process to check and
recheck your implementation of tasks. If anything is not being carried out
properly or is not running on course, you must be aware of it. Second, you
need adequate time to rectify any situation. For instance, you cannot wait
until the last minute to determine if you are off target on your projected
ticket sales. You need to have periodic reviews of sales projections at predetermined points. If sales at the 3-week point are at $900 instead of the
projected $1,500, and if at 2 weeks prior they are at $2,500 instead of the
projected $4,000, you know you are in trouble. You can either lower your
expectations or, preferably, make special efforts to try to get back on target.

Make Extraordinary Efforts

Suppose you have done all you can to try to make your event a success, but you realize you are falling behind. For example, you have distributed your posters announcing the event, you have lined up stores to sell
tickets, and you have organized ticket sellers. But your sales are lagging behind your projections. Can you do more? Now is that moment of truth that

will spell the difference between an event that nets a modest income and one that is significantly successful. Some organizations, when they sense they are falling behind, have been known to have volunteers and staff spend days and nights on the phone soliciting potential customers. Others have reached out for customers by setting up special ticket booths at malls or in downtown areas. Some have made special efforts to contact people who owe them favors or to whom they will eventually owe favors. The common denominator of these extraordinary actions is that they were not planned to happen. They emerged out of the desperation of the situation, and they occurred because the organization members realized the event was in trouble and required corrective action. Be prepared to do all you can—and then be prepared to call upon those inner reserves of your staff and volunteers to do even more—in implementing your event.

Maintain Cash Control

You should pay very close attention to the way cash receipts are handled. While most of your volunteer workers are undoubtedly honest, your safest approach is to have a system of checks and balances where at least two volunteers are involved in every transaction. Depending on your particular situation, you may want to consider having two people be responsible for authorizing payments and signing checks. In any situation, arrange for frequent deposits of receipts and audit the books of your event.

Use a Computer

Keeping track of details can be made considerably easier with the use of the personal computer. Your organization can either buy one, lease one, borrow one from an expert who can show you how to use it, or contract with a computer service company for some of the following services: tracking ticket sales and indicating who is selling how many tickets and in what areas of the community; compiling mailing lists by geographic or demographic categories; printing repetitive letters with inserts of names, addresses, and sentences to make them more personal; tracking income and expenses on a budget sheet and answering "What if . . ." questions; and recording gifts and donations. The value of a good computer program is that it will save hours of volunteer time, as well as enable that time to be put to other uses.

ESTABLISHING A STRUCTURE

Form follows function. This advice—that before you establish your structure you must determine what functions you need to carry out—has long been used in the business community. Obviously, the idea can be readily adapted by nonprofit organizations. Simply stated, before you rush into creating committees, be clear about the tasks that need to be implemented. This principle of form following function means that no universal structure exists for all fund-raising events. The form your structure takes should emerge from your particular situation and grow out of the various activities you need to implement—not the other way around.

Determine the Role of the Board of Trustees

Trustees are responsible for developing the overall policies of the organization, for establishing the strategic plan, and for determining the budget. In addition, one of the primary purposes of trustees is to help in the raising of funds. Some organizations that strongly emphasize events convey, as part of the board of trustees recruitment process, the expectation that trustees will be helping with fund-raising activities, including events. Some even require that volunteers work on the organization's fund-raising events before being considered as trustee. Sometimes, if the event is repeated annually, trustees are purposely recruited because of their potential for making a contribution—for example, as seekers of corporate underwriting or as super organizers. On the other hand, some organizations are reluctant to make trusteeship conditional on helping with events for fear this may frighten some desirable people away. Often trustees are chosen to be on a board for a variety of reasons, and not all trustees join to raise funds or help with an event. You may want them for their general reputation in the community, their accounting or legal expertise, or for other reasons. So use your judgment about making board membership contingent upon involvement in an event.

Form a Fund-Raising Body

Many boards establish a fund-raising body or auxiliary council. If a number of events are to occur in the course of the year, this council in turn may be divided into special events committees. The key to the functioning of a fund-raising body is that its charge is well-defined regarding the expected results and time period within which it must operate. Moreover, the fund-raising body must be clear about when it can make autonomous decisions and when it must seek approval from the trustees. Finally, ground rules must be explicitly established about when it must coordinate its efforts with other units of the organization. For example, requests for corporate funding may need to be submitted to the development unit or publicity plans to the marketing unit of the organization to insure proper coordination.

Develop Well-Managed Committees

Well-managed committees have the advantages of increasing member loyalty and commitment to the organization, heightening motivation to implement plans that have been developed, dividing responsibilities so that tasks are shared, permitting pooling of experience and wisdom, and using members' talents and skills. Moreover, through the committee process you provide a continuity of organizational work. The ongoing structure helps to offset volunteer turnover.

Effectiveness and efficiency are the basis for well-managed committees. The following general guidelines can increase the effectiveness and efficiency of your committee structure:

Select a strong chairperson.

Select members on the basis of what you eventually want to accomplish. If your project is likely to be an event intended to draw more than 1,000 people, then your committee may consist of potential ticket-sellers who have a large number of contacts. If you want to attract corporate support, then your committee should have some members with corporate connections. If your project is intended to appeal to young adults, then you will want them represented on the committee. If you are not certain about what your event is likely to be, but want something different, then select people with a flair for creative and imaginative ideas. If the event is to appeal to a cross-section of the community, then you will want to have broad-based representation that includes, for example, unions, minorities, and business people. Hence, carefully select members on the basis of what you eventually want to achieve.

Delineate a set of planning objectives as discussed in Chapter 2. The well-managed committee knows what it wants specifically to accomplish.

Establish deadlines for each of the committee's major activities and tasks as discussed in Chapter 2. Time schedules push people to make the project a priority compared with other demands on their time.

Create an executive or steering committee, if a large group is involved. The group should meet frequently to exchange information and set overall plans for the event. The group should be limited to 10–15 people to facilitate discussion and decision making.

Note that not all work has to be carried out through the committee process. Often one or two highly responsible people can accomplish far more than a dozen vaguely committed volunteers. Sometimes speedy actions rather than long deliberations are required by the situation. Certainly, for some creative, entrepreneurial go-getters, the committee process can be frustrating and time-consuming.

Consider Special Structures

In keeping with the theme that form follows function, under some circumstances you may need to consider special structures. Sometimes these are ad hoc—they are created for a time-limited period to carry out a specific purpose and disband when their function is completed.

Example: You want to sponsor a large community festival and you need endorsements from various community institutions, such as political parties, unions, the chamber of commerce, and women's groups. You create a committee of 100 people who represent the support and endorsement of these and other organizations.

Example: You want to put on a major bazaar in your community, but you lack the people to implement it. You invite member organizations to rent booths. They participate as a coalition in the planning process while you remain in a coordinating role.

Example: You want to recruit participants from dance classes around the community for a dance-a-thon. You involve the instructors of each of these classes as an advisory committee in the planning of the event.

The common element of these examples is that, based on your analysis of what needs to be done, you have figured out a way of involving the appropriate people in these specially created structures.

DEVELOPING LEADERSHIP

The leadership of an event can often make the difference between mediocrity and a memorable and successful fund raiser. In developing leadership, consider the important qualities to seek in a leader, how to go about recruiting a chairperson, and the transfer of leadership.

Leadership Qualities

Leadership qualities are not easy to define because they generally emerge out of a particular situation with a particular group. Some people are leaders in one situation and followers in another. Still, there are certain leadership characteristics that contribute to the successful running of most events. Look for these qualities in potential leaders:

Enthusiasm. Leaders have a sense of excitement and zest for their groups and their projects. Leaders enjoy meeting the challenge of obstacles. They believe in what they are doing so that they can encourage others to share their enthusiasm and verve.

Ability to work well with people. Leaders make people feel good about the work they are doing for the cause. They are cheerleaders, giving much encouragement and a minimum amount of criticism. They recognize that volunteers work for "psychic pay," and they know that volunteers' primary rewards come in the form of genuine appreciation. They are willing to delegate responsibility and not try to do it all themselves. Leaders provide volunteers with a sense of belonging. They are willing to share their plans openly with volunteers and to be open to their suggestions. Leaders are enthusiastic about every idea—even if they have already thought of it. In short, leaders do not treat volunteers as objects to be manipulated but as people to be respected for their contributions. They inspire people to expend extra efforts. And they make people feel good about their participation by not being dogmatic and authoritarian.

Ability and willingness to give time. Because most events consume considerable time, leaders have high energy levels, are able and willing to work long hours, and do not feel overwhelmed with the enormity of the undertaking. Frequently, leaders are already involved in other leadership roles, so they have to be willing to make this new project a priority of their time.

Organizational Skills. Leaders visualize how all the pieces of a project mesh together and develop a work plan and timetable so that at all times there is an awareness of whether activities are on target. Leaders operate well under pressure and in a crisis atmosphere.

Willingness to take prudent risks. Leaders have an inner confidence that grows out of past achievements. They have gotten results before and know they can do so again. They realize that there is chance of failure, but they welcome the challenge of solving problems to prevent failure. They are willing to try new approaches and new ways of doing things if they think these innovations will improve the event. They have both the inner confidence that they can succeed with the event and the boldness to convince others—volunteers, donors, civic leaders—to join them in achieving their vision.

Dedication and commitment. These words connote the idea of getting the job done—whatever it takes. In addition to delegating and monitoring, some leaders take on tasks because, for various reasons, others cannot.

They are not afraid to take on the "grunt jobs"—getting a mailing out at 2 a.m. to meet a deadline, personally taking on ticket-selling responsibilities, helping to clean up. People respond to leaders who commit themselves to getting the task done at whatever cost.

Entrepreneurial approach. The most impressive leaders appear to operate as if they were running their own business. They care, they worry, and they act as if the event will affect their personal reputation. If necessary, they will work 12- and 14-hour days. They move quickly and expeditiously to troubleshoot and solve problems. In fact, once the process gets rolling and they are under time pressures, they can become impatient with meetings and processing decisions through committees.

In summary, leaders strive to achieve a proper balance between being sensitive to volunteers' needs and feelings on the one hand and, on the other hand, working to complete tasks in order to achieve success.

Recruitment of Leaders

Usually you will seek leadership for an event from within your organization. Sometimes, though, to obtain the best possible person, you may need to go outside your organization. The preferred way to recruit a chairperson is through personal contact. The least effective ways are to contact someone by letter or phone. If you are striving for the best candidate, make an appointment to see the individual personally. When making the call for an appointment, avoid telling the person why you want to meet, so the candidate does not turn you down over the phone. Explain that it is something important enough to justify lunch or an hour of the person's time. You can, of course, be refused face to face, but that is much more difficult, especially when the person calling upon your prospect is well respected and possibly someone to whom favors might be owed.

If you think that the candidate might accept but is still hesitant, consider these approaches:

> Stress that the person will have a chance to be associated with something meaningful and worthwhile.
>
> Emphasize that this is an important, visible assignment that will be well-appreciated in the community.
>
> Identify several other community leaders who are willing to work on the event and who would respond to the person's leadership.
>
> If lack of time is the person's concern, offer a list of specific, time-limited responsibilities. Indicate the availability of sufficient staff and volunteer backup.
>
> If the person is reluctant to accept sole responsibility, suggest that a co-chairperson be selected as your candidate's

first official act. In arranging for co-chairpersons, be careful that the two leaders do not shirk responsibilities by
expecting the other to perform. Ideally, the two should
have complementary skills.

As you contemplate your possible candidates, keep your list confiden-
tial. If you are then turned down by your first choice, you can proceed to
the next as if that person were your prime choice.

If you want to attract business support for your event, seek as a chairperson someone as high in the corporate structure as possible. But do not
despair if you cannot obtain a president or a chief executive officer. Look
for up-and-comers on the rise in their companies with a good reputation in
your community to chair your event.

Transfer of Leadership

In many instances, organizations do not have to undertake the recruitment of new leaders. They provide for an orderly transfer of leadership through a rotation process in which last year's vice-chairperson
becomes this year's chairperson, and the previous year's chairperson is
designated as an official adviser. This procedure works well for events that
are fairly complicated and require an apprenticeship. The special value of
building in the transfer of leadership is that the organization is not dependent on any one person year after year. By sharing leadership tasks and
establishing the orderly transfer of responsibilities, the group can avoid
leadership burnout or failure if the one and only leader suddenly is not
available. Of course, if events change annually, or if you require as the
head of your event a corporate official, then the leadership may have to be
new each year.

WORKING WITH VOLUNTEERS

You cannot put on an event without the enthusiastic commitment of
volunteers. Yet most potential volunteers are already overcommitted in
a variety of home, business, and civic activities, and you must compete
for their time. To attract and keep good volunteers, you must understand
what motivates them, know how to recruit them, match their assignments
and responsibilities, and devise approaches to sustain their motivation.

The Motivation to Volunteer

People volunteer for a variety of reasons, including the following: to
commit themselves unselfishly to a cause, to make new friends, to break
away from the humdrum routine of daily activities, to gain personal recog-

nition, to gain exposure to possible employment opportunities, to return a favor to another volunteer who supported their cause, and to comply with a request of the organization's leadership to fulfill a responsibility of membership. The point about this brief listing is that motivation is not one-dimensional. The recruiting of volunteers and keeping them will, in part, be affected by your assessment of what brings them to the organization in the first place.

Recruitment of Volunteers

A natural source of volunteers is from your own board of trustees and from your membership. These volunteers, presumably, are people who are highly invested in your organization and its cause.

You can also seek volunteers from companies that allow their employees release time to do community service work. Most companies are not eager to loan employees for large amounts of time, but many business, law, and accounting firms encourage employee participation.

Certain organizations exist in almost every community to provide volunteers. Most urban communities have community volunteer bureaus, volunteer action centers, or service organizations for retired persons. Check your Yellow Pages under "Social Services" or call your United Way. For more information on how to identify, recruit, and work with volunteers, contact the National Center for Citizen Involvement, 111 North 19th Street, Suite 500, Arlington, Virginia 22209, (703)276-0542 or the Association for Volunteer Administration, P.O. Box 4584, Boulder, Colorado 80306, (303)497-0238.

Depending on the event, service organizations can be another source of volunteers. Examples include street clubs, business organizations, and women's auxiliaries. This source can be especially helpful if the event will benefit a neighborhood or community and if the various organizations feel a sense of ownership and loyalty to the sponsoring agency.

Whatever the source, there is one best way to recruit volunteers: personal communications. If you do not know the person well, bring someone with you who does. PEOPLE RESPOND TO PEOPLE. If you are turned down, do not give the potential volunteer a difficult time. The person may be truly overcommitted or genuinely feel the lack of commitment to your request. Next year may be another opportunity.

Matching Assignments and Responsibilities

To be most effective in recruiting volunteers, it is necessary that you pinpoint how many volunteers you need for each function in the overall project, what they will do, and when they will be needed. If possible, each chairperson of an activity should complete a chart similar to the one below and submit it to the volunteer chairperson:

Request for Volunteers Chart (Partial)

Assignments	Responsible Person	Number of Volunteers Needed	Dates Volunteers Needed
Corporate Underwriting	N. Henderson	4	6/17–8/1
Ticket Sellers	D. Mikita	25	8/1–9/15
Publicity	B. Mosby	4	7/15–8/15
Arrangements	J. Sapacian	15	9/1–10/1

You obviously want to assign the most qualified people to get the job done. To make this proper match, you must have sufficient information about both your volunteers and your tasks.

You may want to write volunteer job descriptions so that volunteers will know precisely what is expected of them, by when their tasks must be completed, and to whom they will report. Sometimes average weekly hours or total hours are also identified. Many volunteers have full-time jobs and their time is precious. But by identifying segments of time they can take on manageable assignments. Hence, if at all possible, designate volunteer job descriptions in writing, including specific assignments that can be completed within a particular time frame.

Some organizations avoid providing specific job descriptions and anticipated hours for fear of frightening prospective volunteers away. After all, if volunteers know in advance all the demands that are likely to be made of them, they may not commit themselves. But once volunteers begin their work, the excitement and the challenge of their involvement may tap a reservoir of time and energy. This may be true in part, yet for the long-term credibility of the organization, the preferred method is to provide the assignments in a concise way with clear completion dates.

To determine what volunteers prefer to do, simply ask them. Identify the various assignments either verbally or in writing so that they can indicate their preferences. You may be surprised to learn that people with certain talents do not necessarily want to use these talents as a volunteer. For instance, the last thing a secretary may want to do is to type at night on a voluntary assignment. On the other hand, some volunteers may be very eager to apply their skills. Certain tasks may be boring to some people, but to others the tasks may be appealing. Some volunteers may be willing to help out during their lunch hours while others cannot do this but may be willing to spend weekends preparing for the event. So when asking people to volunteer, pinpoint what they will be doing.

Assume that the best volunteers are always going to be busy and very selective in the assignments they accept. The people who are attracted to your organization as volunteers are also attracted to other groups. Because their time and talents are in demand, it is imperative that you give them assignments that can be handled quickly and easily within their busy schedules. You need to convey that once the assignment is accepted, there will not be a flood of new responsibilities.

Although you will want to give volunteers an opportunity to determine what their contribution will be, you may have to steer them to other assignments—tactfully. Some people have exaggerated ideas of their skills, so do not let them volunteer for work you know they cannot handle.

Sustain Volunteer Motivation

Locating motivated persons, recruiting them, and assigning them responsibilities are significant efforts. But the job of working with volunteers cannot stop there. Considerable thought and energy must go into sustaining volunteer motivation; otherwise you run the risk of losing their efforts and enthusiasm. The success or failure of a fund-raising event is determined by the dedication and energy of volunteers who plan, organize, and execute the work. Keep in mind the following ways to sustain volunteer motivation:

Encouraging participation in planning. A well-accepted tenet of both business and nonprofit organizations is that people work harder to achieve the success of a project if they have participated in the decisions. In the development of events where only a few volunteers are involved, there is ample opportunity to participate in planning. Even when an event involves many volunteers, opportunities exist for people to convey their ideas. There are a myriad of decisions in which they can have the opportunity to express their thoughts. Although your steering committee may not accept all of them, you can convey that they are being taken seriously. Under some circumstances volunteers can play a very far-reaching role in decision making regarding such issues as how the proceeds from the event will be used. This participation in decisions fuels their enthusiasm. Volunteers must feel that they are genuine partners, truly sharing a mutual and worthwhile endeavor—not just "free help."

Providing authentic involvement. People usually develop a sense of loyalty and commitment to an organization when they are authentically involved and feel a sense of ownership and identification with the organization and its activities. The word "authentic" is used purposely because volunteers detect when they are given make-work assignments. If you plan a small-scale event requiring only 10 people, do not add 30 more for the sake of keeping volunteers busy. Do not mobilize an army of volunteers, particularly if you might need more extensive involvement later.

On the other hand, do not concentrate the work in the hands of too few people if more are needed. Sometimes the few doing the work think it is easier to handle everything on their own than to try to manage and monitor others. Then these few wonder why they feel so tired and overwhelmed. If people are not given responsibility, they will passively sit back and let others work. This is especially true if newer people are not being involved, since they can easily be made to feel useless if they are not given meaningful tasks to complete.

Promoting upward mobility. People like to know that if they work hard and show leadership ability, they will have opportunities to advance. For example, they may start out as an event committee member, chair a committee the next year, and serve as the chairperson of the event the following year. To some volunteers, promotion and a variety of experiences involving increasing responsibility are important.

Offering recognition. People like to be thanked and to have their efforts acknowledged publicly. Overt appreciation is one of the best ways to motivate volunteers. You can never say thank you too often. Committee chairpersons will get best results by making volunteers feel important and needed and that they are doing a significant job, no matter how menial. If, for example, a group of volunteers has spent six hours preparing a mailing, be sure to let them know what a vital role they are playing for the event.

Letters of recognition, special parties honoring volunteers before or after the event, or even gifts, are among the ways of conveying appreciation. Remember that a volunteer's reward is a sense of achievement and personal satisfaction. Make sure that the person receives large doses of both. Look for ways to feature contributions made by the volunteers.

Making the experience fun. To keep interest and motivation high, build in ways to make the volunteers' experience enjoyable. Do not schedule long, boring, nonessential meetings. Nothing kills enthusiasm quicker than disorganization and drift. Keep meetings short and to the point. Combine meetings with an opportunity for socializing. Organize group sessions at which members can work together, informally chat, and enjoy coffee and cake. On some occasions, involve spouses and other guests. Have drawings for small gifts. Arrange for volunteers to have special privileges, such as allowing them to shop one day in advance of the rummage sale or attending a pre-event cocktail party or dinner. In short, take time out to provide fun for your volunteers.

Communicating. Good communication involves a steady exchange of information between leaders and volunteers. Prior to the event, volunteers should be given a complete schedule pinpointing the place and time they will be working. If appropriate, offer orientation or training sessions for carrying out specific tasks. As a general procedure, anticipate problems that volunteers might encounter and possible solutions. Make certain that your volunteers know who to contact if they meet unexpected difficulties that they are unable to solve on their own. Print a list of all the committees and who is responsible for what tasks. Also, print a timetable so people can see how their tasks relate to the overall success of the event. Send postcards to remind volunteers of deadlines. Periodically arrange to have volunteers' progress monitored. They will generally be pleased that you consider their role important, and they will have a feeling of being accountable. If you determine that one or more members are not doing the job, diplomatically propose that they may have more to do than is reasonable. Given their circumstances, offer to find someone who will help. Transmit progress reports or newsletters so that there is public knowledge about efforts that are on target and efforts that are falling behind.

Caveats for Working with Volunteers

It is difficult to anticipate the many causes that can diminish volunteer involvement. But some of the more common "red flags" are these:

Hiring professional resource development staff.   Organizations that hire fund-raising staff may face a cost-benefit trade-off. On the one hand, such additional staff permit concentrated fund-raising efforts, especially for direct solicitation and endowment campaigns. On the other hand, hiring staff may reduce volunteer efforts. Volunteers may see the paid person taking on the drudgery of mailings, phone contacts, and other activities. Staff have to resist this and see their function primarily as coordinating and mobilizing volunteer efforts.

Penny-pinching.   There exists an understandable tendency to want to do everything as inexpensively as possible. This offer leads to extensive use of volunteers. Sometimes, however, you may find that a better use of resources is to pay for services, thereby avoiding unnecessary burnout of your volunteers. Your assessment of your volunteers and the demands of the situation may, for example, result in your using a computerized mail service instead of having volunteers manually process several thousand invitations. Or secretarial service may be worth the costs. Carefully weigh the advantages of purchasing services with the financial demands these may present to you.

Resistance.   On some occasions volunteers may lack enthusiasm about participating in a fund-raising event; this may be symptomatic of deeper problems with the organization. For example, volunteers may be resistant because they see the leadership of the organization as unnecessarily autocratic, because the cause that is benefiting from the fund-raising event is controversial or is not viewed as significant, or for other reasons. The best advice for this situation is to delay the event until there is resolution of the underlying problems. If people are resistant, they are conveying an important message that must be heard. Generally, it is better to abort your event efforts than to go ahead with what might end up as a fiasco.

In summary, consider the following questions in assessing volunteer motivation:

> Do you consider what motivates your volunteers?
>
> Do you involve volunteers in planning the event and take their ideas seriously?
>
> Do you involve them in meaningful activities, trying to match their interests and talents with the tasks that need to be done?
>
> Do you provide them with new and challenging opportunities?
>
> Do they know in clear detail what is expected of them?
>
> Do you give them sincere praise and recognition, realizing that this is their "psychic pay?"
>
> Do you try to liven up their experience with fun activities, including refreshments, interesting settings, etc.?
>
> Do they have assignments in which they feel a real sense of accomplishment?
>
> Do you provide constant communication of progress?
>
> Do you avoid assigning too many tasks to one person to prevent overload?

DETERMINING THE ROLE OF STAFF

Most organizations sponsoring events rely almost entirely on volunteers. Some organizations, of course, do rely to some limited extent on staff involvement. Consider the following observations about staff participation in the event process:

Professional staff hired primarily for resource development are more likely to concentrate on the more lucrative fund-raising efforts, such as direct solicitation and planned giving. Events frequently are considered a secondary function.

One of the major values of staff is that of providing continuity over a period of several years. When staff members have been involved in events (even peripherally) over several years, they can often recall previous mistakes and build on earlier experiences.

The role of staff should be to provide limited consultation and to perform certain tasks that volunteers may be reluctant to do, such as taking minutes and preparing thank-you letters in the chairperson's name. Of course, organizing volunteers can entail tremendous staff time and energy.

Staff must restrain themselves from taking over the chairperson's role and avoid doing tasks that volunteers could do. The role of staff is to encourage volunteers to do their jobs, and volunteers should be the ones to receive credit for a successful event—not staff. It is important that staff develop the conviction that the ownership, and therefore the responsibility, for the event reside with the volunteers.

USING CONSULTANTS

The cost of hiring a consultant should be built into your event budget if you think the expenditure will help you achieve higher income and have a more successful event. Consider hiring a consultant for the following reasons:

> The event is big enough to warrant paying a consultant's fee.
>
> You lack skilled expertise in the staff or volunteers.
>
> You may not have carried out a particular event previously or were dissatisfied with earlier results.
>
> Volunteer assistance is very limited and you need a powerhouse person to identify assignments and lead people to carry them out.
>
> A consultant has the know-how to negotiate better arrangements regarding publicity, catering, music, and other matters.
>
> Your organization does not want to be diverted from its main activities.
>
> A consultant, based on previous contacts, can add names to your mailing list for invitations and provide other services you could not otherwise obtain.

If you decide to hire one, contact potential consultants as soon as possible to discuss your needs. In talking to a consultant, you should try to be explicit about your expectations and about the strengths and weaknesses of your organization. Avoid seeking a consultant to bail you out of a desperate financial situation.

The following are ways in which you can involve a consultant:

One-time exploratory consultation. The purpose is to determine whether a match exists between your objectives and the talents of the consultant. Be candid about your expectations. Usually consultants will not charge a fee for a one-time exploratory meeting.

Feasibility analysis. The consultant devotes 3 to 4 days to determine the feasibility of the proposed event. The analysis includes the commitment of volunteers to work on the event, projections of income and expenses, and preliminary plans for implementation. An hourly rate or flat fee is charged.

Strategic consulting. Hired on a retainer basis, the consultant commits to so many hours or days over a period of several months. The consultant attends strategy meetings and advises on key issues, such as ticket prices, segmenting the market, maximizing profits, and implementing plans.

Implementation consulting. The consultant is involved in all aspects of the event from beginning to end. The consultant works very closely with the chairperson and, if mutually agreed upon, functions as a quasi-chairperson by setting meeting agendas or even chairing meetings and delegating responsibilities. The consultant is expected to do considerable prodding of volunteers and staff to do their jobs. The consultant walks a fine line between performing as a chairperson and helping the chairperson do the job.

Before you hire a consultant, keep in mind the following considerations:

> Check out references to determine the consultant's ability to perform and to be accurate about income and expense projections. You want to know that you are dealing with someone who is realistic and is not overselling.

> Determine if the consultant is overextended. Most consultants cannot take on more than two or three major events and two smaller projects in a year. A good consultant will begin a major project at least 8 months in advance.

> Clarify the consultant's relationship to staff and volunteers. Typically, you want someone who, with your chairperson, is able to delegate assignments and can then oversee that tasks are carried out in a positive and noncritical fashion.

> Select a consultant who has creative ideas but who is willing to listen and to defer to others—someone who is articulate but does not need to be the center of attention.

To avoid later misunderstandings, a contract with the consultant should be developed that specifies what is to be done, by whom, by what date, and at what cost. Agree on fees and reimbursement of expenses, such as travel, meals, and supplies. Select a date when both parties will assess the progress made or not made (this is the time when the contract can be changed or terminated). And state the desired result against which the consultant will be evaluated. Have an attorney review the contract before signing it.

A consultant's fee depends on the anticipated size of the event, the number of people attending, the net amount to be raised, and the time commitment. Some consultants charge a flat fee, while others charge a fee that is based upon hours or days worked up to an agreed-upon maximum. It is unethical for a consultant to base the fee on a percentage of the monies raised. This is because a percentage might cause the consultant to push too hard to achieve a financial goal and in the process not keep the best interests of the organization in mind. To cut down on the costs of hiring a consultant, you might hire someone who is just starting out as a consultant. Also, you might pay less for free-lance consultants than for those who work for a firm, because of lower overhead costs.

If you do not think you can afford to hire a consultant, there are ways to obtain free consultation. For instance, you can contact your local United Way to determine if it sponsors a Management Assistance Program (MAP) in your community. Usually you do not have to be a United Way agency to obtain free fund-raising consultation services. If MAP does not already have a pool of volunteer professionals, ask them to find someone who has put on an event similar to what you have in mind. Also, you can directly contact agencies that have development staff, such as hospitals, universities, health organizations, and large voluntary agencies. You will find them willing to offer suggestions, particularly if you are reaching out to a different constituency.

MOPPING UP

When the event is over, there is still plenty of work to be done. Mopping up entails paying bills, preparing detailed records, expressing appreciation, and evaluating results.

Pay Your Bills

Paying your bills is one of the most obvious activities you have to do when the fund-raising event is over. Do not delay this important task. Your vendors depend upon your prompt payment, and because you may be seeking their business at some future time, you do not want to have the reputation for being a late payer.

Prepare Detailed Records

Prepare detailed records of the event as a guide for the next time the event is offered. These records should include complete and precise organizational details regarding such matters as the number of volunteers, organizational structure, comparison of actual expenditures and income with budgeted projections, list of supplies, and schedule of activities.

The outgoing chairperson should take responsibility for providing updated information on committee chairpersons and members, businesses that donated goods and services, volunteers with special skills, mailing lists, and people with special connections. All these materials should be organized in a notebook or folder. Duplicate copies should be made, and a permanent copy should be locked in a file to ensure that records are not lost.

As part of your record preparation, identify people who attended the event but are not already members of your organization. Have their names and addresses added to card files or, preferably, to a computerized mailing list so they can be advised of future events, solicited for memberships, and informed of organization activities.

Express Appreciation

Immediately after the event, chairpersons of each unit should be asked to write thank-you letters to their volunteers. Writing prompt and personal thank-you notes is one of the most important activities you can do. Do not procrastinate. Remember, appreciation is the "psychic pay" for your volunteers. Send thank-you letters to all those who have donated their services and supported the event. Contributors who did not attend should receive a copy of the printed program. Include with it a tax exemption certificate, indicating the financial donation.

If you have to send a large number of personalized thank-you letters, an inexpensive, fast, and error-free approach is called the print and fill-in method. You type the body of the letter on a plain sheet of paper, use a copy machine to reproduce it on your letterhead, and then fill in the individual's name, address, and salutation. If you do not have your own copy machine, take the job to an offset printer. Of course, if you have access to word processing equipment, you can arrange to have each letter individually typed with an inserted sentence or two reflecting the particular individual's contribution. If you are unable to individualize your letters and must send a form letter, then at least add a personalized, handwritten note to each.

Evaluate the Results

Review the event as soon after it takes place as possible. The longer you delay, the less vivid will be your memories and impressions. Review

what happened in an objective, frank manner. Try to avoid individual ac-
cusations. Invite ideas on how problems can be dealt with the next time.
Your primary approach is to elicit ideas for improvement and determine if
mistakes or miscalculations are correctable. Ask for ideas for new activities.

If the organization has previously laid the groundwork by setting objectives and determining action plans, activities, and tasks, then evaluating
results will occur more easily and with greater sophistication. The evaluation process should consist of two parts: monitoring tasks and assessing
the achievements of objectives.

Through a monitoring process you can determine whether and to
what extent tasks were carried out as planned. Below are some of the questions to ask:

> Should the timetable have been altered to permit an earlier
> start and better sequencing of tasks?
>
> Were there sufficient funding resources and volunteers to
> do the job?
>
> Did the expected expenditures for tasks match the budget
> projections? If not, what are the explanations for the dis-
> crepancies?
>
> Did all the committees function to accomplish what they
> were supposed to?
>
> Was there a proper number of volunteers assigned to
> tasks? Can imbalances (e.g., too many tasks for some
> persons; too few for others) be identified?

These kinds of questions will help you review your ability to implement the activities and tasks that you had planned. If you detect deficien-
cies, you can determine what remedies you will take next year.

As stressed in Chapter 2, setting both financ1al and nonfinancial objectives is crucial because these become the standards against which you
can measure results following the event. In assessing the results, it is possible that you might conclude your event was partially successful and should
be repeated, even though you did not achieve your financial objectives.
Suppose, for example, you had hoped to raise $5,000 net profit but only
raised $2,000. If your primary objective was financial, then you would not
consider the event a success. But if you had determined you wanted the
event to achieve greater organizational visibility, generate member enthusiasm, and identify potential givers, then, though the financial objective
fell short, the event might be considered partially successful.

If the organization did achieve its financial objectives, these questions
should be asked:

Were the objectives set too low? Given what you now know about the response to the event, should higher objectives be established next year—or do you think you have reached a plateau?

Although the financial objective was achieved, were other important nonfinancial objectives accomplished as well? If people generally seemed bored, if demands on volunteers were too exhausting, if the hope for good public relations was not fulfilled, then these factors may be sufficient to force you to reconsider the event in the following year.

Do the results reflect that the volunteer time and effort and the expenses incurred were worth the results? Consider the following examples:

You rented five telephones costing $300 to make calls to encourage increased attendance. But you calculate only $700 more in ticket sales was raised toward the total income of $2,200. Was the additional expenditure for the telephones worthwhile?

You felt fortunate in being able to have a celebrity for your event. But since the fee was so high and you only sold 70 percent of your tickets, your expenses just about matched your income. Would you hire as popular—and as expensive—a star next year?

You held a party in a lovely park. The setting attracted a good crowd, but your expenses turned out to be astronomical because you had added costs of electricity, portable bathrooms, and bus transportation from parking lots. Was the gross profit of $12,000 worth the $8,000 in expenditures?

You decided to add a raffle to your dinner dance, but the top prize of a special trip, which you obtained at a discount, cost you $2,400. By adding $2,400 in costs and not increasing the ticket price of $30, you required an additional 80 people above what you would otherwise have in attendance. But you calculate after the event that although you had sufficient attendance, only 60 of the additional people attended because of the raffle. Was the extra expense of the raffle prize worthwhile?

Hence, it is possible to be successful in achieving the general financial objective and still want to alter the event or seek a different one based on other considerations.

If the event did not achieve its financial objective, these questions should be asked:

Was the financial objective set unreasonably high? Perhaps this was a first-time event and you "guesstimated" incorrectly. Perhaps there were unforeseen and unique circumstances that were unpredictable.

Were adequate resources available to accomplish the event? Were there enough ticket sellers, backup staff, and up-front money?

Was the timetable appropriate? Would an earlier start-up time ensure better results? Could the tasks be scheduled better?

Although the financial objective was not achieved, were other equally important, nonfinancial objectives accomplished? This is perhaps the most difficult assessment to make. Frequently, groups that do not achieve their financial objectives rationalize that the good public relations, the esprit de corps of volunteers, the identification of new members, or the leadership development compensate for the poor financial results. In fact, the achievement of these and other objectives may be sufficient to overcome the limited financial results. Only you and your group can make that highly subjective assessment.

The review of an event's success, partial success, or failure provides a springboard for further decision making. You can use this opportunity to determine what changes you want to consider for the future. Perhaps you need to rethink whether events are a preferred method of fund raising over other possible alternatives. Perhaps you may want to modify your objectives in light of this experience. Perhaps the way you organize and the timetable you establish need to be modified. Through this review you are in a position to learn from your experiences, to consider revisions, and then to take corrective action. This willingness to base future decisions on a critical review of changing circumstances is central to your decision-making process.

RESOURCES

Ardman, P. & Ardman, H. *Woman's Day book of fund raising.* New York: St. Martin's Press, 1980, pp. 53–57, 228–229.

Brody, R. *Problem solving: Concepts and methods for community organizations.* New York: Human Sciences Press, 1982, Chapters 3 & 9.

DeSoto, C. *For fun and funds: Creative fund-raising ideas for your organization.* New York: Parker Publishing Co., 1983, p. 202.

Drotning, P. T. *500 ways for small charities to raise money.* Chicago: Contemporary Books, Inc., 1979, pp. 4–6, 24–31, 54–55, 73, 147.

Flanagan, J. *The grass roots fundraising book.* Chicago: Contemporary Books, 1982, pp. 9, 59, 63–66.

Fottler, M. D. & Fottler, C. A. The management of volunteers in nonprofit organizations. *The Nonprofit World Report*, September–October 1984, pp. 19–20.

Gaby, P. V. & Gaby, D. M. *Nonprofit organization handbook* (Englewood Cliffs, NJ: Prentice-Hall, Inc., 1979), p. 108.

Honig, L. The cost of people—Evaluating fundraising events. *Grassroots Fundraising Journal*, October 1983.

London, M. Effective use of volunteers: Who, why, when and how. *Fund Raising Management*, August 1985, pp. 18, 20.

Lord, J. G. Thirty-five essentials every trustee should know. *The raising of money.* Cleveland, OH: Third Sector Press, 1983.

Lovelock, C. H. & Weinberg, C. B. *Marketing for public and nonprofit managers.* New York: John Wiley & Sons, 1984, p. 167–170.

Musselman, V. W. *Money raising activities for community groups.* New York: Association Press, 1969, pp. 22, 23.

Pritchard, J. H. *There's plenty of money for nonprofit groups willing to earn their shares—How to do it successfully*. Phoenix: Cornucopia Publications, 1984, pp. 20–22, 29, 33–34, 46–60, 70–76.

Raebel, J. Volunteers from business. *The Grantsmanship Center Reprint Series on Corporate Funding*, 1980, pp. 3–11.

Schleck, R. S. Building a quality board. *Nonprofit World*, September–October 1985.

Schneiter, P. H. & Nelson, D. T. *The thirteen most common fund-raising mistakes and how to avoid them*. Washington D.C.: Taft Corporation, 1982, pp. 54–58.

Sheerin, M. *How to raise top dollars from special events*. New York: Public Service Materials Center, 1984, pp. 13, 14, 19, 29, 34–35, 46, 48.

Strawhecker, P. The process of developing innovation and leadership. *Fund Raising Management*, March 1985, pp. 28, 32.

Swanson, A. *Building a better board: A guide to effective leadership*, Washington, D.C.: Taft Corporation, 1984.

SUMMARY OF 25 MAJOR
STRATEGIC POINTS

1. Fit the fund-raising event within an overall strategic plan so that the event complements other fund-raising activities.
2. Establish both financial and non-financial objectives.
3. Think creatively and uncritically about a variety of event possibilities, and then conduct a feasibility analysis to narrow your choices.
4. Use a market-oriented approach in selecting your event: Determine to what audience or customers you are trying to appeal.
5. Engage in comprehensive and careful planning.
6. Your cause is important, especially to your supporters, but it is a secondary reason for most people attending the event.
7. Even successful events can lose their appeal over time; be prepared to modify.
8. Put sizzle and zest in your event by giving old ideas a new twist, holding the event in a unique place, conducting pre-event activities, or selecting an appealing theme.
9. Prepare a contingency plan in case something goes wrong.
10. Make clear to your contributors what portion of their donation can be considered a charitable gift and what portion is a nondeductible purchase of goods or services.
11. Be aware that both internal and external competition are quite possible.
12. Keep accurate records.

13. Base pricing decisions on profit expectations, competition, and how customers perceive the value of goods or services received.

14. Consider whether you should penetrate your existing market, attract new market segments, alter your event, or diversify through both new events and new markets.

15. Consider ways to increase income from an event by establishing different ticket price categories.

16. Be committed to spending as little as possible on expenses.

17. Seek corporate funding, but do not become unduly dependent on it.

18. Develop a promotions plan.

19. Form follows function: Structure your committees to fit the event.

20. Seek leaders who have these qualities: enthusiasm, the ability to work well with people, the willingness to commit sufficient time, organizational skills, the willingness to take prudent risks, a strong dedication, and an entrepreneurial approach.

21. Understand and build upon the various motivations of volunteers.

22. PEOPLE SELL TO PEOPLE.

23. Pay attention to details in implementing the event.

24. Be prepared to take corrective actions and allow enough time to exert extraordinary efforts when mistakes or unanticipated situations occur.

25. Evaluate your results to determine what modifications, if any, you would make next time.

PART II

PROGRAMS FOR SUCCESS

INTRODUCTION TO PROGRAMS

This part of the book is divided into five chapters that contain 21 categories of fund-raising events. Chapter 9, *Communitywide Events*, discusses fairs, sales, shows and exhibits, tours, and products and services. Chapter 10, *Competition Events*, covers contests and games, pledge events, sports competitions, and sports tournaments. Chapter 11, *Entertainment Events*, describes local productions, professional productions, professional sponsorships, and special performances. Chapter 12, *Gala Events*, highlights auctions, benefits, dinners, luncheons, breakfasts, and parties. Chapter 13, *Gambling Events*, focuses on bingo, casino nights, nights at the races, and raffles.

All of these events offer the following advantages:

They have significant profit-making potential.

They are adaptable to almost any organization and its level of resources, although the magnitude of the event may vary.

They can attract a good deal of free publicity if the organization seeks coverage, thereby providing valuable visibility and excellent exposure.

They offer all interested members of the organization the opportunity to volunteer their efforts.

They can evolve into annual events if they are successfully presented the first time—attracting increased publicity, attendance, and profits each year as the expertise of the organization and the excellent reputation of the event grow together.

These events also entail a number of cautions:

> They are extremely ambitious undertakings that require careful planning and an enormous amount of very detailed work. Therefore, an organization that is a novice in planning any of these events must be able to devote a considerable amount of preparation time to the event.

> They require significant volunteer involvement in addition to staff time.

> They may be very similar to other frequent or pre-claimed events in your community that already compete with one another. Some communities are saturated with certain types of events, and there may not be room for yet another one unless its theme is new or it is uniquely presented.

The time frame for planning, promoting, and implementing these events ranges from 2 to 12 months, depending on the particular event, the organization's experience in presenting it, and the organization's available resources. To determine the time frame for a specific event, it is necessary to develop an activities list and prepare a timeline chart, as discussed in Chapter 2. Also, seek advice from people who have had experience in planning similar events.

Each of these events requires the selection of an individual to function as the event chairperson. The major responsibilities of an event chairperson include the following: Plan meetings, prepare agendas, identify decision-making issues, and distribute materials; conduct meetings firmly but flexibly, keeping the discussion on track; define objectives and tasks for every committee by meeting with each committee chairperson to identify responsibilities and expectations; oversee that costs are held within the budget; keep the rest of the organization informed of the event; and provide troubleshooting assistance to those who need backup.

In addition to the event chairperson, other volunteer leaders are necessary to successfully plan and implement an event. Most events will require the leadership of volunteers to handle arrangements, acquisitions, printed materials, promotions, the program agenda, reservations, special features, sponsorship and underwriting, ticket selling, financial matters, and volunteer coordination. Of course, not every event will have to fill all of these leadership roles, while some events may require additional roles. Consider the following leadership areas in determining which volunteers are needed for a particular event:

Arrangements. Responsibilities of the arrangements chairperson include securing a location for an event, determining the layout for the event, renting all necessary equipment and supplies, arranging for lighting and sound systems, hiring security, and overseeing cleanup. Depending on the nature of the event, the arrangements chairperson may also work with a caterer, decorator, or other professionals.

Acquisitions. The solicitation, contracting, pickup, and storage of items (e.g., for an auction or rummage sale) should be handled by the acquisitions chairperson. Obtaining prizes for an event is another responsibility of this volunteer leader.

Printed materials. The design and distribution of printed materials for an event are the responsibilities of this volunteer leader. As discussed in Chapter 7, printed materials include promotional pieces (e.g., brochures, fliers, and posters) as well as invitations, tickets, and program books.

Promotions. The promotions chairperson or communications coordinator, as described in Chapter 6, organizes all promotions—from news/public affairs coverage to advertising—for the event.

Program agenda. Responsibilities of the program agenda chairperson include developing the content of an event and making all of the necessary arrangements—from hiring a speaker, to finding entertainment, to selecting a master of ceremonies.

Reservations. Taking advance reservations, arranging seating plans, and sending tickets through the mail are the major responsibilities of the reservations chairperson.

Special features. Responsibilities of the special features chairperson involve organizing any additional activities that are included in the event, from a refreshment stand to a pre-event cocktail party.

Sponsorship and underwriting. Responsibilities of the sponsorship and underwriting chairperson include actively contacting corporations, merchants, and others who might be willing to make contributions to the event.

Ticket selling. The organization and supervision of the sale of individual and/or table tickets is the responsibility of the ticket-selling chairperson. Depending on the type of event, tickets can be sold in advance, at the event, or both.

Financial matters.   The treasurer or financial matters chairperson of the event plans the budget and keeps track of all expenses and income. When monetary transactions are required at the event itself (e.g., at an auction or a fair), this volunteer leader must supervise those activities as well. Financial matters that must be dealt with following the event (e.g., paying bills) are also this person's responsibility.

Volunteer coordination.   Committees must have sufficient volunteers to carry out their activities. The volunteer coordinator recruits volunteers and assigns them to committees according to the volunteers' interests and skills.

All of the volunteer leaders involved in an event should form a steering committee that meets regularly.

You may choose to have an honorary chairperson—in addition to the working chairperson—to add prestige to your event. In selecting the best person for this role, keep in mind that the honorary chairperson should be a well-known community leader, able to meet with the steering committee at least once before plans are announced, willing to write necessary letters on the honorary chairperson's own business or personal stationery, and willing to review certain materials, including letters that go out in the honorary chairperson's name, the final financial statement, and the final report. Your organization may wish to create a small group of honorary co-chairpersons who will lend their names to the event.

Although the activities involved in planning and implementing each of these events vary, certain activities are common to all of them. These pertain to developing a name and theme for an event and choosing a location.

A name and theme should be chosen to give an event a unique identity that, if possible, somehow relates to the organization and its cause. For instance, one benefit that was planned to aid the renovation of an entertainment complex and held during a Memorial Day weekend was called *A Star-Spangled Spectacular*. Try to develop an exciting name and theme that will make the event unique and enticing to your intended audience, thereby increasing the event's likelihood of being a success. Then carry out the name and theme through the publicity and advertising, invitations, decorations, menu, music, entertainment, and dress of those attending.

Note that many organizations use the same name and theme year after year. For example, one organization's annual flea market is call *Serendipity*, which refers to the ability to discover valuable or desirable items by accident. Other organizations use the same name every year with a different theme. For instance, although the name of one zoo's annual auction is always *Zippity Zoo Doo*, the theme is determined according to which zoo project or exhibit will benefit from that year's auction proceeds. Some organizations select a different name and theme for each event, as in *Three-Ring*

Fling, which was the name given to an art organization's annual party whose theme that particular year was a three-ring circus.

When choosing a location for an event, consider the following factors:

Size—The location must be able to accommodate all of the features of the event and its guests.

Accessibility—The location should be easily accessible to volunteers and guests, including handicapped persons.

Costs—Determine the rental fees, parking costs, tipping requirements, union labor charges, and other expenses.

Flexibility—The owner or manager of the facility should be accommodating and easy to work with. A flexible schedule for setup and cleanup, permission to select your own caterer or other workers, and the ability to use your own volunteers in any capacity are desirable factors.

Novelty—People like to attend events that are held in unusual or new locations, such as shopping malls, museums, zoos, penthouses, corporate headquarters, new buildings, mansions, and warehouses. Keep in mind that a novel location can lead to the creation of the event's theme and assist in attracting underwriting for the event.

Practicality—The location should offer sufficient parking, good acoustics and lighting, and other necessary features that are specific to the event, such as kitchen facilities for a dinner or a dance floor for a party.

If possible, try to obtain the use of a location for free—as a tax deductible contribution from its owner or manager.

Be sure to check with your county clerk to make sure that zoning laws do not prohibit the event from being held at the location you select. Then contact your local fire department to determine the crowd capacity of the location and its safety regulations. Also talk to your local police department to see whether certain licenses and permits are required to hold the event there. In addition, consult with your organization's insurance agent to find out if liability insurance must be purchased for the event.

In addition to developing a name and theme for an event and choosing a location, numerous activities are involved in planning and implementing a particular event. An overview of these activities is provided in each section. For the first-time organizer of an event, more detailed information and sample materials will be needed. Refer to the resources listed at the end of each chapter for further assistance.

Chapter 9

COMMUNITYWIDE EVENTS

FAIRS

A fair is a local celebration that includes a potpourri of games and contests, foods and beverages, entertainment, and rides. Money can be raised at a fair through general admissions fees and ticket sales for individual activities. A fair is also referred to as a festival or carnival.

Special Advantages

In addition to the general advantages listed in the Introduction to Programs, a fair offers the following special advantages:

> The entire community—people of all ages and at all income levels—can show its support for your organization by attending a fair.

> A fair can attract people who may have no interest in your organization but want to participate for their own amusement. Of course, visitors from surrounding areas who do attend will have the opportunity to learn about your organization and community.

> This type of event can generate spontaneous business from people who just happen to be passing by.

Special Cautions

Keeping in mind the general cautions listed in the Introduction to Programs, the following special cautions about a fair should be carefully considered as well:

A huge amount of space is generally required for a fair.

Many of the costs that a fair entails must be paid for up-front.

The ability to promote a fair throughout the entire community is necessary so that as many people as possible become aware of the event.

To make a fair a success, large crowds are necessary, since each person in attendance probably will not spend a significant amount of money at the event.

Large crowds sometimes include rowdy groups. Your organization must be willing and able to deal with this situation if it occurs.

Good weather is an important ingredient for the success of a fair.

Expenses

A fair can entail the following expenses for your organization: site rental fee—rental fees for tents, booths, tables, chairs, portable restrooms, cooler trucks, trash compactors, and other equipment—sound and lighting system rental fees—electrical power costs—technicians' fees—labor fees—storage costs—purchase of food, beverages, and refreshment supplies—entertainment fees—purchase of merchandise for sale and for prizes—purchase of decorations—purchase of licenses and permits—purchase of liability insurance—security costs—printing costs—postage costs—promotion costs. Donations and discounts should be sought for these expenses, many of which require up-front payment.

Volunteer Requirements

The volunteer leaders needed to plan and run a fair include the event chairperson, arrangements chairperson, acquisitions chairperson, printed materials chairperson, promotions chairperson, ticket-selling chairperson, treasurer, and volunteer coordinator. Their roles are described in the Introduction to Programs. In addition, the following volunteer leaders are needed:

theme chairperson—works on the theme, color scheme, and decorations for the fair so that the event will have a planned, appealing, unified appearance;

booths chairperson—selects the types of booths, assigns them to the appropriate persons, and supervises their operation;

food and beverage chairperson—decides what foods and beverages will be sold, who will sell them, and where they will be sold—supervises the donation, purchase, cooking, and serving of food—oversees the maintenance of health and safety standards—handles the purchase or rental of necessary equipment;

entertainment chairperson—secures all entertainment that will be included in the event—from music, to jugglers, to magic shows, to cooking demonstrations;

contests and games chairperson—arranges all contests and games to be featured at the fair;

special services chairperson—sets up areas for first aid, lost and found, and information at the fair—arranges for traffic police and security;

cleanup chairperson—makes sure that the festival site is left in as good condition as possible.

In addition to these volunteer leaders, many, many more volunteers are needed to help plan and run the fair, including a reserve of volunteers to help in booths that need additional assistance or replacements. The exact number of volunteers, of course, will depend on the size and scope of your event and the number of time shifts that need to be covered.

Selecting a Time

Fairs are often scheduled during the summer so that they can be held outdoors in warm, clear weather. Some organizations choose to hold their fairs during other seasons, though. For example, a winter festival that features such outdoor activities as ice-skating competitions, snowman-building contests, and cross-country skiing might be very successful. Regardless of the season, weekends will attract the largest audience to a fair.

If you are holding an outdoor fair and fear that rain could turn the event into a disaster, consider selecting an alternate date in case of rain. To avoid a potentially devastating situation, you might also decide to house the event in tents or to pay for rain insurance (check with your insurance agency about purchasing rain insurance).

Choosing a Site

The site for a fair must be able to bear the traffic of the workers and their vehicles as well as the general public. It must be able to accommodate all of the booths and activities that you want to feature. It must have room so that people can walk around, participate in the event, and talk to friends. And it must have sufficient seating space for people to eat and rest.

An outdoor site for a fair might be a schoolyard, athletic field, park, churchyard, or parking lot. An indoor site might be a school or civic auditorium, church hall, community center, or convention center.

Designing the Layout

The following points should be considered in designing the layout for a fair:

> To avoid monotony, set up groupings of booths that vary in size, shape, and decoration.
>
> Do not put similar types of booths next to each other.
>
> Foot-traffic lanes should be wide enough to accommodate the anticipated attendance. The lanes should lead naturally from one booth to another.
>
> All wires, ropes, and tent pegs should be well marked.
>
> Restrooms and a first-aid station should be accessible and clearly marked.
>
> Special attractions for children should be scaled down in size and placed in a separate area.
>
> Food and beverage stands, as well as tables and seats, should be spread throughout the grounds in locations where they will not hold up the flow of foot traffic.
>
> Entertainment units should be placed so that the noise from one does not affect any of the others.

To attract people to your event and then keep them there, the fair as a whole, as well as each of it components, must be visible—bold, bright, and colorful. Volunteers should be easy to identify by their badges, hats, or T-shirts that carry out the colors or theme of the event. If possible, a map or scale model of the fair should be placed at each entrance to the event.

Obtaining Booths and Rides

If your organization is planning on running a fair as a one-time event, you should probably rent the booths from a carnival supply company listed in the Yellow Pages. If your organization is planning on holding the fair on an annual basis, you might want to look into building your own booths of wood and hardware or purchasing heavy cardboard booths that come conveniently folded flat and can be quickly assembled and then disassembled for easy storage and reuse. Booths are generally available through carnival supply and paper supply companies listed in the Yellow Pages. The number of booths needed for any fair will depend on the capacity of the site, the number of volunteers available to work at the booths, and the size of the anticipated audience.

Fairs generally include the following categories of booths: games of skill, luck, and chance; refreshments; information and item displays or exhibits; demonstrations of skill; merchandise items for sale; entertainment; and services, such as first aid, lost and found, and information. For specific booth ideas, visit other fairs to see what clever attractions they offer, and check the resources listed at the end of this chapter.

In addition to booths, some fairs feature rides. If they are permitted by local and state ordinances, rides can be rented from carnival supply companies listed in the Yellow Pages. Since rides are in great demand during the summer, you may have to select the date of your fair based on the available dates that you can contract for the use of specific rides. If you cannot afford full-size rides, you might consider renting smaller, less expensive children's rides.

Contracting for the use of rides at a fair generally involves guaranteeing to pay the owner of the equipment a predetermined amount for each ride that the owner brings to your fair, sets up, and operates. The guarantee ensures the owner that all basic expenses will be paid for. Contracting for rides also involves paying the owner a predetermined percentage on all of the rides' ticket sales beyond the amount of the guarantee.

Due to guarantees and sharing of profits from ticket sales, rides generally are not a significant source of income for a fair. But safe rides are an excellent attraction, adding to the excitement and attendance of the event.

Providing Refreshments, Entertainment, and Unique Contests and Games

The food and beverages sold at your fair must be high-quality refreshments. Otherwise, your event's success will be impeded in its first and following years. Make sure that all food and beverages are prepared and served according to local health ordinances.

Entertainment at your fair should be varied. For example, you might include a fortune-teller, clowns, magic shows, fashion shows, puppet shows, and dance demonstrations. Each act should be kept short and repeated frequently so that people can move about. Whenever possible, use local talents, since if they require any fees at all, the amounts will probably be low. Note that entertainment at a fair is often used as a way of attracting people to the event and is provided for free.

Some fairs highlight unique contests and games as main attractions to the event. These features give each fair its own special identification. For example, one fair features a "Bastille Day Waiters' Race" and a "Great American Beer Slide."

The "Bastille Day Waiters' Race," run in timed heats, is a test of speed, skill, and agility. Waiters and waitresses from area restaurants dash through a maze of tables lined with hecklers while balancing a tray bearing a wine glass, corkscrew, napkin, oversize menu, and a raw egg in a doggie bag. Midway through the 250-foot obstacle course, contestants are required to open a wine bottle, pour a glass of wine, add up a typical check, and resume their dash. Points are deducted for mistakes, such as spilling the wine, breaking the egg, or leaving the corkscrew behind.

The "Great American Beer Slide" offers contestants the chance to slide a mug of beer down a specially designed Beer Slide Bar and onto a target painted at the end of the bar. Mugs landing on the bull's-eye win their sliders a chance to participate in the finals where the objective is to land the mug on a dot inside the bull's-eye. The entry fee includes a souvenir mug.

Obtaining Prizes

The less money your organization has to pay for prizes, the greater your potential profit will be from the event. Try to have as many prizes as possible donated. If you must purchase prizes, try to obtain them at wholesale prices, at a discounted rate, or on consignment. Contact carnival suppliers and novelty retailers or wholesalers, which are listed in the Yellow Pages, for advice, as well as the actual merchandise.

Working with Other Organizations

Financially, it is probably more advantageous for your organization to conduct all activities at the fair on its own, rather than to involve other organizations. After all, why share the profits with another group? If you do decide to involve other organizations, however, determine in advance the amount you will be charging to rent booth space, and the percentage of the profits you will be asking for. Make sure that each arrangement is established in a written contract that includes your organization's responsibilities (e.g., providing booths, parking, security, electricity, signs, advertising), the renters' responsibilities (e.g., image, booth setup, uniforms), and joint responsibilities (e.g., cleanup, banking services, and fire prevention).

If your organization feels that it is unable to hold a fair on its own, or if the competition in your area leaves no room for even one more fair, consider piggybacking onto another community fair. In other words, arrange to operate one element of another group's fair to benefit your organization. You might participate in another organization's event—or even in a professional concessionaire's event—by renting and operating food, games, or entertainment booths and keeping all or a percentage of the profit earned at the booths, by running service booths (e.g., first aid, information, or lost and found) for a fee, by serving as ticket sellers and takers for a fee, or by providing cleanup services for a fee. Note that although participation in another group's fair offers money-making potential for your organization, it does not provide much publicity or name promotion for your organization.

Variations

In addition to general fairs, more specialized events can be organized, including children's festivals, ethnic attractions, and food events and competitions.

At a children's festival, all booths and special attractions are geared toward children. Activities might include a bicycle-decorating contest, a bubble gum blowing contest, a treasure hunt, and a karate demonstration. A children's festival can be a special event itself, or it can be a feature of a regular festival.

An ethnic attraction can feature the authentic arts and crafts, costumes, food, customs, and entertainment of a group of any background or country. For instance, an Italian festival might include a bocce ball tournament, pasta- and pizza-making demonstrations, and a drawing for a trip to Italy.

Food events and competitions are often the basis for many fairs. For example, your event might focus on building and then selling a *giant banana split*. Or your event might highlight a *rib burn-off* or a *chili cook-off* as the "hottest event in town," featuring competition among amateur, professional, and celebrity categories of cooks. *Gourmet galas* are also popular food events involving area restaurants or amateur chefs who rent booths to demonstrate the preparation of their famous dishes and sell sample-size portions.

A special kind of food can also serve as the central theme of a fair. For example, *chocolate festivals* are becoming increasingly popular all over the country. These festivals can include such activities as a chocolate fashion show (models dressed in brown and white clothing carry chocolate desserts down the runway as both the clothing and the dessert are described), a chocolate ice-cream eating contest, a chocolate-chip cookie recipe contest, and a chocolate-filled dunking tank.

Many other foods also offer excellent themes for a fair. For instance, a *zucchini festival* in one town featured the sale of such foods as zucchini breads and muffins, a longest-unbroken-zucchini-peel competition, a largest-home-grown-zucchini contest, and a zucchini pancake breakfast.

SALES

A sale involves gathering, displaying, and selling a variety or a single category of donated or specially purchased used or new items to people at bargain prices that are affordable to them. Money can also be raised at a sale by charging minimal admission fees to the event, selling refreshments, and holding a raffle. Some organizations have high-priced, sneak-preview parties or pre-sale events the night before a sale to give special guests a chance to shop first—but within certain limits, so that all of the best items are not sold before the actual sale begins.

A sale that features a large variety of miscellaneous items set up in stalls, booths, or on tables is often referred to as a garage sale, rummage sale, flea market, white elephant sale, nearly new sale, or bazaar. A sale that features a single type of item is usually identified according to the item, such as baked goods, books, crafts, slightly used designer dresses and other clothing, pets, or plants.

Special Advantages

In addition to the general advantages listed in the Introduction to Programs, a sale offers the following special advantages:

> A sale has great appeal for the entire community, since most people enjoy bargains and unusual finds.
>
> This type of event can be organized with limited up-front costs.
>
> Any time of year is a good time to hold a sale.
>
> Anyone can support your organization by donating or purchasing items at your sale. And donations are tax-deductible, although purchases are not.
>
> A sale may attract people from other areas, who will then have the opportunity to learn more about your organization and community.

Special Cautions

Keeping in mind the general cautions listed in the Introduction to Programs, the following special cautions about a sale should be carefully considered as well:

> Large crowds of willing shoppers are necessary for a successful sale since each person will probably spend only a small amount of money.
>
> Two types of communitywide publicity are needed for a sale—one to obtain donations and the other to promote the event.
>
> Collecting the donated items to be sold at a large sale featuring a wide variety of items can be extremely time-

consuming. Some organizations spend a year or even longer locating, gathering, and preparing items for sale.

Expenses

A sale can entail the following expenses for your organization: site rental fee—supplies and equipment rental fees, including booths, tables, and chairs—purchase of donation/appraisal forms, price tags, receipt books, and paper bags and boxes for storing and packaging items—purchase of refreshments—storage costs—purchase of licenses and permits—purchase of liability insurance—security costs—printing costs—postage costs—promotion costs. Try to have as many expenses as possible covered by donations or reduced through discounts.

Volunteer Requirements

The volunteer leaders needed to plan and run a sale include the event chairperson, arrangements chairperson, acquisitions chairperson, printed material chairperson, promotions chairperson, treasurer, and volunteer coordinator. Their roles are described in the Introduction to Programs. In addition to these volunteer leaders, many, many more volunteers are needed to donate, collect, sort, and price items for the sale, as well as work in various capacities at the actual event.

Selecting a Time

The best time of the year to hold a sale that features a variety of used merchandise is during the spring or fall, since that is when people tend to clean out their homes and donate unwanted items. Fall is also a good time to hold this type of sale, because people shop for gifts with the winter holidays in mind. A sale that features just one type of item should be scheduled according to the time of year when people might be most interested in purchasing that type of item. For example, a plant and flower sale that is scheduled close to Mother's Day could be very successful. The best time of the week to hold any type of sale is on a weekend, since Saturdays and Sundays are most convenient for bargain shoppers.

Choosing a Site

A sale can be held in a multilevel parking garage, parking lot, barn, basement, auditorium, gymnasium, fairground, park, arena, building lobby, airplane hangar, theater, or tent. Whatever the location, it must be safe, well-ventilated, and well-lit, since seeing is crucial to buying. If possible, the site for your event should be the same place where you store the collected items. This will eliminate the added step of having to move merchandise from one place to another.

Obtaining Items to Sell

Try to have as many items as possible donated for your sale. If the nature of your event requires you to purchase items, shop around for the best prices and negotiate a purchase or consignment arrangement.

Volunteers should be encouraged to donate some of their own belongings as well as obtain items from friends and relatives. Collecting items tends to snowball, as more and more people make tax-deductible donations and urge others to do so as well. Ask real estate agents to hand out fliers about your sale to their clients, since people often give things away when they are preparing to move.

Arrange to have all donations either picked up or delivered in a manner that is most accommodating to the donor. Picking up merchandise tends to result in larger donations than when donors must transport items themselves. Several cars, station wagons, and vans should be available to pick up merchandise. And very reputable volunteers should be recruited to handle the pickups.

Since many organizations in a community seek donations for sales and other events, it may be necessary to offer an added incentive that will result in donations to your organization rather than another group. For instance, one organization that holds an annual secondhand fur sale attracts donations by offering free appraisals of items (or allowing donors to make their own appraisals) and reimbursing the storage costs of any furs to be donated that are now in storage. Some organizations hold drawings as a way to obtain donations. By donating an item to the sale, a person receives a drawing ticket and the chance to win an appealing prize.

Pricing Items

Items should be sorted, priced, and marked as they are collected. The fewer times that volunteers have to handle the items, the less frustrating the process will be. Volunteers who frequently attend sales and are familiar with the going rates for items should handle the pricing. Remember that prices can always be cut on items that are not selling well as the end of the sale approaches.

Storing Items

As soon as they are received, items should be checked out for resalability, cleaned or repaired if necessary, priced, and then properly tagged and stored. Remember that there is a potential buyer for just about every-

thing. Items that absolutely cannot be sold should be set aside for a follow-up sale or donated to another charity if possible.

A supply of sturdy boxes with lids is needed to store items prior to the
sale. The boxes should be labelled and stacked according to the type of
merchandise they contain. For instance, you might have specific storage
areas for clothing, books, records, kitchen items, toys, jewelry, shoes, lin-
ens, and tools.

Displaying Items

Items should be displayed in an organized and attractive manner with
clearly marked prices so that the selling process runs as efficiently as possible. Folding tables work well as displays since they are easy to set up,
move around, and store. Easily seen signs should be hung that indicate the
type of merchandise for sale at each table and in each area. If yours is an
unusually large sale, you might consider setting up an information booth.
Decorations can be used to tie all of the displays together and turn the sale
into a unified marketplace. Seek the advice of experienced sales planners in
organizing the displays and setting up traffic flow patterns.

Selling Items

Volunteer sellers should be gracious and helpful to all shoppers. They
should be familiar with the merchandise they are responsible for selling,
and able to answer any reasonable questions. They should not pressure
shoppers into buying anything. A "will call" area should be set up so that
shoppers can store their purchases while they continue to look around.
Items that are not sold as the end of the sale approaches can be offered as
part of a special spree or "gambler's sale" where for a small amount of
money (e.g., $1, $5, or $10) shoppers can gather everything that they can
carry or that will fit in one shopping bag. Or the people running the booths
can take a make-me-an-offer approach.

Keeping Track of Sales

It is extremely important to keep track of every transaction that occurs
at a sale. Depending on the size and sophistication of your event, this
can be accomplished with cash registers, receipt books, item tags, or total
sheets. Pocket calculators or adding machines will also be useful. The handling of and security for all money should be determined prior to the start
of the event.

Variations

An organization that does not have the resources to plan and conduct
a sale on its own might consider another option. For instance, it could join

with several other organizations in the community and hold a big sale. Or it could serve in a landlord capacity—providing the location for the sale, renting space to other organizations that wish to participate, promoting the sale, and perhaps even receiving a small percentage of the profits from each organization's sales.

As another option, supermarkets, department stores, and other retailers sometimes schedule sales on special days to help certain organizations raise money for their worthwhile objectives. The organization receives a certain percentage (e.g., 5 or 10 percent) of all sales that take place on the special day. The retailer receives excellent publicity, increased business, and the opportunity to make a charitable contribution by participating in this type of event. A special day must be scheduled as far in advance as possible—usually a weekday. The key to benefiting from a store's sales on a special day is widespread advance publicity. The store should work jointly with your organization on all promotion. This same idea can be applied to restaurants, beauty salons, gas stations, amusement parks, nightclubs, and theaters in your community. Even banks may agree to participate. For example, in one city a large bank agreed to make a contribution to a particular organization every time anybody made a financial transaction using its bank machines.

Money can be raised by working with retailers in other ways as well. For example, one organization sets up sessions for its members in which retailers send instructors to conduct classes on such topics as fashion, needlework, and cooking. Members who then make purchases at the participating stores can arrange for a percentage of their purchases to benefit the organization. Another organization has a special sales slip arrangement with local retailers. This involves an agreement in which the retailer makes a contribution in a certain amount (e.g., $5) every time a member turns in a certain amount in sales slips (e.g., $50) from the store.

SHOWS AND EXHIBITS

A show or exhibit features the display of relatively expensive items, such as fashions, art, or antiques, by one or more merchants or dealers. Money is earned from a show or exhibit by renting booth or table display space to exhibitors and charging admission fees to the general public. When the items on display are offered for sale, that money goes to the merchants and dealers, although the organization may get a commission. Often a show or exhibit includes a private sale for special guests who pay high ticket prices to attend the gala pre-event prior to the opening of the show or exhibit to the public. Items sold at the private sale are generally marked as sold but kept on display for as long as the show or exhibit is open to the public.

Special Advantages

In addition to the general advantages listed in the Introduction to Programs, a show or exhibit offers the following special advantages:

People from throughout the community are attracted by the opportunity to see the same type of item at one time since this makes browsing and purchasing easier.

The extended hours of a show or exhibit provide flexibility to the general public and contribute to increased attendance.

A show or exhibit can familiarize an entirely new audience with your organization and community.

The site for a show or exhibit (e.g., a department store for a fashion show or a community park for an art exhibit) will often help publicize the event.

This type of event can be presented any time of the year.

Exhibitors' fees can be increased with the success of a show or exhibit.

An organization does not have to worry about collecting the merchandise for a show, as it does for a sale.

Special Cautions

Keeping in mind the general cautions listed in the Introduction to Programs, the following special cautions about a show or exhibit should be carefully considered as well:

People generally are not willing to pay high admission fees for a show or exhibit, so a large attendance may be necessary to earn a profit.

Up to 12 months may be needed to plan a show or exhibit featuring many representatives since seeking exhibitors is a time-consuming process.

Make sure that the type of show or exhibit you sponsor will be able to draw a crowd in your community. The event must appeal to the interest of your intended audience. It must also be widely promoted.

If you are presenting a show or exhibit for the first time, it may take a great deal of work to convince exhibitors that participation in your event will be worth their while.

Also, it may be difficult to charge high exhibitor fees for
a first-time event.

A show or exhibit that is not successful its first year will
have a difficult time attracting merchants and dealers to
display their wares the following year.

Expenses

A show or exhibit can entail the following expenses for your organization: site rental fee—display tables and booths rental fees—lighting and
sound equipment rental fees—catering costs or the purchase of refreshments—entertainment fees—purchase of licenses and permits—purchase
of liability insurance—security costs—printing costs—postage costs—
promotion costs. Often the site for a show or exhibit will be provided at no
cost in exchange for widespread publicity. Underwriting should be obtained for as many other costs as possible.

Volunteer Requirements

The volunteer leaders needed to plan and present a show or exhibit
include the event chairperson, arrangements chairperson, printed materials chairperson, promotions chairperson, program agenda chairperson,
reservations chairperson, special features chairperson, ticket-selling chairperson, treasurer, and volunteer coordinator. Their roles are described in
the Introduction to Programs. In addition to these volunteer leaders, the
volunteer involvement in a show or exhibit will vary according to the type
of event. For example, a fashion show that your organization is producing
itself will require many more volunteers than a fashion show that your organization is sponsoring but not producing. A 5-day art show featuring
hundreds of exhibitors will require enormous volunteer involvement compared to a 1-day event featuring a handful of local artists.

Choosing a Site

The best site for a show or exhibit will depend on the type of event.
For example, a fashion show will require a site that has a stage or runway,
a lighting system, a sound system, dressing rooms, mirrors, and space to
hang clothes. An art show will require a park, public school grounds, or a
large building with booths and tables for displays. Attend shows that are
similar to yours to see where and how they are set up.

Seeking Exhibitors

A person with thorough knowledge of the topic of your show or exhibit, as well as an understanding of the community's awareness and pref-

erences, should lead the effort of seeking exhibitors. To obtain the names of potential exhibitors, contact local and regional sources. For example, if your organization would like to have an art show, talk to local museums, artists, and art associations first. Also, visit other shows in the area and compile a list of exhibitors who participate. And consider placing ads about your event in trade magazines and newsletters that specifically address the topic of your show or exhibit. For instance, if you plan on organizing an antique car show, place notices in classic car collectors' publications 6 to 12 months before the event.

Exhibitors must be contacted as far in advance as possible so that they can hold the date and compile enough inventory to exhibit. In fact, some organization scouts are dispatched nearly a year before the event in an attempt to seek and select participants. When contacting exhibitors, make sure that you are able to describe your show, including the date, the location, any fees they will be required to pay, and the anticipated attendance. Exhibitors must be convinced that your event will present them with an excellent opportunity to sell their items.

Exhibitors who agree to participate should sign a contract. Reconfirmation by letter or phone call should be made to exhibitors right up to a few days before the show. Although prepaid exhibit fees generally decrease the chances of exhibitors cancelling out, consider recruiting an extra 10 percent of exhibitors to compensate for last minute no-shows.

Note that participants in some annual shows are often rotated so that the public gets a variety from year to year. At any event, exhibitors should offer a wide range of choices and prices to your audience.

Offering Additional Features

To attract greater attention and increased attendance, a show or exhibit can offer additional features, including entertainment, refreshments, free or discounted admission for certain groups (e.g., students or senior citizens), guided tours, and demonstrations, lectures, or workshops that pertain to the topic of the event. For example, one art show holds art workshops for children while their parents are attending the show.

Some shows include an auction whereby each exhibitor contributes one of their works or products to be auctioned off to attendees. The auction can be held all at once or it can be spread throughout the entire event to catch different potential buyers at each mini-auction. All items to be auctioned should be prominently displayed in a common area. In addition to an auction, any type of show or exhibit can include a raffle.

Variations

Many different types of shows and exhibits can be organized, including fashion shows, holiday tree shows, theme shows, and touring exhibits.

A *fashion show* features the modeling of clothes. It is often held in conjunction with a luncheon or a tea. The merchandise at a fashion show is sometimes sold from the floor. A fashion show can be planned, organized, and produced by your organization or by a professional coordinator from a retail store, wholesale house, magazine, or other high-fashion organization. Either your volunteers or a paid expert must create a theme, select the clothing and accessories, provide the models, prepare and deliver the commentary, and arrange the musical program, which is an important component of any fashion show.

Themes can range from a particular designer, to the season of the year, to an aspect of fashion (e.g., travel, work, or parties), to celebrities' outfits, to historical costumes. Fashion shows can even be held on skates. The theme of one fashion show was "Crimes of Fashion." Guests searched for clues and prizes throughout the department store where the show was held. Consider your audience when determining the theme, price range, and type of clothing to be modeled.

Sometimes the models will be provided by the sponsor of the fashion show, and sometimes your organization will have to provide volunteer models. The use of nonprofessional, volunteer models will keep expenses down. Models can include women, men, teenagers, young children, and mother-daughter teams. Rehearsals must be scheduled for all models.

A good commentator is needed to run a fashion show. This should be a poised, knowledgeable person with an ability to describe clothes and ad-lib when necessary. A scriptwriter may be necessary to prepare the commentator's descriptions. Backstage, a person is needed to give the models their walk-on cues. People are also needed backstage to help the models dress.

To increase profits, a fashion show can feature "escort angels"— people who make significant donations to underwrite the event for the privilege of escorting the models down the runway.

A *holiday tree show* features a showcase of splendidly decorated Christmas trees. Each decorated tree is sponsored by an individual, a corporation, or another organization. The trees are sold during a preview night event. Then the trees are left on display for the general public to view after paying an admission fee. Many of the purchased trees are actually donated to another charity after the event.

Individuals, corporations, and organizations that sponsor trees can select their own decorators or let your organization arrange for the decorating. Possible decorators might include florists, artists, and interior designers. Although they are not paid for their efforts, decorators do receive free publicity from the event since their names, along with the sponsors' names, are printed on plaques that are placed at the base of each tree.

In addition to the trees, such items as wreaths, gingerbread houses, and quilts can be displayed. A gift boutique, penny candy store for children, and refreshment area can easily be added to this type of event.

And entertainment, craft demonstrations, a North Pole Post Office, and hands-on activities for children can be featured.

A *theme show* can be organized based on just about anything, including animals, antiques, art, autos, boats, bridal fashions, farms, homes, and sports.

An *animal show*, such as a horse or dog show, can include exhibits, demonstrations, and competitions involving a wide variety of the type of animal featured.

Reputable dealers who control their own merchandise can participate in an *antique show*. This type of show can feature furniture, china, glass, jewelry, clothing, and bric-a-brac.

An *art show* can include graphics, wood carvings, sculpture, jewelry, photography, oil paintings, watercolors, prints, cartoons, handicrafts, and ceramics. It can feature the works of one artist or of many artists, of name artists or of young artists who are not yet widely recognized. Some art shows give the public the chance to commission an artist, with the sponsoring organization receiving a percentage of the commission.

New cars, racing cars, old cars, or just about any type of vehicle can be featured at an *auto show*. Vehicle owners can pay registration fees and enter competitions. Work closely with nearby auto dealers and clubs on organizing the event. A flea market of auto parts and memorabilia is a natural addition to this type of show.

A *boat show* can be popular in areas where boating is a major form of livelihood or recreation. A boat show might include representatives of retail boat dealers, marinas, marine hardware companies, boating apparel retailers, and sporting goods stores.

The main attraction in a *bridal show* is a fashion show of bridal gowns, bridesmaid dresses, and tuxedos. The show can also include exhibits by caterers, photographers, florists, and travel agents.

A *farm show* can feature farm equipment manufacturers, grain supplies, seed distributors, and individual farmers who market their own goods. Animal exhibits can also be included in this type of show.

Builders, furniture dealers, appliance dealers, hardware stores, remodeling businesses, roofers, plumbers, electricians, painters, carpet and tile dealers, interior decorators, and any other type of merchant whose products or services are needed by people building, remodeling, or buying a home can be included in a *home show*. When space and time permit, model rooms and even model homes can be constructed at a home show.

Sports professionals, demonstrations, equipment, and supplies can all be included at a *sports show*. Local athletes and retailers should be asked to participate. A banquet honoring area athletes—from students to professionals—can be an attractive pre-event to a sports show.

A *touring exhibit* is a special presentation that your organization can sponsor and charge the general public an admission fee to attend. It can be put together by a gallery, museum, estate, or collector. Items included in a touring exhibit are not for sale. Any kind of collectible item—from art to political memorabilia—can be the theme for a touring exhibit. A touring exhibit involves a great deal of responsibility for the sponsoring organization. The event must be held in a fireproof location that prohibits smoking, and there must be adequate insurance coverage.

TOURS

A tour provides public access to a number of gardens or homes, or one decorators' showcase, at a given time for a reasonably priced admission fee. Tickets can be sold in advance of and at the event. A tour can be run every day during its duration or just on particular days, such as weekends. It can last 1 week, 2 weeks, or even a month. Refreshments and gifts are often sold at a tour, and a program book with advertisements is usually featured. A high-priced gala event held the day before the tour is opened to the public can be an additional money-maker.

Special Advantages

In addition to the general advantages listed in the Introduction to Programs, a tour offers the following special advantages:

> Since the admission fee to a tour is generally reasonably priced, almost any member of the community can support your organization by taking the tour.
>
> Members of the general public are often attracted to a tour, since the event offers them access to places that they normally would not have the opportunity to see. People are always interested in seeing how others live.
>
> People from surrounding areas may be attracted to a tour, particularly a decorators' showcase. While taking the tour they can become more familiar with your organization and community.
>
> A tour can help your organization build its mailing list if you provide a guest book for people to sign.

Special Cautions

Keeping in mind the general cautions listed in the Introduction to Programs, the following special cautions about a tour should be carefully considered as well:

The timing of a tour is usually limited to comfortable weather seasons during the year.

Trusted volunteers who can control and safeguard a tour are critical, since if something is damaged or stolen, the feasibility of a similar event in the future may be jeopardized.

Since a tour is open to the general public, a huge amount of publicity and advertising are needed to promote the event.

To be successful, a tour requires very large attendance since the admission fee is not high.

A decorators' showcase, which requires the cooperation of interior designers, is difficult to plan unless the area is affluent and the customer potential for the designers is great.

At least 9 to 12 months are needed to plan a tour. To recruit just five homes or gardens may require approaching 40 or 50 owners, and this can take a long time as well as a considerable amount of persistence and negotiation. To prepare a decorators' showcase professionally can be a very lengthy undertaking as well.

Expenses

A tour can entail the following expenses for your organization: purchase of refreshments—purchase of gift shop items—purchase of licenses and permits—purchase of liability insurance—security costs—printing costs—postage costs—promotion costs. As many of these costs as possible should be donated in exchange for free publicity.

Volunteer Requirements

The volunteer leaders needed to plan and conduct a tour include the event chairperson, arrangements chairperson, printed materials chairperson, promotions chairperson, special features chairperson, ticket-selling chairperson, treasurer, and volunteer coordinator. Their roles are described in the Introduction to Programs. In addition to these volunteer leaders, a large number of volunteers are needed to sell tickets and serve in shifts as tour supervisors, guides, and security staff, as well as refreshment stand and gift shop workers.

Planning a Garden Tour

A garden tour is relatively simple to plan and conduct, although its tickets may not be that easy to sell, since members of your community may not be particularly interested in seeing other people's gardens. So try to feature only unique and unusually attractive gardens in your tour. Ask your members about their own gardens or about those of their friends and relatives. Once you have identified a sufficient number of lovely gardens, determine that their owners are willing to open them to the public under the supervision of responsible members of your organization. Agreements with owners should be put in writing.

The best dates for a garden tour are during those periods when gardens are at the peak of their attractiveness. This can vary according to the type of garden, so all of the gardens that you select for your tour should have in common the same time period when they look their best. Rain dates should be reserved for a garden tour so that tickets sold in advance do not have to be refunded.

Garden tours are usually organized so that people can visit the gardens in any order that they wish, traveling in their own automobiles or in buses provided by your organization. This setup, of course, requires ample parking facilities and volunteers from your organization who can be present at each site throughout all of the tour hours.

A map of the garden locations and their exact addresses should be handed out to people when they purchase their tickets for the event— whether they purchase them in advance or on the day of the tour at any of the garden sites. Prominent signs should be placed at each site so that they can be easily identified. Tour pathways at each site should be carefully marked according to the owner's suggestions so that guests do not stray from the garden.

Volunteers from your organization who will serve as guides should meet with the garden owners prior to the event so that they can learn about the gardens. Guests will ask questions and your volunteers should be able to answer them.

To raise additional money at a garden tour, with the owner's permission, consider selling refreshments as well as plants, flowers, and garden supplies provided by a local nursery.

Planning a Home Tour

In seeking sites for a home tour, consider your own members' homes and the homes of people they know. Approach people who have allowed their homes to be part of other tours and have enjoyed the experience as well as people who have never participated in a home tour. Sometimes people who are trying to sell their homes may be willing to be part of the tour, since their homes are already in the proper condition to be shown to outsiders and any guest on the tour could become a buyer. When recruiting home owners to become part of your tour, you must be able to assure them that the following conditions will be met:

Their homes, grounds, and possessions will be safe.

A sufficient number of volunteers from your organization will be present during the tour to protect each owner's property.

Your organization will assume full responsibility for any losses or damages that occur during the tour.

Volunteers from your organization will help prepare the home to be shown.

All guests will be conducted through the home by volunteer guides from your organization—they will not be permitted to roam freely about the home.

Guests will be allowed only into those rooms that are included in the tour according to the owner's wishes.

Volunteers from your organization will clean up the home and grounds following the tour.

Often people are reluctant to share their homes with the public. If they agree to do so, it will be because they believe in your organization enough to give up their time and privacy and because they are confident in the safeguards you have assured them.

As with a garden tour, a map should be developed of the home tour so that guests can determine their own beginning and ending points within the hours of the tour. The map can be part of a descriptive program book of the tour.

Planning a Decorators' Showcase Tour

A decorators' showcase tour features the donated, outstanding efforts of interior decorators on a large refurbished home (usually a mansion) or other site with unusual character. Generally, a different decorator is responsible for each room of the showcase, as determined through a drawing for rooms.

Preparing for a decorators' showcase requires exclusive access to the site for the number of months that the decorators need to do their jobs. Preferably, the site should be vacant, but if it is a home and people do live there, arrangements must be made for them to reside elsewhere or in just one section of the home during the preparation and presentation period. In addition, the current furnishings in the home may have to be placed in storage.

The owner of a potential location for a decorators' showcase will usually be convinced to participate by the fact that the property will be in much better condition after the event than before due to the decorators' work.

The same assurances regarding security and assistance should be given to the owner of a decorators' showcase as the owner of a home that is included in a home tour.

Decorators will be attracted to participating in a showcase because the event will provide them with excellent recognition, free publicity, and a large number of potential customers. The expenses that they incur through their participation can be a tax-deductible charitable contribution. Work with the local chapter of the American Society of Interior Designers in recruiting decorators.

Security is vital to the success of a decorators' showcase. There must be around-the-clock security throughout the preparation and the presentation of the showcase.

A silent auction for many of the furnishings of the decorators' showcase can be held at a preview party for the event. The program book for a decorators' showcase can include the floor plan of each room and before-and-after pictures of the different rooms.

Variations

A *garden tour* can feature springtime wildflowers or the changing colors of autumn leaves. Actual *group trips to the countryside* can be arranged by your organization, or maps of the tour can be sold to people who wish to take the tour on their own. Volunteer hosts and hostesses on the trips or printed materials distributed with the maps should describe the flowers, plants, trees, leaves, and wildlife to be seen. Your organization might consider selling box lunches—or including them in the ticket price—as an additional money-maker.

A *home tour* can feature historical homes, contemporary condominiums, bachelors' apartments, a developer's model homes, the homes of well-known people in your community, homes designed by one or more notable architects, artists' homes, interior decorators' homes, waterfront homes, energy-efficient homes, homes decorated for the Christmas season, homes that are decorated as they were in a bygone era, homes that include various types of collections, special rooms (such as romantic bedrooms, nurseries, dining-room table settings, or spectacular kitchens), or alternative homes (such as private yachts, guest houses, farm houses, or corporate executive suites). If yours is an annual home tour, consider featuring the most popular homes from previous years' tours.

A home tour can also be combined with an art show. This type of event features one or two well-known artists at each home on the tour. In addition to touring the homes, guests have the opportunity to purchase artwork with a percentage of the proceeds going to the organization.

A *decorators' showcase* can focus on such unique settings as new homes in a particular builder's development (with each home decorated to appeal to a different life-style, from young professional couples to families with teenagers) or a restored theater (with each dressing room decorated by a different interior designer).

A *haunted house* at Halloween is another type of specially decorated tour. Try to find an old, spooky, structurally sound house with a lot of rooms that can be decorated and equipped appropriately with volunteers playing Halloween roles in each room.

One organization actually built its own decorators' showcase. A new home was built by local contractors in 7 days in a shopping mall's parking lot. It was then decorated by various stores in the mall, opened for the general public to tour, and finally raffled off to a single winner who decided where to have the house permanently moved.

Tours can be extended beyond gardens, homes, and decorators' showcases to *local excursions* featuring art galleries, museums, theaters, ocean liners, factories, businesses, nightclubs, Christmas lights, places of culinary interest, or areas of ethnic interest. *Theme tours* can be planned, such as a health and beauty tour (featuring stops at a fitness center, hairstyle salon, and boutique) or an insomniacs' tour (featuring late night and early morning stops at a racetrack, a daily newspaper's headquarters, and a bakery factory). Through further expansion, *actual trips* can be sponsored, such as ski weekends, camping outings, and longer vacations. When arranging trips, work with a reputable organization that plans trips or a travel agent. Allow sufficient time to sell your package so that if you do not obtain the required minimum, you can still cancel.

PRODUCTS AND SERVICES

In addition to planning special events, many organizations sell products and provide services as ways to meet their organizational and financial objectives. These moneymaking endeavors can provide a continuing, dependable source of income for the organization. Although they can require a good deal of time and a considerable amount of work, staff and volunteers gain excellent experience through their involvement, and the organization builds recognition throughout the community and sometimes beyond.

Special Advantages

In addition to the general advantages listed in the Introduction to Programs, selling products or providing services offer the following special advantages:

> Any size organization can work at its own pace, starting
> with a small inventory or program and growing at a rea-

sonable rate. The investment of time, money, and volunteers can be small at first with increased commitment as efforts expand.

An appropriate role can be found for every volunteer—from advertising to selling to instructing to bookkeeping. And volunteers can learn valuable and marketable job skills.

Support for your organization can be obtained from almost anybody in the community who purchases your products or services. People who neither give to charity nor attend events may be willing to buy a product or pay for a service that they can use.

Special Cautions

Keeping in mind the general cautions listed in the Introduction to Programs, the following special cautions about selling a product or providing a service should be carefully considered as well:

Depending on the magnitude of the effort, selling a product or providing a service can be costly in terms of up-front money.

These endeavors sometimes have a slow return on the investment.

Competition can occur when more than one organization in the community is selling a certain type of product or providing a certain type of service.

Expenses

The expenses involved in selling a product will depend on the quality, production methods, and size of inventory. For example, it could cost an organization thousands of dollars to develop a community cookbook when the book is professionally designed, typeset, pasted up, printed, and bound. Costs can be significantly reduced when the entire production process is handled by the organization. Going to a printing company that specializes in printing cookbooks for fund raisers is another way to cut costs. The expenses involved in providing a service will depend on the type of service and the number of customers to be served. Generally, volunteer involvement and donations of needed supplies and equipment will keep the expenses down. Promotional costs, including printing, postage, and advertising, should be taken into account for any product or service.

Volunteer Requirements

The volunteer involvement in selling a product or providing a service is determined by the nature of the particular effort, including its level of complexity and the size of its intended audience. Talk to organizations that sell products or provide services to gain a sense of the volunteer requirements for your effort.

Deciding What Product to Sell and How to Sell It

Salable products can be items that will appeal mostly to your members. Possibilities include lapel buttons, bumper stickers, and T-shirts. Or salable products can be items that will appeal to the general community and sometimes beyond. Possibilities include food, posters, cookbooks, calendars, greeting cards, craft items, local directories, historical publications, coloring books, and maps.

Whenever possible, a product should be unique and have special appeal to your intended audience. For instance, a community calendar could feature photographs of your organization or community, birthday and anniversary dates of your members and other local residents, meeting dates, and special-event dates. Advertisements purchased by local businesses might be included as well. Or a nursing home calendar might feature photographs of the residents and their environment to demonstrate the vitality, humanity, and beauty that can exist in nursing home life. A community cookbook could feature dessert recipes from local restaurants and well-known area cooks' kitchens. Or instead of selling homemade candy for Valentine's Day, an organization might sell "Breakfast in Bed Valentine Baskets" filled with fresh bagels and pastries, cream cheese, jelly, and coffee for two.

Certain products are particular to a single organization. For instance, a community group that was trying to raise funds to restore the town's clock tower sold chocolate bars in the shape of the clock tower to earn money. A nature center sold birdseed to its members and others in the community throughout the fall and winter. A women's organization sold banners to be kept in automobile glove compartments that said "Call Police."

Some organizations sell manufacturers' products, such as candy, holiday cards, board games based on the community, and entertainment coupon books. The disadvantages of selling another firm's goods are that your volunteers merely function as a virtually free sales force for another company and your organization earns only a small percentage of the profits. On the other hand, selling a company's products requires only an investment of time—not money. In addition to providing the inventory, the company generally supplies instructors on sales techniques, order forms, and forms for keeping records. Carefully check out a company under consideration and its products. Also, make sure that all unsold items are returnable so that your organization does not end up paying for them.

When deciding what type of product to sell, define your potential customers so that you can choose a product that will appeal to them. Also, try to select a product that buyers will want to purchase for themselves and others or that they will consume and need again. Otherwise, think about changing products from year to year so that you always have something new to sell.

Seek advice from other nonprofit organizations that sell products, top retailers in the area, attorneys, experts in marketing, and financial advisors. You might also talk to people who tried to sell products but were not successful.

Products can be sold retail or wholesale or both. Retail items are sold directly by members of your organization to the purchasers. Or you can sell your products at retail prices through another entity. For example, in one community, several organizations sell Christmas cards every year. As a gesture of goodwill, a large bank with many branches displays and provides order forms for each organization's cards. This centralizes the selling and purchasing, making the process easier for everyone involved. Wholesale items are sold by your organization in large quantities and at a discount to buyers who then resell them at retail prices to individual purchasers. You can also sell your products wholesale to mail-order catalogs. Choose a number of catalogs that might be interested in your product, write to them, and then call them to determine their interest in purchasing your product.

Promoting the Product

All products can be promoted in several ways to progressively larger audiences. These include marketing them in person, on the telephone, or through the mail, to your own members and their friends and relatives, marketing them to the general public, selling them from booths at other events, selling them through retail stores, selling them through mail-order catalogs, and placing advertisements for telephone or mail orders in numerous publications.

You might want to hold a special event to kick off your promotion campaign. For example, you could plan a luncheon to introduce and launch the sale of a community cookbook. The menu could feature dishes made from recipes printed in the cookbook. The invitation list could include all contributors to the cookbook, representatives of the press, and supporters of your organization.

Processing the Sales

Processing the sales for a successful product can be a full-time job. Orders must be filled, delivered, and billed, inventory must be controlled, and bookkeeping records must be maintained. To minimize the billing process, request payment at the time that the product is purchased. If the product is ordered in advance, insist on payment when the order is placed rather than when the product is delivered.

Benefiting from the Sale of Others' Products

Arrangements can be made so that the proceeds from the sale of a particular product at various locations benefit your organization. For example, in one community, two retired chief executive officers formed a company to manufacture men's fragrances. Although retailers carry the product, all proceeds go to a particular charity. As another example, two women completed a craft book for children and determined that all proceeds from the sale of the product at local book and craft stores go to a children's hospital. As a third example, a national health organization receives a percentage of the proceeds from the sale of a certain brand of frozen pizzas. The pizzas are sold over the phone, and the organization's name is included in the sales pitch.

Deciding What Service to Provide

Deciding what service to provide requires learning what skills and talents your members have, determining their willingness to volunteer their time and abilities, and matching the options to the interests and needs of the community. Services can range from providing talent to labor to education. Talent possibilities include entertaining, catering, and giving parties. Labor possibilities include washing cars, gardening, baby-sitting, making deliveries, cleaning houses, painting, wrapping gifts, walking dogs, and running errands. Education possibilities include teaching classes, tutoring, running workshops, and arranging demonstrations.

Services can be provided as an ongoing activity, for a few weeks or months, or just for a single day. Some organizations provide a single service, while others set up talent banks and provide a variety of services.

Promoting the Service

Services should be promoted through publicity, letters, phone calls, and such printed advertising materials as posters and fliers. The intended audience might be individuals, other groups and organizations, or even businesses and corporations.

Serving the Public

Services should be made readily available and offered graciously to the general public. Prices should be competitive with similar services that are offered in the community. Customers should either pay a flat fee or an hourly rate—depending on what is appropriate—and they should receive good value for their money.

RESOURCES FOR FAIRS

Alberti, C. E., Macko, G. S., & Whitcomb, N. B. *Money-makers: A systematic approach to special events fund raising.* Ambler, PA: Whitcomb Associates, 1982, Supplement 3, pp. 1–25.

DeSoto, C. *For fun and funds: Creative fund-raising ideas for your organization.* West Nyack, NY: Parker Publishing Co., 1983, pp. 132–145.

Drotning, P. T. *500 ways for small charities to raise money.* Chicago: Contemporary Books, Inc., 1979, pp. 88–94.

Gaby, P. V. & Gaby, D. M. *Nonprofit organization handbook.* Englewood Cliffs, NJ: Prentice-Hall, Inc., 1979, pp. 82–86.

Hay, J. T. *534 ways to raise money.* New York: Simon & Schuster, 1983, pp. 23, 39, 73–77.

Leibert, E. R. & Sheldon, B. E. *Handbook of special events for nonprofit organizations.* New York: Association Press, 1972, pp. 158–165.

Musselman, V. W. *Money raising activities for community groups.* New York: Association Press, 1969, 17–160.

National Council of Jewish Women, Inc., *The raiser's edge.* New York: National Council of Jewish Women, Inc., p. 58.

Olney, J. The Last Word. *Chocolatier,* Summer 1985, p. 97.

Pritchard, J. H. *There's plenty of money for nonprofit groups willing to earn their shares— How to do it successfully.* Phoenix: Cornucopia Publications, 1984, pp. 251–255, 289–298.

RESOURCES FOR SALES

Alberti, C. E., Macko, G. S., & Whitcomb, N. B. *Money-makers: A systematic approach to special events fund raising.* Ambler, PA: Whitcomb Associates, 1982, pp. 3.1– 3.27, 4.1–4.14.

Ardman, P. & Ardman, H. *Woman's Day book of fund raising.* New York: St. Martin's Press, 1980, pp. 174–182.

Drotning, P. T. *500 ways for small charities to raise money.* Chicago: Contemporary Books, Inc., 1979, pp. 105–116.

Flanagan, J. *The grass roots fundraising book.* Chicago: Contemporary Books, Inc., 1982, pp. 173–181, 217–224.

Gaby, P. V. & Gaby, D. M. *Nonprofit organization handbook.* Englewood Cliffs, NJ: Prentice-Hall, Inc., 1979, pp. 96–99.

Hay, J. T. *534 ways to raise money.* New York: Simon & Schuster, 1983, pp. 33–34, 122–141, 172.

Leibert, E. R. & Sheldon, B. E. *Handbook of special events for nonprofit organizations.* New York: Association Press, 1972, pp. 153–157.

Musselman, V. W. *Money raising activities for community groups.* New York: Association Press, 1969, pp. 75–138, 205–215, 225–229, 240–241.

National Council of Jewish Women, Inc., *The raiser's edge.* New York: National Council of Jewish Women, Inc., pp. 21–22, 26–28, 41–44, 56.

Pritchard, J. H. *There's plenty of money for nonprofit groups willing to earn their shares— How to do it successfully.* Phoenix: Cornucopia Publications, 1984, pp. 257–263, 285–300, 374, 389–390, 392–393.

Warner, I. R. *The art of fund raising.* New York: Bantam Books, Inc., 1984, pp. 82, 83, 89.

RESOURCES FOR SHOWS AND EXHIBITS

Alberti, C. E., Macko, G. S., & Whitcomb, N. B. *Money-makers: A systematic approach to special event fund raising.* Ambler, PA: Whitcomb Associates, 1982, Supplement 2, pp. 1–27.

Ardman, P. & Ardman, H. *Woman's Day book of fund raising.* New York: St. Martin's Press, 1980, pp. 182–184, 194–197.

DeSoto, C. *For fun and funds: Creative fund-raising ideas for your organization.* West Nyack, NY: Parker Publishing Co., 1983, pp. 68–69, 92–96, 107–108.

Drotning, P. T. *500 ways for small charities to raise money.* Chicago: Contemporary Books, Inc., 1979, pp. 85–86, 98, 104–105.

Gaby, P. V. & Gaby, D. M. *Nonprofit organization handbook.* Englewood Cliffs, NJ: Prentice-Hall, Inc., 1979, pp. 86–87, 99–101.

Guercio, G. F. Festival of trees brightens hospital's fund raising year. *Fund Raising Management,* January 1985, pp. 38–43.

Hay, J. T. *534 ways to raise money.* New York: Simon & Schuster, 1983, pp. 70–73, 78–81.

Hughes, T. M. Horse shows raise funds, promote civic cooperation. *Fund Raising Management,* February 1985, pp. 70–78.

Leibert, E. R., & Sheldon, B. E. *Handbook of special events for nonprofit organizations.* New York: Association Press, 1972, pp. 135–152, 211–212.

Mirkin, H. R. *The complete fund raising guide.* New York: Public Service Materials Center, 1981, pp. 113–114.

Musselman, V. W. *Money raising activities for community groups.* New York: Association Press, 1969, pp. 229–231, 234, 238–239.

National Council of Jewish Women, Inc., *The raiser's edge.* New York: National Council of Jewish Women, Inc., pp. 9–13, 47–49.

Pritchard, J. H. *There's plenty of money for nonprofit groups willing to earn their shares— How to do it successfully.* Phoenix: Cornucopia Publications, 1984, pp. 153–159, 223–233, 388–389, 418–419.

Sheerin, M. *How to raise top dollars from special events.* New York: Public Service Materials Center, 1984, pp. 85–89, 91–96.

Vogel, C. Show business. *New York Times Magazine,* April 28, 1985, pp. 78–80.

RESOURCES FOR TOURS

Alberti, C. E., Macko, G. S., & Whitcomb, N. B. *Money-makers: A systematic approach to special events fund raising.* Ambler, PA: Whitcomb Associates, 1982, pp. 6.1–6.13.

Ardman, P. & Ardman, H. *Woman's Day book of fund raising.* New York: St. Martin's Press, 1980, pp. 211–213.

DeSoto, C. *For fun and funds: Creative fund-raising ideas for your organization.* West Nyack, NY: Parker Publishing Co., 1983, pp. 40–55, 61–62, 87–88.

Drotning, P. T. *500 ways for small charities to raise money.* Chicago: Contemporary Books, Inc., 1979, pp. 79–85.

Flanagan, J. *The grass roots fundraising book.* Chicago: Contemporary Books, Inc., 1982, pp. 189–191, 231–235.

Fund-Raising Institute. Risk-free "Dream House" tour raises gifts and publicity for hospital. *FRI Monthly Portfolio,* June 1981.

Gaby, P. V. & Gaby, D. M. *Nonprofit organization handbook.* Englewood Cliffs, NJ: Prentice-Hall, Inc., 1979, p. 91.

Hay, J. T. *534 ways to raise money.* New York: Simon & Schuster, 1983, pp. 174–181.

Leibert, E. R. & Sheldon, B. E. *Handbook of special events for nonprofit organizations.* New York: Association Press, 1971, pp. 85–91, 166–168.

Musselman, V. W. *Money raising activities for community groups.* New York: Association Press, 1969, pp. 243–246.

National Council of Jewish Women, Inc., *The raiser's edge.* New York: National Council of Jewish Women, Inc., pp. 16, 38, 59.

Pritchard, J. H. *There's plenty of money for nonprofit groups willing to earn their shares— How to do it successfully.* Phoenix: Cornucopia Publications, 1984, pp. 143–151, 393–394.

Vogel, C. Show business. *New York Times Magazine,* April 28, 1985, pp. 78–80.

RESOURCES FOR PRODUCTS AND SERVICES

Alberti, C. E., Macko, G. S., & Whitcomb, N. B. *Money-makers: A systematic approach to special events fund raising.* Ambler, PA: Whitcomb Associates, 1982, products: Supplement 2, pp. 1–17.

Ardman, P. & Ardman, H. *Woman's Day book of fund raising.* New York: St. Martin's Press, 1980, products: pp. 218–222; services: pp. 215–216.

DeSoto, C. *For fun and funds: Creative fund-raising ideas for your organization.* West Nyack, NY: Parker Publishing Co., 1983, products: pp. 19, 79, 90–91, 98; services: pp. 28–29, 66–72, 79–81.

Drotning, P. T. *500 ways for small charities to raise money.* Chicago: Contemporary Books, Inc., 1979, products: pp. 157–160; services: pp. 149–155.

Flanagan, J. *The grass roots fundraising book.* Chicago: Contemporary Books, Inc., 1982, products: pp. 129–136; services: pp. 136–139.

Gaby, P. V. & Gaby, D. M. *Nonprofit organization handbook.* Englewood Cliffs, NJ: Prentice-Hall, Inc., 1979, products: p. 101; services: p. 95.

Hay, J. T. *534 ways to raise money.* New York: Simon & Schuster, 1983, products: pp. 48–49, 113–120, 124–139; services: 39–41, 65, 142–151, 181–184, 187–188.

Honig, L. Fundraising events, Part four: Starting at home. *Grassroots Fundraising Journal,* December 1982.

Mulford, C. *Guide to student fundraising: 129 ways to raise money.* Reston, VA: Future Homemakers of America, 1984, products: pp. 50–51, 55–56.

Musselman, V. W. *Money raising activities for community groups.* New York: Association Press, 1969, products: pp. 233, 235–236.

National Council of Jewish Women, Inc., *The raiser's edge.* New York: National Council of Jewish Women, Inc., products: pp. 31, 62, 87–89; services: pp. 73–74.

Pritchard, J. H. *There's plenty of money for nonprofit groups willing to earn their shares— How to do it successfully.* Phoenix: Cornucopia Publications, 1984, products: pp. 108–118, 177–181, 339–358, 375, 383, 397, 399–401; services: pp. 133–137, 359–364, 376–383, 391–392, 396, 398, 400.

Zien, L. Tao House calendar. *Grassroots Fundraising Journal,* February 1985, pp. 10–12.

Chapter 10

COMPETITION EVENTS

CONTESTS AND GAMES

A contest or game can stand on its own as a special event if it is able to attract sufficient funds through entry fees from participants, admission tickets for spectators, and sponsorships by local businesses. A contest or game can also be used to promote another special event. For instance, an Elvis Presley look-alike contest might be held the month before a dance with a 1950s theme. The highly publicized winner of the contest would then greet the guests at the dance.

Special Advantages

In addition to the general advantages listed in the Introduction to Programs, a contest or game offers the following special advantages:

- It can be easy to keep the expenses down in planning a contest or game. And if sponsorships are obtained, then the event may not have any up-front costs.
- A contest or game can be a fun and exciting event for participants and spectators.
- An appropriate contest or game can be selected for any time of year, any type of weather, and any age group.
- This type of event can be organized relatively quickly.

Special Cautions

Keeping in mind the general cautions listed in the Introduction to Programs, the following special cautions about a contest or game should be carefully considered as well:

> Imaginative efforts are needed to plan and promote a contest or game that is appealing enough to earn sufficient funds.

> A contest or game generally is not a huge moneymaker.

> Volunteers are needed who have the ability to recruit participants for the event, to seek contributions from potential sponsors, and to sell tickets to spectators.

> Valuable and desirable prizes must be obtained to attract participants.

> A top-notch master of ceremonies is critical to running a successful contest or game.

Expenses

A contest or game can entail the following expenses for your organization: site rental fee—purchase of prizes—production and presentation expenses that are specific to the specific contest or game—purchase of licenses and permits—purchase of liability insurance—security costs—printing costs—postage costs—promotion costs. Try to seek sponsorship for the event from local businesses.

Volunteer Requirements

The volunteer leaders needed to plan and run a contest or game include the event chairperson, arrangements chairperson, printed materials chairperson, promotions chairperson, sponsorship and underwriting chairperson, ticket-selling chairperson, treasurer, and volunteer coordinator. Their roles are described in the Introduction to Programs. In addition, a contest or game requires the involvement of a recruitment chairperson to seek participants for the contest or game and a rules and regulations chairperson to develop all of the instructions for entering and participating in the contest or game. Additional volunteers are needed to assume responsibilities particular to the contest or game. Generally, the number of volunteers required is not overwhelming.

Considering Ways to Earn Money

Money can be earned from a contest or game in a variety of ways. These include charging entry fees for participants in the event, asking local businesses to sponsor the event in exchange for free publicity, and selling admission tickets to spectators in advance and at the door of the event.

Great effort is often required to recruit participants for a contest or game. Generally, at least 2 to 4 weeks should be focused on this activity. Publicity, advertising, and direct contacts are essential for obtaining participants. Fliers, posters, and announcements in local newspapers can be used to invite contestants as well. The information provided should include a description of the event, the cause that it will benefit, when it will be held, contestants' qualifications, what the prizes include, where an application can be obtained, the deadline for submitting an application, and the entry fee.

When seeking sponsors, it is important to explain how their contributions will help their businesses and your charitable cause. Develop a portfolio that includes a description of the event, as well as a description of your organization, and how it will use the profits from the event. Sponsorship contracts should also be included in the package.

Volunteers responsible for seeking sponsors should first approach businesses and individuals they know. This is because they are less likely to be turned down by acquaintances, early successes can be used to influence other potential sponsors, and the experience gained in selling to acquaintances will be useful when the time comes to sell to strangers. Once sponsors are obtained, feature them in all promotions for the event. Also, design a program book to be distributed at the event that lists the sponsors. If any of the sponsors donate prizes for your event, acknowledge their generosity in the program book and announce their donations as the prizes are awarded.

Most contests or games attract spectators. Friends and relatives of contest or game participants can usually be counted on to purchase tickets, as well as members of your organization and residents of the community. Do not be overly generous with complimentary admissions, since it is likely that you will be counting on ticket sales as part of your profit.

Establishing Rules and Regulations

The official rules and regulations for a contest or game should be established before efforts are made to recruit participants for the event. The rules and regulations should be included in promotion materials so that interested people can be certain about what their involvement will entail. For instance, specifications for a talent contest might cover the following areas:

when and where the contest will be held, qualification requirements, sponsorship procedures, number of contestants to be accepted, judging criteria, prizes, entry fee amount, contestants' obligations, causes for disqualification, and the entry deadline.

Considering Legal Matters

Verify the legality of running any contest or game in your area by contacting your state attorney general's office. That office will be able to tell you whether the event is legal and what licenses or permits are required to conduct the event—if any. If an event is not legal, then modify it. Otherwise, do not pursue the activity.

If your contest or game is based on a television show or a manufacturer's product, you must abide by their copyright and trademark restrictions. Generally, your contest or game should be at least 40 percent different in content and name than existing contests or games.

Offering Prizes

Bigger and better prizes will add to the amount of public interest in your contest or game. More contestants will want to participate and more spectators will want to watch the competition. So try to obtain exciting prizes for your event. Seek donations from members of your own organization and from local businesses in exchange for recognition of the donation in all publicity. If you cannot obtain prizes for free, ask for discounts on any purchases you must make or shop at wholesale houses.

Selecting a Master of Ceremonies

The master of ceremonies is a crucial component in the successful presentation of a contest or game. The master of ceremonies sets the tempo of the event, holds the attention of the audience, and keeps the event running smoothly. Try to recruit a local celebrity with experience for the role.

Variations

A contest or game can be developed around just about any imaginable activity as long as it is designed to capture the interest of potential participants, sponsors, and spectators. This means that it should be unique to your community and not just a duplication of an event that is presented by another organization. Types of contests or games that may be appropriate for your organization to pursue include beauty contests, board game tournaments, card game tournaments, eating contests, million-dollar contests, photo contests, races, road rallies, scavenger hunts, talent contests, and treasure hunts.

A *beauty contest* can be conducted independently at the local level and focus on women, men, teenagers, young children, or babies. Money is raised by charging entry fees for contestants, who are often sponsored by local businesses, and admission fees for the audience. A beauty contest can also be conducted as a franchise or licensee of a national contest. The fees for conducting a preliminary beauty contest can be high. Contact the national organizer of the major contest you are interested in for information.

Rather than entry and admission fees, certain types of beauty contests can raise money though contributions. For example, you might want to establish a "Most Beautiful Waitress Contest" in your community whereby people vote for their favorite waitress by making contributions over a month-long period at restaurants that officially sponsor the contest. The waitress who receives the most "votes" (i.e., the largest contribution) is the winner of a grand prize.

A *board game tournament*, such as checkers, chess, backgammon, Monopoly, Scrabble, or Trivial Pursuits, can be staged for just about any age group. Participants pay entry fees, businesses sponsor portions of the game (e.g., the Boardwalk square in Monopoly), and observers pay admission fees. Games that involve both skill and luck tend to be the most appealing. The skill component allows players to compliment themselves when they win. And the luck component allows players to place the blame elsewhere when they lose.

You can organize your own board game tournament or participate in a national tournament. Contact the company that makes the game you are interested in to obtain permission to use its trademark or to determine whether it will be running a national tournament. Most companies are happy to participate in newsworthy events that promote their games, and any basic board game tournament or marathon can be somewhat newsworthy. But to capture greater coverage, it may be necessary to add a unique element to the event. For example, some groups organize giant, life-size (or bigger) board games. The players in one chess tournament were people dressed in costumes who moved about on a giant chessboard. The board for a Monopoly game was the size of a gymnasium, and the playing pieces included an actual wheelbarrow, a giant thimble (a turned-over garbage can), and an oversized shoe.

A *card game tournament* can be organized for one or more types of card games, including bridge, canasta, hearts, pinochle, poker, or rummy. This type of event can be held one time, weekly, or monthly. Rules, regulations, and tournament instructions for most card games can be obtained by writing to the United States Playing Card Company, Beech Street and Park Avenue, Norwood, Ohio 45212, (513) 396-5700.

An *eating contest* can feature any type of food—from pizza to ice cream to pies to ribs—and any age group, weight division, or technique category (e.g., one-handed or using chopsticks). Participants pay entry fees or obtain the fees from sponsors, businesses donate the food, and observers pay admission fees.

In a *million-dollar contest*, the winner of the event—if there is a winner—receives $1 million (usually in equal payments over a number of years). The ability to offer a prize of $1 million is obtained by purchasing a special premium on your insurance policy. Check with your insurance agent for details. Since the premium can be extremely expensive, you should be quite certain that you can raise enough money from the event to cover the cost of purchasing the premium and all other expenses and still yield a profit. Or try to find a business to purchase the insurance premium as a contribution to your organization. Contests that offer million-dollar prizes are easy to publicize since such an enormous prize immediately draws the attention of the media.

One example of this type of event is a *million-dollar fishing contest* which involves selling fishermen the chance to reel in a specially marked fish for $1 million. The event requires a nearby lake that is well stocked with fish and frequently used by fishermen. One fish in the lake is obtained and tagged so that it can easily be identified if it is caught. Check with your state department of fish and game before planning this type of event.

In a *photo contest*, amateur photographers pay a fee to enter their photos. Professional photographers and other local experts serve as judges. Prizes for different categories of photographs should be donated. Photo contests can feature certain themes (e.g., nature, children, night shots), have restrictions according to age and equipment, or focus on general categories of shots. An exhibit of all of the photographs can serve as an additional fund raiser if admission fees are charged.

A *race* that is unusual is generally easy to promote. For instance, *hot air balloon races* can be arranged in cities that have balloon-flying clubs. Ask the members of the club to participate in the race, seek sponsors for each balloon, and sell admission tickets to the audience. Or if you live near a river or lake, plan a *crazy craft race* featuring homemade vessels that are hand-built of wood and milk cartons.

Any city can accommodate a *balloon launch.* This involves selling tickets in advance of and at the event. Purchasers can then exchange their tickets for balloons that are all released at the same time. Each balloon carries a card with the purchaser's name on it and instructions to the person who finds the balloon to return it to the organization. The person who returns the balloon from the farthest place receives a prize as does the purchaser of the ticket for that balloon.

Another unique race is a *lobster race.* Sponsored by area restaurants, this event involves celebrities who prod live lobsters down a short watery track to the finish line.

A *road rally* involves a certain type of vehicle, such as motorcycles, sports cars, vans, or snowmobiles, and combines a race and a treasure hunt. Contestants usually enter a rally in teams consisting of a driver, a navigator, and sometimes additional passengers.

A road rally tests the timing and navigational skills of its participants. Each participating team is given a list of directions to the final destination. Included in the directions may be a list of questions that must be answered correctly along the way. The winner of the rally is the team that completes the route in the shortest time and answers the most questions correctly. The starting and finishing times and mileage of each team must be recorded to determine the winner.

Rather than answer a list of questions, a rally might involve checkpoints that require certain activities. For example, in one rally, five checkpoints were set up. At every checkpoint, each team was required to pay for a draw of a playing card. The team that held the best poker hand at the end of the rally won the grand prize. Instead of playing cards, participants in another rally drew dominoes at each checkpoint. The team with the highest number of domino points at the end of the rally was the winner.

A *scavenger hunt* can be a fun event for teams of people who pay entrance fees to participate. Each team is given the same list of items—from the ordinary to the unusual—that must be found by a certain time. The winning team is the one that finds all items on the list first. Check with other organizations that have arranged scavenger hunts for unique ideas.

A *talent contest* is one of the simplest forms of stage presentations. However, the event still requires an experienced production coordinator to handle the auditions, staging, sequencing, lighting, sound, and other details of a show. Local talent contests often attract large audiences who are willing to pay reasonable admission fees. Also, sponsors can be sought for the various acts.

Auditions for the contest should be well publicized so that you can choose the very best from a variety of acts to participate in the contest. Auditions should be conducted as early as possible to allow time to find more and better acts if needed, for improving upon acts that do not quite meet the contest's standards, and for determining the format and sequence of the contest. Performers should be asked to present their acts at the audition exactly as they would present them during the contest. Notes should be taken at the audition, and a stopwatch should be used to time each act. This information will be useful when the time comes to put the show together.

After the auditions, the director of the event must package the variety of acts into a tight, well-balanced, and fast-paced contest. At least one rehearsal should be scheduled to run through the whole show. This will allow each act to find out how it will be staged and which act it will follow. And it will allow musical accompanists and members of the stage crew to coordinate the technical aspects of the show.

A *treasure hunt* involves participants who pay their entry fees and then obtain maps and clues (often written in verse) for finding the treasure, which is usually a certificate representing the grand prize. The first person or team to find the treasure is the winner.

To encourage the advance purchase of entry tickets, many treasure hunts permit participants who buy their tickets early to start the treasure hunt a certain amount of time (e.g., 1 hour) before participants who pay for their tickets on the day of the event. The offer of a head start on a treasure hunt is an excellent incentive for advance ticket sales.

When planning a treasure hunt, make sure that only one or two persons involved in planning the event know where the treasure is hidden. This will minimize the chances of the information somehow slipping out. Also, see that clues are placed in areas that are not near properties that might be damaged or residents who might be disturbed. And be sure to notify the appropriate city authorities about the event, its routes, and the general time periods when participants will be in certain areas.

PLEDGE EVENTS

A pledge event is an activity where people sign up—and sometimes pay an entry fee—to take part in an activity and obtain sponsors who pledge financial support for the entrants' participation. Sponsors agree to contribute a specific amount (from cents to dollars) for each segment of the event that the participant completes (e.g., $2 per mile, $1 per lap, 50¢ per basket, or 10¢ per minute). At the end of the event, each participant's monitored efforts must be officially validated to avoid fraud. Then the person can collect all pledges and turn the money over to the organization. Whenever possible, a pledge event is held in conjunction with a major company that underwrites the event and assists in other ways. Admission fees are sometimes required of spectators at a pledge event. Many pledge events are called "_____-a-thons" (e.g., bike-a-thons, bowl-a-thons, dance-a-thons, skate-a-thons, and swim-a-thons).

Special Advantages

In addition to the general advantages listed in the Introduction to Programs, a pledge event offers the following special advantages:

> Money can be raised from a pledge event through entrance fees, sponsorship pledges, and spectator fees. Also, refreshments and souvenir items can be sold for a profit.

> People of all ages and at all income levels can take part in a pledge event.

A pledge event does not require too much up-front money. And, if necessary, entry fees can be charged to defray any advance expenses.

Corporations often help in underwriting and promoting a pledge event.

All pledges are tax deductible.

The enormous participation that a pledge event can attract may make a strong statement in support of your organization's cause.

This type of event can simultaneously be held in numerous locations (e.g., a swim-a-thon that takes place in every high school pool in the community at the same time).

Special Cautions

Keeping in mind the general cautions listed in the Introduction to Programs, the following special cautions about a pledge event should be carefully considered as well:

Enormous promotional and volunteer efforts are usually necessary to recruit enough participants, sponsors, and spectators to make a pledge event successful.

Participants must have enough time before the event to seek pledges.

The weather can greatly affect the success of an outdoor pledge event.

Not all pledges are collectible—usually 75–80 percent are received.

The best time to hold a pledge event is on a Saturday or Sunday.

Expenses

A pledge event can entail the following expenses for your organization: site rental fee—costs of entry and sponsorship forms, certificates of achievement, receipt books, and other materials—purchase of identification and souvenir items, trophies or other prizes, and refreshments for participants—purchase of licenses and permits—purchase of liability insurance—printing costs—postage costs—promotion costs. Try to have as many expenses as possible underwritten by a major company in exchange for considerable free publicity.

Volunteer Requirements

The volunteer leaders needed to plan and conduct a pledge event include the event chairperson, arrangements chairperson, printed materials chairperson, promotions chairperson, sponsorship and underwriting chairperson, treasurer, and volunteer coordinator. Their roles are described in the Introduction to Programs. In addition, a pledge event requires the involvement of a participant chairperson to recruit as many people as possible to be in the pledge event and to encourage everyone who has entered to obtain as much pledge support as possible. Every available volunteer is needed for a pledge event as well—either to help out, to participate, or to make a pledge.

Obtaining Permission to Hold the Event

Permission must be obtained for pledge events that are to be held on public property, such as walk-a-thons and bike-a-thons. Contact the appropriate person in your local government as early in the planning process as possible for advice, permits, and cooperation. Special arrangements may also have to be made with the facility that is going to serve as the location for an indoor pledge event. For example, an activity that is planned to last a long time (e.g., a 24-hour dance-a-thon) will require special permission from the facility.

Seeking Corporate Sponsorship

Try to find a major company to sponsor your pledge event. In addition to providing financial support, a corporate sponsor can be of great assistance in obtaining participants for the event, in supplying prizes, and in offering refreshments. For instance, if your corporate sponsor is a fast-food chain, it may be possible to arrange for the distribution of entry forms at the various restaurants, to obtain free food coupons as prizes, and to offer complimentary snacks to participants. A corporate sponsor also may be able to help publicize the event. All arrangements with a corporate sponsor should be finalized in a written contract.

Recruiting Participants

In recruiting participants, publicize the pledge event as widely as possible throughout your community, using printed materials and the media. Also ask for assistance from any companies that may be underwriting the event and from local businesses that may be interested in the event (e.g., bicycle shops for a bike-a-thon, or exercise classes for an aerobics pledge event). Check with local schools and universities to see if they would like to become involved, since pledge events often appeal to teachers and students and can be taken on as class projects. And check with local corporations since they are often willing to put together teams of participants for pledge events. Recruit participants according to the type of event. For instance, a rock-a-thon (using rocking chairs) could easily involve nursing home residents.

Seeking local, regional, or national celebrities to participate in your pledge event may add to the happening's appeal and popularity. At the local level, media celebrities are often quite willing to take part in a pledge event. Their involvement will greatly increase your chances for media coverage of the event.

Preparing Materials for Participants

Each person who signs up to participate in a pledge event should receive a kit containing a sponsor listing/pledges earned record sheet, instructions about how to get sponsors initially and how to collect money after the event, a date/time/location reminder, a set of rules, a list of prize categories, maps (if applicable), a fact sheet on your organization, and any other relevant information. Participants should also be provided with identification cards and other items (e.g., T-shirts or caps) that can also serve as souvenirs after the event. A punch card that hangs from each participant's neck can be used to identify walkers in a walk-a-thon. The punch card should have a border of numbered blocks so that each block represents one of the miles along the route. When the walker arrives at the end of a mile, a volunteer punches a hole in the appropriate block on the card to verify the walker's accomplishment.

One organization designed a sponsor listing sheet that was in the form of a scavenger hunt. The sheet contained 50 sponsor descriptions with associated point values. For example, participants were instructed to find a sponsor who was over 6 feet tall (10 points), who had been married at least 25 years (20 points), who was a medical professional (5 points), and who recently lost at least 10 pounds (15 points). Each participant who signed up enough sponsors to equal at least 100 points was eligible for a door prize drawing after the event.

Developing a Route

If your pledge event is a long-distance, outdoor activity (e.g., a run-a-thon or bike-a-thon), you must develop one or more circular routes that are safe, simple, accurately marked, scenic, easily viewed by the public, and fun. Along the routes there should be checkpoints with volunteers to supervise and validate the progress of the participants, medical aid, mechanical assistance, and police patrols.

Routes are often measured by kilometers rather than miles, since a pledge per kilometer will result in more money than a pledge per mile. For example, a pledge of $1 per mile for 20 miles equals $20. A pledge of $1 per kilometer for 32 kilometers (equivalent to 20 miles) equals $32.

Offering Prizes

Prizes will help attract participants to a pledge event. They can be awarded for achievements in numerous categories, including outright winners, male and female winners, winners according to professional group, and different age-group winners. They can be awarded for the highest number of sponsors signed up and the greatest amount of pledges collected. Try to have all prizes donated from the major company that may be sponsoring your event and from local businesses.

Consider holding a party after the event and awarding the prizes there. Or, after all pledges have been collected and given to the organization, you might want to hold a special drawing for prizes open to everyone who turned in a certain minimum amount of money. For instance, at one high school each time a student brought in $25 in pledges following a walk-a-thon, the student received a ticket for a chance to win a car in a drawing that was held 2 weeks after the event. The car was donated by a local dealer. Placed on display (and even driven around and through the school) a few weeks before the walk-a-thon, the car served as a great incentive for increasing participation in the walk-a-thon, obtaining sponsors, and collecting pledges.

Collecting Pledges

Participants should be given a deadline for collecting and turning in their pledges after the event (e.g., within 1 or 2 weeks following the event)—the sooner the better. They should be told whether pledges are to be handed in personally or mailed. If they are to be mailed, indicate that only checks or money orders are acceptable, and provide each participant with a pre-addressed return envelope. The name and phone number of a person to contact with questions should be provided. You might also give participants certificates of achievement to prove that they took part in the pledge event and receipt books so that their sponsors can have their contributions verified.

Variations

The variety of pledge events is huge and always growing. Your organization may want to think of a new idea or consider one of the following activities as the basis of a pledge event: walking, running, swimming, bicycling, skating, dancing, singing, shooting baskets, playing a musical in-strument, twirling a baton, marching in a band, dieting, reading books, rocking in a chair, sleeping on a water bed, staying awake, exercising, playing volleyball, bowling, constructing jigsaw puzzles, playing a board game, jumping into a pool of gelatin, golfing, jumping rope, or playing hopscotch. Also, consider adding unique features to your pledge event. For example, an exercise competition might include a fashion show of leo-tards, tights, and warm-up suits.

Another type of pledge event involves *working out a special arrangement with a professional sports team* whereby anyone can pledge to make a dona-tion to your organization each time the team accomplishes a specific goal. For example, if your town has a baseball team, it might be possible to give people the opportunity to pledge to donate a certain amount of money to your organization for every homerun hit or base stolen. With a football team, donations could be based on touchdowns or field goals.

Mock arrests are a unique type of pledge event. In a mock arrest, people make donations to have citizens "arrested" at their homes or places of busi-ness by off-duty police officers at a certain time of the day of the event. The "prisoner" is then taken to a specially set up "jail" and given a specific "bail" that must be raised through telephone calls before the prisoner is re-leased. The bail, which is donated to the organization, is pledged by the prisoner's friends, relatives, coworkers, and business associates. Some-times the person who is arrested knows about the situation in advance and sometimes the arrest is a complete surprise. Each prisoner is "arraigned" for a variety of comical charges (e.g., inciting to have a good time, at-tempted dieting, or reckless bicycling) and usually stays in jail for 1 or 2 hours. Be aware that some people may not be comfortable with being arrested—even for humorous and charitable reasons.

Events featuring mock arrests have been conducted by many non-profit organizations under various names. For example, the American Can-cer Society calls its event "Jail-N-Bail," the American Heart Association runs a "Cardiac Arrest," and the Cystic Fibrosis Foundation holds a "Lock Up."

Pledge events can also be presented in the form of *adoption events* where funds that are needed for a specific cause are gained through adop-tions of that cause. For example, one community that was plagued by street potholes organized an "Adopt-A-Pothole" campaign. The commu-nity made it possible for citizens to adopt a pothole in one of three sizes—small, medium, or large. The money donated to adopt each specific pot-hole was then used to repair it. Every person who adopted a pothole re-ceived a certificate. Another community designed an "Adopt-A-Dancer" program for members of its ballet company. Since most of the company's ballet dancers came from out of town for the 6-month season, they needed sponsors to make them feel at home during the period of their temporary residence. The "Adopt-A-Dancer" program recruited donors who contributed substantial amounts for the privilege of supporting an individual dancer. Each donor then carried out many activities over the 6-month period to make their dancer feel at home, such as inviting the dancers to holiday celebrations.

SPORTS COMPETITIONS

A sports competition can involve organizing a participatory athletic event, such as a 10-kilometer run, in which individuals or teams pay entry fees to participate. Or it can involve organizing a spectator competition, such as a softball game between your organization's team and a local television station's team, in which spectators pay admission fees to watch. Often an awards ceremony or party is held at the end of a sports competition. A sports competition differs from a pledge event in that competitors do not seek sponsors to make financial contributions in support of their participation.

Special Advantages

In addition to the general advantages listed in the Introduction to Programs, a sports competition offers the following special advantages:

A sports competition is a fun and exciting event for both participants and spectators.

As more and more people become increasingly conscious of good health and weight control, the appeal of a sports competition grows as well.

People of all ages are attracted to a sports competition.

Community spirit is stimulated and friendly competition is encouraged through this type of event.

This type of event can be held any time of year.

When a sports competition includes teams, it can often attract the involvement of corporations, businesses, professional groups, and other organizations.

Special Cautions

Keeping in mind the general cautions listed in the Introduction to Programs, the following special cautions about a sports competition should be carefully considered as well:

Unless the number of participants and/or spectators is quite large, a sports competition may not be a significant money-maker since individual entry and admission fees are generally small.

It is important to select a sports competition that will appeal to individuals in your community who have some athletic aptitude, and that will require no more than a minimal amount of training.

A sports competition may have to compete with professional and interscholastic athletic events in your area.

Expenses

A sports competition can entail the following expenses for your organization: rental fees for supplies and equipment particular to the type of event—purchase of refreshments—purchase of souvenir gifts and prizes—purchase of first-aid supplies—rental fees for tables, chairs, and portable toilets—purchase of licenses and permits—purchase of liability insurance—printing costs—postage costs—promotion costs. Try to have as many expenses as possible underwritten. For example, a business may be willing to pay for T-shirts as the giveaway gift at your event if the name or logo of the business can be printed on the back of each shirt. Also, try to seek sponsorship from likely supporters, such as sporting good stores or health clubs.

Volunteer Requirements

The volunteer leaders needed to plan and run a sports competition include the event chairperson, arrangements chairperson, printed materials chairperson, promotions chairperson, reservations chairperson, sponsorship and underwriting chairperson, treasurer, and volunteer coordinator. Their roles are described in the Introduction to Programs. In addition to these volunteer leaders, depending on the type of sports competition, volunteers may be needed to serve as timers, course directors, aid station workers, registration workers, finish line workers, refreshment table workers, drivers, medical assistants, coaches, judges, referees, ticket sellers, and ticket takers. Note that the size of the volunteer involvement in a sports competition depends on the size of the event. For instance, a bicycle race that attracts 200 participants will require fewer volunteers than a 10km run that attracts 2,000 participants and a large crowd of spectators.

Determining the Entrance Fee

The entrance fee for a sports competition should be determined based on the financial objectives of the event, the number of individual or team participants you anticipate, the number of spectators you hope to attract, the going rate for similar events in your community, and the types of souvenir gifts and prizes you will be offering. Usually participants expect better gifts (e.g., T-shirts) and prizes (e.g., silver trophies) with higher entrance fees. Of course, an entrance fee that is too high will discourage participation. Consider charging a lower fee for advance registrations than for day-of-the-event registrations. If your sports competition is a team event that mostly involves participants from corporations, businesses, professional groups, and other organizations, then you can consider setting much higher fees.

Recruiting Participants

The best way to recruit individual participants for a sports competition is through widespread publicity and advertising. To recruit team participants for a sports competition, it will be necessary to directly contact corporations, businesses, professional groups, and other organizations. You may want to group the teams according to profession or similar interests to add another level of competition to the event. For example, you might establish competitions among teams of doctors, dentists, lawyers, insurance agents, real estate agents, bankers, and teachers.

Designing a Course

If the type of sports competition you are organizing requires a course, such as a walking, running, or bicycling route, usually a loop type of course is desirable so competitors can start and finish the event at or close to the same point. This sort of setup simplifies transportation and parking arrangements for participants and spectators.

The course must be measured for accuracy, and on the day of the event each mile of the route (or other unit of measurement) should be carefully marked. Try to seek corporate sponsorship for each marker as well as the starting and finishing lines. Prior to the event the course should actually be tested for adequacy, and spots for aid stations should be selected. Emergency vehicles should have quick access to any point on the course. Once the course is designed, it should be approved by local authorities and permits should be obtained if necessary. A map of the course with landmarks and aid stations indicated should be prepared for distribution to participants in advance of and at the event.

Setting Up a Registration Area

The registration area should be carefully organized in advance of the event to avoid confusion, congestion, and criticism at the event. It should have tables and chairs set up for predetermined categories (e.g., age, alphabet, preregistered, or not preregistered). Registration kits should be given to each participant. The kit might include instructions, a map of the course, an identification number to be worn, and souvenir gifts.

Setting Up Aid Stations

Sports competitions that cover long distances require that aid stations be set up. The purpose of the aid stations is to provide water and medical assistance during the event. The number of aid stations to be set up will depend on the type of competition, the time of year, the time of day, and the location of the event. Each aid station should be equipped with medically trained volunteers, water, ice, and first-aid supplies. Beverages should be provided at the finish line as well. Try to seek corporate sponsorship—in exchange for free publicity—for the aid stations.

Variations

A sports competition that involves individual competitors who pay entry fees to participate might focus on walking, running, bicycling, cross-country skiing, swimming, Frisbee throwing, skating, or even a combination of these events. Including local celebrities as participants will add to the event's appeal. A sports competition that focuses on team participation might feature a combination of such contests as a basketball shoot, obstacle course, tug-of-war, one-mile relay, and standing-long-jump relay.

A sports competition that involves spectators who pay admission fees to watch the event should be the type of event that easily attracts and accommodates a large number of spectators. For example, football, baseball, basketball, soccer, hockey, tennis, or track and field events have great spectator appeal. A bowling competition, which may have great appeal, probably would not be a good moneymaker, since bowling alleys do not have much room for spectators.

Sports Tournaments

A sports tournament involves either organizing a participatory event featuring members of your community as participants, or sponsoring a spectator event featuring celebrities or professional athletes as participants. The most popular types of tournaments generally involve golf or tennis. Money is raised in a participatory tournament through entry fees. In a spectator tournament, money is raised through admission fees. Corporate sponsorship is usually an important element in any type of tournament. A sports tournament often includes a breakfast or luncheon and is followed by a dinner and awards presentation. Entertainment and a raffle can be provided as well, and a program book with advertisements can be prepared as an additional moneymaker. Sometimes sports tournaments are referred to as classics or invitationals.

Special Advantages

In addition to the general advantages listed in the Introduction to Programs, a sports tournament offers the following special advantages:

> In exchange for free publicity, businesses are often willing to underwrite a sports tournament or at least sponsor teams or individual participants.
>
> Amateur athletes are usually happy to participate in a sports tournament that will provide them with an opportunity to display their skills.
>
> With corporate sponsorship and great participation, a sports tournament can be a large moneymaker.

Special Cautions

Keeping in mind the general cautions listed in the Introduction to Programs, the following special cautions about a sports tournament should be carefully considered as well:

> The particular sport that you select for your tournament should be popular in your community; otherwise, people will not want to participate in or watch the event.
>
> Entry fees for a sports tournament are generally high, restricting the number and types of participants to people who can afford the event.
>
> Corporations are often inundated with requests to underwrite or sponsor sports tournaments.
>
> Volunteers must be willing to recruit participants for a sports tournament.

Expenses

A sports tournament can entail the following expenses for your organization: country club fees—purchase of food and beverages—purchase of prizes and souvenir gifts—rental fees for supplies and equipment—purchase of licenses and permits—purchase of liability insurance—printing costs —postage costs—and promotion costs. Efforts should be made to have the entire event sponsored by a corporation or at least to have as many of these expenses as possible underwritten.

Volunteer Requirements

The volunteer leaders needed to plan and run a sports tournament include the event chairperson, honorary chairpersons, arrangements chairperson, printed materials chairperson, promotions chairperson, program agenda chairperson, reservations chairperson, special features chairperson, sponsorship and underwriting chairperson, ticket-selling chairperson, treasurer, and volunteer coordinator. Their roles are described in the Introduction to Programs. In addition to these volunteer leaders, volunteers are needed to seek participants for the tournament and to help run the actual event.

Selecting a Site

Most sports tournaments are held at country clubs—the more prestigious, the better, since people are attracted to country clubs to which they normally do not have access. Contact a country club as early as possible. A considerable amount of time may be necessary to determine the country club's willingness to accommodate your event, to find out whether or not the event fits into the country club's regulations and bylaws, and to select a date for the event. If possible, try to involve a prominent member of the country club in your planning efforts. Also, recruit the assistance of the country club's sports professional in planning the day and developing rules of play for the tournament. Note that an annual tournament might be held at a different country club every year so as not to inconvenience the club's members more than once and to attract participants to a different location every year.

Instead of a country club, a tennis tournament might be held simultaneously on private courts through the community. One organization plans an annual tennis event that involves a mixed-doubles, round-robin, 2-day tournament played on private residential courts with the semifinal and final rounds played at a local tennis club. Lunch is donated by the court owners and served to the players at each site. A party for all participants is held the evening of the first day of the event.

Obtaining Corporate Support

Many types of corporate support can be arranged for a tournament. Under the best of circumstances, you may be able to find a corporation that is willing to underwrite the entire event. Otherwise, seek corporate sponsorship of players or other components of the tournament. For example, in a golf tournament, each green and tee could be sponsored by a different corporation in return for recognition, publicity, and a certain number of tickets so that representatives from the corporation (e.g., top officers and major clients) can participate in the tournament.

Setting the Entry Fee

The amount that you charge participants to take part in your sports tournament will depend on the amount of money you hope to raise, the expenses you anticipate in holding the event, the going rate for sports tournaments in your community, and the number of participants you hope to attract. For the most part, sports tournament entry fees are high, especially when corporate sponsorship of teams of participants is likely. Arranging for professional players to participate in the event as team members or captains will add to the appeal of the event and permit you to charge even higher fees for the privilege of playing with pros.

To increase the participation—and therefore the number of entry fees—in a sports tournament, schedule more than one starting time or encourage group participation. For instance, a golf tournament could have two tee-off times (e.g., 8 a.m and 1 p.m.) to include twice as many people as well as double the possibilities of corporate sponsorship. Or a golf tournament could include groups of four players. To make the tournament move more quickly, every foursome could play from its best shot each time.

Organizing a Spectator Tournament

Organizing a spectator tournament involves either sponsoring or being the beneficiary of a professional athletic event. Sponsorship is usually arranged on a limited guarantee basis whereby your organization pays a minimum amount plus a percentage of the receipts to the professional participants. Daily admission tickets can be sold, as well as packages of quantities of tickets for all or portions of the tournament. Note that it is difficult to be selected as either the sponsor or beneficiary of a professional sports tournament, since the competition is usually great among charitable organizations wishing to make money from the event.

Variations

If your organization decides to plan a golf or tennis tournament, consider adding unique elements to your event, such as friendly betting, a hole-in-one golf contest, Mulligans, and privilege cards.

Friendly betting can add to the funds earned at the event when all of the money goes to the organization. In a golf tournament, this may require a volunteer's presence at each hole to keep tabs on the betting.

A *hole-in-one golf contest* is a very exciting opportunity that involves offering a grand prize, such as $10,000 in cash or a new car, to the first person who makes a hole-in-one at a specified hole or during a specified period of time. Check into purchasing a hole-in-one insurance premium to guarantee the grand prize in case someone actually wins. Contact the National Hole-In-One Association, 728 Campbell Centre, Dallas, Texas 75206-1679, 214-691-6911, 1-800-527-6944 (national), or 1-800-442-6061 (Texas). The Association's Sporting Contest Division can provide information on a prize promotion for sporting events other than golf, too. Or contact the Sports Achievements Association, 12431 Lewis Street, Suite 202, Garden Grove, California 92640, 714-740-1563, 1-800-421-8522 (national), or 1-800-421-3148 (California). Consider asking a corporation to purchase the hole-in-one insurance as a donation to your organization.

A *Mulligan* is a ticket that is good for a replacement shot during a golf tournament. Usually only one Mulligan can be purchased per person, although it can be used on the tee, on the fairway, in the rough, in the sand, or on the green—anywhere that an erratic shot can spoil a great game. The idea of a Mulligan may be adaptable to another type of sports tournament.

A *privilege card* entitles the purchaser to cross-country ski or play golf or tennis at a number of courses or courts for free on certain days and at certain times. Consider selling privilege cards to participants in your tournament and other sports enthusiasts. Although a good deal of work is involved in recruiting courses or courts to participate, the resulting package can be very attractive to potential purchasers. An appreciation event can be held at the end of the season for all course and court owners.

RESOURCES FOR CONTESTS AND GAMES

Alberti, C. E., Macko, G. S., & Whitcomb, N. B. *Money-makers: A systematic approach to special events fund raising.* Ambler, PA: Whitcomb Associates, 1982, Supplement 1, pp. 1–22.

DeSoto, C. *For fun and funds: Creative fund-raising ideas for your organization.* West Nyack, NY: Parker Publishing Co., 1983, pp. 120–124.

Hay, J. T. *534 ways to raise money.* New York: Simon & Schuster, 1983, pp. 35–37, 43–44.

Pritchard, J. H. *There's plenty of money for nonprofit groups willing to earn their shares— How to do it successfully.* Phoenix: Cornocopia Publications, 1984, pp. 183–194, 317–322, 329–338, 373, 375–376, 396–398.

Reid, R. Monopoly turns fifty. *Republic,* September 1985, pp. 82–91.

RESOURCES FOR PLEDGE EVENTS

Alberti, C. E., Macko, G. S., & Whitcomb, N. B. *Money-makers: A systematic approach to special events fund raising.* Ambler, PA: Whitcomb Associates, 1982, pp. 8.1–8.4, 9.1–9.5

Ardman, P. & Ardman, H. *Woman's Day book of fund raising.* New York: St. Martin's Press, 1980, pp. 200–206.

DeSoto, C. *For fun and funds: Creative fund-raising ideas for your organization.* West Nyack, NY: Parker Publishing Co., 1983, pp. 110–118.

Fund-Raising Institute. Pothole Club raises funds for Columbus. *FRI Monthly Portfolio,* July 1984.

Gaby, P. V. & Gaby, D. M. *Nonprofit organization handbook.* Englewood Cliffs, NJ: Prentice-Hall, Inc., 1979, pp. 106–107.

Metsker, R. How to produce a profitable walk-a-thon. *FRI Bulletin* May 1982.

Mulford, C. *Guide to student fundraising: 129 ways to raise money.* Reston, VA: Future Homemakers of America, 1984, pp. 62–64.

Nonprofit Executive. Syndicate arrangement helps raise funds. *Nonprofit Executive,* September 1984, p. 5.

Pritchard, J. H. *There's plenty of money for nonprofit groups willing to earn their shares—How to do it successfully.* Phoenix: Cornucopia Publications, 1984, pp. 125–132.

Reid, R. Monopoly turns fifty. *Republic,* September 1985, p. 86.

Sainsbury, J. A. *The beginner's guide to advanced fund raising.* New York: Jan Arthur Sainsbury, 1985, pp. 19–20.

RESOURCES FOR SPORTS COMPETITION

Alberti, C. E., Macko, G. S., & Whitcomb, N. B. *Money-makers: A systematic approach to special events fund raising.* Ambler, PA: Whitcomb Associates, 1982, pp. 12.1–12.14.

DeSoto, C. *For fun and funds: Creative fund-raising ideas for your organization.* West Nyack, NY: Parker Publishing Co., 1983, pp. 124–127.

Drotning, P. T. *500 ways for small charities to raise money.* Chicago: Contemporary Books, 1979, pp. 145–147.

Hay, J. T. *534 ways to raise money.* New York: Simon & Schuster, 1983, pp. 160–171.

Pritchard, J. H. *There's plenty of money for nonprofit groups willing to earn their shares—How to do it successfully.* Phoenix: Cornucopia Publications, 1984, pp. 139–142.

RESOURCES FOR SPORTS TOURNAMENTS

Alberti, C. E., Macko, G. S., & Whitcomb, N. B. *Money-makers: A systematic approach to special events fund raising.* Ambler, PA: Whitcomb Associates, 1982, pp. 13.1–13.24.

Ardman, P. & Ardman, H. *Woman's Day book of fund raising.* New York: St. Martin's Press, 1980, pp. 224–226.

National Council of Jewish Women, Inc., *The raiser's edge.* New York: National Council of Jewish Women, Inc., pp. 71, 72.

Plessner, G. M., Golf Management Manual. In *The Encyclopedia of Fund Raising* (vol. 2). Arcadia, CA: Fund Raisers, Inc., 1986, pp. 7–108.

Pritchard, J. H. *There's plenty of money for nonprofit groups willing to earn their shares— How to do it successfully.* Phoenix: Cornucopia Publications, 1984, pp. 383–384, 417–418.

Chapter 11

ENTERTAINMENT EVENTS

LOCAL PRODUCTIONS

A local production involves providing amateur entertainment for the community that members of your organization put together and star in. Types of local productions include variety shows, musicals, and plays.

Special Advantages

In addition to the general advantages listed in the Introduction to Programs, a local production offers the following special advantages:

Admission to a local production is generally inexpensive so that just about anybody in the community can attend the event and support your organization.

Producing a local show can provide a great deal of fun and unique involvement opportunities for volunteers.

Special Cautions

Keeping in mind the general cautions listed in the Introduction to Programs, the following special cautions about a local production should be carefully considered as well:

People will not pay very much money to see a local production. To make a profit, your organization must be able to sell a large number of tickets since they will be relatively low-priced.

Producing a local show requires the time-consuming involvement of unusually talented volunteers. It is important to involve people with theatrical experience in producing a local show.

If you cannot get production and technical people with theatrical experience to volunteer their efforts, you will have to pay them, since their expertise is crucial to the success of your show.

You must have access to a performance facility that is large enough to hold the size audience that you hope to attract to your local production.

You may be faced with competition from schools and community theater groups that also produce local shows.

Expenses

Producing a local show can entail the following expenses for your organization: production and technical experts' fees—costume rental fees or manufacture costs—site rental fee—orchestra fee—rental fees and royalties for manuscripts and scores—set construction costs or rental fees—union labor costs—sound and lighting equipment rental fees—purchase of liability insurance—printing costs—postage costs—promotion costs. Try to have the entire production underwritten, or at least have as many expenses as possible donated.

Volunteer Requirements

The volunteer leaders needed to produce a local show include the event chairperson, arrangements chairperson, printed materials chairperson, promotions chairperson, sponsorship and underwriting chairperson, ticket-selling chairperson, treasurer, and volunteer coordinator. Their roles are described in the Introduction to Programs. In addition, you will need the following volunteers:

production experts—members of this group can include the producer, director, writers, musical director, choral director, choreographer, staging director, scenic director, costume designer, makeup artist, props manager, stage manager, and their assistants;

technical crew—these technicians can include electricians, sound experts, lighting experts, carpenters, and stage hands;

cast—the number of cast members will be determined by
   the type of production;

orchestra—if your production requires live music, an orchestra of the appropriate size will be needed.

Requirements for further volunteer involvement will depend on the nature
and magnitude of your production.

Choosing a Show

When choosing a show to produce, consider how well-known the
show is, since the production must be appealing to your potential audience. Also, keep in mind the capability of your production staff, technical
crew, and cast—they must be able to stage and perform a quality show.
And carefully investigate the rental and royalty payments due on the
show. Popular shows are more expensive.

Unless a stage production is in the public domain (i.e., it was never
copyrighted or the copyright has expired), you must obtain permission
from the author to present the musical or play, and you must pay rental
and royalty fees to the owner of the property. Generally this is handled
through the author's agent. To find out about available properties and their
rental and royalty terms, contact the following sources:

Music Theatre International
810 Seventh Avenue
New York, New York 10019
(212) 975-6841

Tams-Witmark Music Library, Inc.
560 Lexington Avenue
New York, New York 10022
(212) 688-2525

The Dramatic Publishing Company
4150 North Milwaukee Avenue
Chicago, Illinois 60641
(312) 545-2062
Catalog available upon written request

Dramatists Play Service, Inc.
440 Park Avenue South
New York, New York 10016
(212) 683-8960
Catalog available upon written request

Samuel French Inc.
7623 Sunset Boulevard

Hollywood, California 90046
(213) 876-0570

Samuel French Inc.
45 West 25th Street
New York, New York 10010
(212) 206-8990

Bakers Plays
100 Chauncy Street
Boston, Massachusetts 02111-1783
(617) 482-1280
Catalog available upon written request

Selecting the Cast

Selecting the cast generally takes place after the show has been chosen or written and the producer or director has compiled a complete list of cast requirements. Each actor and actress must, of course, fit their role and be able to perform well. Local talent is usually easy to find. Community performers usually enjoy offering their talent to benefit a worthy case and to gain experience. If your organization does not have access to sufficient talent for a production, then place an ad in a local newspaper for open auditions.

Organizing the Rehearsals

The number of rehearsals will depend on the nature and complexity of the show, as well as the experience of the production crew and cast. For example, plays will require more rehearsals than variety talent shows. Generally, 3 to 4 weeks of rehearsals on a regular basis are necessary, followed by intense rehearsals the last few days before the performance.

Determining the Number of Performances

More than one performance is usually presented to achieve the greatest financial results from the enormous effort that producing a local show entails. To determine the number of performances to present, balance the expenses involved in each show (additional performances are relatively inexpensive to present) with your ability to attract large audiences to all performances.

Arranging Additional Activities

In conjunction with bringing in funds through ticket sales, the production of a local show can include additional moneymaking activities, such as creating a program book with ads and selling refreshments and souvenirs at the show.

PROFESSIONAL PRODUCTIONS

A professional production involves arranging and financing a major performance for a large audience. Responsibilities can include selecting the performer and the facility and negotiating their respective contracts, handling the technical aspects of the production, and selling as many tickets as possible to the show. All income from ticket sales—beyond the expense of producing the show—benefits the organization.

Special Advantages

In addition to the general advantages listed in the Introduction to Programs, a professional production offers the following special advantages:

People of all ages like to attend professional productions.

You can introduce the many people who attend the event to your organization and perhaps establish future affiliations and support.

The successful production of one professional show can lead to increased opportunities to handle other profitable productions.

Special Cautions

Keeping in mind the general cautions listed in the Introduction to Programs, the following special cautions about a professional production should be carefully considered as well:

Producing a professional show can be extremely time-consuming and expensive. Gaining access to nationally known performers can be a difficult, lengthy process. Also, considerable up-front money may be required.

It may be necessary to hire a professional consultant to produce a professional show.

Often, up to 12 months are needed to book a performer and a facility. Lengthy communications and negotiations are often required to decide on a date and financial arrangements.

Once a show is booked, there is really no way for you to get out of it. Even if you do get out of it, your future efforts may be thwarted, since word travels about unreliable producers.

Numerous circumstances may be beyond your control, such as performers who get sick before the show, who are stranded due to transportation difficulties, or who simply cancel.

Expenses

Producing a professional show can entail the following expenses for your organization: site rental fee—legal fees—sound and lighting equipment rental fees—performer's fee and expenses—production consultant's fee—union workers' wages—purchase of liability insurance—security costs—printing costs—postage costs—promotion costs. These expenses can require a considerable amount of up-front money. Efforts should be made to obtain them for free or to have the production underwritten.

Volunteer Requirements

The volunteer leaders needed to produce a professional show include the event chairperson, arrangements chairperson, printed materials chairperson, promotions chairperson, sponsorship and underwriting chairperson, ticket-selling chairperson, treasurer, and volunteer coordinator. Their roles are described in the Introduction to Programs. In addition, producing a professional show requires the involvement of the following people:

sound and lighting system coordinator—rents the equipment and hires the technicians to set it up and operate it;

stage manager—makes sure that everyone is working on schedule, that the stage is set up properly, and that any backstage problems during the show are handled immediately (the stage manager must be experienced, so if you cannot find a volunteer with this experience, then hire someone);

lobby manager—supervises the ticket takers and the setup of any table displays;

house manager—supervises the ushers and handles any seating problems;

security coordinator—hires the security workers, gives them their assignments, and deals with any problems they cannot solve;

box office manager—sells tickets at the door;

first-aid specialist—assists in any medical problems or
  emergencies that arise;

Many more volunteers are needed to assist these specialists with the detailed work that producing a professional show involves.

Using a Consultant

Producing a professional show can be extremely difficult. If you have
never done it before, consider using a consultant. But try to get a professional producer to volunteer the necessary expertise to your event. Be sure
to mention the professional assistance you will be receiving when you contact a performer. Since charitable performances are notorious for being
poorly produced, this information may influence the performer's decision
to do your show.

Selecting a Performer

Before starting your search, decide if you want a local performer, who
may be less expensive, or a national performer, who may attract a larger
audience. Whether local or national, the performer must be somebody who
is appropriate for your organization.

To find a local performer, ask local promoters and club owners for
their ideas. Then go to the clubs where the performers are booked and
check out their popularity. Also, ask members of your organization and
your friends for their suggestions.

To find a national performer, read the entertainment sections of newspapers, magazines, and trade magazines of the entertainment industry. By
studying these publications you will find out which performers participate
in fund-raising events and what issues are of interest to various performers.

Once you have a list of performers in mind, make your final decision
based on your connections, the performer's draw, the performer's fee, and
available dates. Then find out what the performer's needs and expectations
will be and have a written contract drawn up.

Nationally known performers who have a reputation for doing fund-
raising events are deluged with requests. Often their decision to do a particular show is the result of a personal connection. Try to find someone in
your organization who somehow has access to the performer you want—
or who knows someone who has access. If you are absolutely sure that no
one in your organization has any connections, then you must be willing to
take the time to develop them yourself. Contact the performer's record
company, manager, or agent with letters and phone calls as a first step in

determining the performer's interest and availability. Or try to find a way to contact the performer directly. Make sure that your communication highlights what the performer will gain from doing a show for you (e.g., personal gratification, exposure, or publicity).

The best person to contact, other then the performer, is the performer's manager. Unlike an agent, who books the entertainer's dates and receives a percentage of each performance, a manager is involved in the development of the performer's career and is aware of the performer's interests. Managers are more likely than agents to be interested in fund-raising events.

The following resources will assist you in selecting a performer for your production:

> *Performance Magazine* (1020 Currie Street, Fort Worth, Texas 76107, 817-338-9444)—This magazine publishes monthly schedules of performers touring the U.S. and abroad. It also lists concerts that various groups have performed, including the date, the facility, the capacity, the ticket price, and how many tickets were sold.
>
> *Billboard Publications* (9107 Wilshire Boulevard, Beverly Hills, California 90210, 213-273-7040)—This is the trade magazine of the music industry.

In determining if the performer can draw the number of people you would like to attend the event, consult with local promoters and radio station disc jockeys for their opinions. Check the performer's record sales, and find out the average attendance for the performer's shows.

Take special note of exactly when the performer last appeared in your area. If the appearance was within the last 6 months, or if the appearance is scheduled to be within the next 6 months, the performer's commercial contract may not allow any other shows within a particular geographic radius and for a particular length of time. Even if there are no contract restrictions, a performer who has appeared in your area within the last 6 months may not have much drawing power.

Because it is so expensive to produce a professional show, the only way your organization may be able to make a significant profit—without charging exorbitant ticket prices—is by having the performer's fee underwritten or by convincing the performer to give up at least a portion of the fee, perhaps in exchange for covering expenses. Of course, even this type of arrangement can be quite costly. If you do agree to cover the performer's expenses, make sure that you know precisely what those expenses will involve. For example, determine the exact number of people whose airfare, hotel rooms, and rental cars you will be paying for. After you have found a performer whose fees are within your budget and who is willing to do your show, decide on a date. This will depend on the performer's availability and on your organization's preferences.

Determine the performer's needs and expectations well in advance of the show so that you can prepare to meet them. The performer may have specific requests regarding accommodations, transportation, and the schedule for the visit (e.g., times and places of media interviews, party or meal attendance, and free time requirements).

Well in advance of the show you should also let the performer know what you will need. For example, you will probably want biographical material, photographs, a list of suggested interview questions, and any other press material. And you will need the performer's sound, lighting, and staging requirements, instructions, and cues. Ask the performer how many free tickets you should set aside, obtain a list of the people the performer will allow backstage, and find out how the performer wants to be introduced. If you want the performer to say something special about your organization, prepare the material and deliver it to the performer at least several hours before the show.

With the help of an attorney, draw up a written contract for the performer as soon as possible. In its simplest form, a contract can be a letter of agreement that states the date, time, place, type, and length of the performance, as well as the performer's fee and expenses. Or it can be a much more complicated document. If the performer sends your organization a contract, review it carefully with an attorney before signing it. A contract between your organization and the performer is absolutely necessary before you start spending money on the event.

Choosing a Facility

At the same time that you are trying to select a performer, you must decide on a facility. Consider the following factors in choosing a facility for your show: size, cost, unions, acoustics and lighting, stage, and seating.

Select a facility based on an estimate of the number of people you think will attend the event. If you have no idea, find out how many people have attended the performer's show in a city of size similar to yours and under similar circumstances. If your estimated figures cover a wide range, try to choose a facility that can accommodate the middle of the range. If that is not possible, then opt for a smaller facility rather than a larger one. With a smaller facility, the financial risk and anxiety for your organization will be less, and the audience will have the sense of seeing a sold-out performance rather than a poorly attended one. Also, the performer probably will not object to working in what may be a smaller facility than usual, since the performer who has not exhausted the potential audience can return to the area to do a commercial performance for a larger audience.

Clubs often make excellent small facilities. A club owner may offer your organization use of the club on a night when it is normally closed, perhaps on a regular basis. And the owner may not charge you a rental fee, choosing instead to take all of the proceeds from the sale of drinks and to leave all ticket income to your organization. Clubs also offer the advantage of having sound and lighting systems already in place. The appeal of the arrangement to the club is free publicity, increased business, and goodwill in the community.

It may be possible to do two shows in a small facility—either on the same night or on consecutive nights. The advantage of doing two shows on the same night is that the additional costs will not be as great as doing two shows on different nights. The disadvantages of doing two shows on the same night are that the performer and crew may be extremely tired, the two shows will not be as long as a single show might be, and the house will have to be turned over quickly and efficiently. In contrast, doing the same show on two consecutive nights has the advantage of the performer being less tired and able to do a longer show each night. Doing the same show on two consecutive nights has the disadvantage of costing you more money.

If your only choice is a facility that will probably be too large, you may be taking quite a risk in using it. Large facilities usually charge high rental fees, and they are difficult to sell out. You could end up losing money. Try to negotiate the rental fee, and consider closing off a portion of the facility, such as the balcony, to make the house seem fuller. Another method for filling a house is to arrange for a free ticket promotion with a local radio station.

Before entering into an agreement with any facility, make sure you know exactly what it is going to cost you. For example, in addition to the price for using the facility, which may be a flat fee or a flat fee plus a percentage of the gross, there may be additional costs, including the following: use of tables in the lobby, cleanup, stage door guards, use of the box office, use of the marquee, liability insurance, use of sound and lighting equipment, and hall ushers. Ask a lot of questions to uncover any possible hidden costs. And check with other groups who have used the facility to learn about their experiences.

Determine if the facility is a union facility and, if so, what jobs are union controlled. If the facility is unionized, you probably will not be able to use any workers who are not union members. When working with a unionized facility, find out what the minimum crew requirements are and try to use just the minimum. Ask if you can supplement the minimum union crew with your own people. And make sure you know what the union regulations are regarding working hours and overtime.

Be certain that the facility has good acoustics and lighting. Otherwise your show could be a disaster. Regarding acoustics, try to avoid places with high ceilings, such as churches and gymnasiums. And remember that glass makes sound bounce, while heavy carpeting and draperies absorb sound. Check to see if the facility has sufficient power to run your sound system and lights. Locate the electrical outlets to make sure there are enough of them in the necessary spots.

Determine if the stage's length and width are adequate for the type of show that will be presented. For example, a dance troupe will need more space than a singer. Also, determine if the stage is high enough for everybody in the audience to see.

Find out how many seats are in the house and subtract the number that are not usable due to poor visibility or sound. A facility with too many bad seats will detract from your potential profit by preventing you from selling every ticket in the house.

Once you have selected a facility, ask for a contract. The contract should guarantee the date, the hours that you have access to the facility, the cost, and any special arrangements that you have agreed to. Review the contract carefully with an attorney before signing it.

Selling Tickets

Selling tickets is crucial to the success of a production. But before the actual selling begins, a number of decisions must be made, including whether to sell tickets in advance or just at the door, whether to sell general admission or reserved seating, and whether to use a professional ticket agency or to sell the tickets yourself through ticket outlets.

Decide whether you want to sell tickets in advance, at the door, or both. The advantages of selling tickets in advance include the following: You will always have a sense of how large the attendance will be, you will have cash flowing in before the show, you will not have long lines of people at the ticket office the night of the show, people will know for sure that they can get in, there will not be too much cash at the ticket office the night of the show, and if you have a no-refund policy and the show is cancelled due to the weather or some other reason, you will still make some money. The advantages of selling tickets at the door include these: Special advance tickets will not need to be printed, the expense of paying ticket outlets a commission will be avoided, and you will not have to worry about keeping track of sales and handling money over an extended period of time.

Most organizations sell tickets in advance as well as at the door. If you decide to offer both options, then you must determine whether you will charge more for the tickets sold at the door. This tactic may encourage people to buy their tickets early. On the other hand, it may penalize people who do not have the money in advance, or who decide to attend at the last minute.

Advance tickets should go on sale about a month before the show.

Ticket locations and a phone number for additional information should be included in your publicity. The ticket itself should state the name of the show, price, date, time, location, and the name of your organization. Every ticket should be numbered so that you can easily keep track of how many have been sold.

If you decide to let people order tickets through the mail, you can request that they include a self-addressed, stamped envelope so that you can mail them their tickets. Or you can hold all tickets at the door so that you will not have to worry about tickets getting lost in the mail. However, you may be faced with a long line of people waiting in line to pick up their tickets just before the event.

Do not offer every seat for sale, since you will need to save some seats to accommodate certain sound and lighting equipment, to give away as complimentary tickets to special guests, to give to the performer and crew, and to give to the media. If possible, hold all complimentary tickets at the door rather than hand them out in advance. That way you can try to sell any tickets that are not picked up. Also, you can avoid being frustrated by the person who received a free ticket from you and then gave it away or even sold it to somebody else.

Decide whether to sell general admission or reserved seating. General admission means that everyone pays the same amount and can sit wherever they want to, on a first-come, first-served basis. Reserved seating means that a person purchases a specific seat for a price that may vary according to the seat location. Reserved seating eliminates the situation of people arriving early to stand in line so that they can get a good seat. And reserved seating may result in greater profits, since some of these tickets are generally more expensive. Reserved seating, however, is more costly, because you must pay to print seat numbers on the tickets and recruit ushers to show people to their seats. If you decide to have reserved seating, consider selling the tickets from just one outlet, or using a professional ticket agency so that you do not have to worry about distributing the tickets in an equitable seating manner among numerous locations.

Whether general admission or reserved seating, advance tickets can be sold by a professional ticket agency or by your organization through ticket outlets that you have selected. The advantages of using a professional ticket agency are that people are used to buying tickets that way, people can use their credit cards, the agency will print the tickets from their own computer, the agency will be responsible for bounced checks or any other fraud, the agency computer will accurately keep track of the number of tickets sold, your volunteers will not have to sell tickets, and the agency may publicize your event. The advantages of selling tickets on your own through ticket outlets that you have selected are that you have access to incoming money from ticket sales at all times, you can choose outlets in geographic areas that you particularly want to reach, and you can get good publicity from the outlets while providing them with publicity as well. The disadvantage to using either a professional ticket agency or ticket outlets is that they may expect a commission or service charge from the ticket sales.

Note that a seller's commission is quite different from service charge. A seller's commission is taken out of the ticket price by the ticket seller. A service charge is added to the ticket price by the ticket seller. Because a service charge is paid directly to the ticket seller by the customer, this would be the most advantageous arrangement for your organization.

If you decide to sell tickets on your own through outlets that you have selected, be sure to establish a contract with your outlets. The contract should state the ticket prices, the number of tickets given to the outlet, the selling dates and times, the commission or service charge the outlet is taking, how and when the commission or service charge will be paid, and who is responsible for missing tickets and money problems.

Selecting your ticket outlets is an important strategic decision. The locations of the outlets should be over a wide area to make ticket buying easier for your intended audience and to help publicize the event in an effort to attract new audiences. The outlets should be easy to recognize, such as a chain of record stores or bookstores.

Do not use too many outlets. And start out by giving each outlet a small number of tickets. Then give larger batches of tickets to those outlets that are selling the most tickets. Keep track of every ticket distributed to the outlets. Design a special sheet to indicate which tickets each outlet has (e.g., bookstore A has numbers 1–50 and bookstore B has numbers 51–100).

If your organization is planning to produce other shows, after the performance you should evaluate each outlet's ticket sales and try to establish some patterns. For example, determine how many tickets each outlet sold, why some sold more than others, and when most of the tickets were sold. This information will help you plan the ticket outlets, promotion, and cash flow for your next show.

Make sure that ticket sales and locations are advertised in the section of your local newspapers that normally advertise such performances and on the radio stations that play your performer's music. Otherwise, the performer's fans in your area may never find out about the event. If tickets sales are doing poorly just days before the event and you are able to determine that you will lose less money by canceling the show than by presenting it, then cancel.

Designing the Sound and Lighting Systems

Because the sound and lighting systems are extremely important to the success of any performance, it is a worthwhile expenditure to hire experienced professionals to set up and supervise these systems. The technicians should attend a performance and test the equipment at the facility where you hope to hold the event before you make a final commitment to the facility.

The following points should be kept in mind about sound and lighting equipment, whether it is provided by the facility or rented from a separate company: the equipment should be appropriate for the size and layout of the facility, the number of people it holds, and the type of performance; the equipment should meet the performer's requests; and every piece of rented equipment should be checked before it leaves the rental store to make sure it works.

A meeting should be held at the performance facility a few weeks before the day of the show. At this time the sound system and lighting system technicians can again look over the equipment at the facility. In addition, the stage manager can get a general idea of how the stage will be set up, the lobby manager can determine where table displays will be located, the house manager can review the seating structure, and the security coordinator can get a feel for the layout of the facility.

PROFESSIONAL SPONSORSHIPS

A professional sponsorship involves guaranteeing (i.e., assuming financial responsibility for) a show that is scheduled to be presented in your area by a professional production company. It also involves realizing a percentage of the show's profits (beyond the amount of the guarantee) in return for your investment. Sponsoring a professional show may or may not entail your organization's participation in the ticket-selling process, depending on the arrangement between your organization and the production company. Types of professional productions that can be sponsored include big-name bands and orchestras, carnivals, circuses, ice shows, individual performers, lecture series, musicals, and plays.

Special Advantages

In addition to the general advantages listed in the Introduction to Programs, a professional sponsorship offers the following special advantages:

Sponsoring a professional show is much easier to plan and implement than producing a professional show since your organization does not have to be responsible for the actual production.

A range of sponsorship options exists, depending on the amount of effort your organization is willing to invest in the event, the degree of financial risk it wants to take, and the amount of profit it hopes to earn.

Special Cautions

Keeping in mind the general cautions listed in the Introduction to Programs, the following special cautions about a professional sponsorship should be carefully considered as well:

- Considerable up-front money is required when the production company requests your organization to fully or partially guarantee the show.
- Although sponsoring a professional show is much easier than actually producing a show, its profit-making potential may be less, since the income from the event must be split between the production company and your organization.
- If ticket sales do not bring in enough income to exceed the amount of the guarantee, then your organization will not recoup the guarantee amount and will actually lose money.

Expenses

A professional sponsorship can entail the following expenses for your organization: the full or partial guarantee amount that the production company requests—purchase of liability insurance—printing costs—postage costs—promotion costs. These are up-front costs that require funds from your organization prior to the event.

Volunteer Requirements

The volunteer leaders needed to sponsor a professional show include the event chairperson, the promotions chairperson, the ticket-selling chairperson, the treasurer, and the volunteer coordinator. Their roles are described in the Introduction to Programs. The additional volunteer involvement required for sponsoring a professional show depends on the role your organization agrees to take in promoting and selling tickets to the show. The greater your organization's promotion and ticket-selling responsibilities, the greater the volunteer involvement.

Finding Out About Possible Sponsorships

The two ways of finding out about the possible sponsorship of a professional show are when a production company comes to you or when you seek out a production company. Special considerations should be kept in mind for each approach.

If your organization is prominent in your community, or if your cause is extremely appealing, a professional production company may approach your organization with an offer for sponsorship. Consider the offer with caution. Find out why they are making the offer. Check to see what other sponsors the production company has worked with in your community, and ask those sponsors what their experiences have been with the company. Determine the exact amount of work and money that will be expected of your organization, and whether the effort and expense will be worth your while. For example, will your organization be expected to sell tickets to the event, or will the production company sell the tickets and just use your organization's name in the publicity? And decide if you really want your organization's name affiliated with the event.

If you decide to approach a production company, you must first find out what professional productions are coming to your area, and whether a scheduled production already has sponsorship. Contact the management of the facilities where such productions are normally presented. These people should be able to tell you well in advance what the shows are, when they are scheduled, and how to get in touch with their production companies. Also, contact the special events coordinator at a nearby college or university. Productions that want to come to town often send information and proposals to these institutions. It is important to find out as early as possible what shows are coming to town and when, since by the time an event is announced to the public, any type of local sponsorship has probably already been arranged.

As soon as you hear about an interesting, appropriate professional production that is scheduled for your community, contact the production company. Ask if the company would be willing to allow your group to sponsor the show. Some productions will be interested in your inquiry— either for humanitarian or financial reasons—while others will not even consider your offer.

In deciding whether to sponsor a certain type of show, consider the following factors:

> *Facility*—Your community must have the proper facility to house the show.

> *Timing*—Your organization must have sufficient time to plan your role in the event, and promote it.

> *Novelty*—A production that has never come to your community, or at least has not been there for many years, may draw large audiences and offer greater moneymaking potential.

Before making your final decision, attend the show—even if you must travel a long distance to do so. Check all the details of the show (e.g., size, length, scenery, cast, and name performers), and then obtain the production company's written guarantee that the exact same show will be presented in your community. Review the production portion of the contract carefully with your attorney before signing it.

Deciding on the Type of Sponsorship

Sponsorship of a professional show by your organization can involve full guarantee sponsorship, partial guarantee sponsorship, and no guarantee sponsorship. These options vary according to financial investment and profit-making potential.

Full guarantee sponsorship requires the greatest financial investment from your organization and offers the greatest profit-making potential in return for that investment. This option usually occurs when your organization approaches a production company with a request to bring a show to town that otherwise would not have been scheduled. Under full guarantee sponsorship, your organization must guarantee the production a specific amount of money to come to your community. The amount of the guarantee should equal the show's production expenses. In addition, an agreement must be reached on an equitable split between the production company and your organization of all income from the event. Full guarantee sponsorship can be risky for an organization. If income from the event does not exceed the amount of the guarantee, then the organization loses money. So, before signing a contract that commits your organization to full guarantee sponsorship, try to be as certain as possible that the event will bring in more money than the amount of the guarantee. Of course, if your organization can get the guarantee underwritten, then you will eliminate the risk of losing money.

Partial guarantee sponsorship requires a smaller financial investment from your organization and offers less profit-making potential. This option occurs when the production company agrees to a guarantee amount that is actually less than the cost of bringing the production to your town. Production companies are likely to agree to the option of partial guarantee sponsorship when they strongly feel that the show will do well in the community. Because the production's risks increase through partial guarantee sponsorship, the company may take a larger percentage of the income in excess of the guarantee amount. Although the profit-making potential for an organization may be less through partial guarantee sponsorship, the risk of losing money on the guarantee is also less.

No guarantee sponsorship requires no financial investment from your organization and offers limited profit-making potential in return. This option generally occurs under one of two sets of circumstances. First, the production company just uses your organization's name in promoting the event and pays your organization a small share of the income for use of your name. Second, the production company gives your organization the responsibility of selling tickets to the event and, in return for your efforts, gives you a percentage of the income above a specified amount (that amount is generally equal to what the guarantee figure would have been under full or partial guarantee sponsorship) or a commission on each ticket sold. No guarantee sponsorship, obviously, presents no financial risk to your organization.

Regardless of the type of sponsorship your organization agrees to, make sure that the arrangement is written as a formal contract and reviewed by your attorney before you sign it. The sponsorship portion of the contract should detail all financial conditions (e.g., guarantee amounts, income distribution formulas, and commissions) and all responsibilities (e.g., selling tickets, promoting the event, and keeping records).

SPECIAL PERFORMANCES

A special performance entails selecting a show or movie that is coming to town, purchasing anywhere from a block of tickets to the entire house of one performance at a discounted rate, and then selling the tickets at a higher price—mostly to friends and supporters of your organization—to benefit your organization. A special performance often includes additional features before or after the show, such as cocktails, dinner, dessert, a cast party, a door prize drawing, or a raffle. These features, of course, are reflected in the price of the ticket.

Special Advantages

In addition to the general advantages listed in the Introduction to Programs, a special performance offers the following special advantages:

> A special performance is a glamorous, attractive, exciting, fun event that people like to attend any time of the year.

> Your organization has no responsibilities regarding arranging or financing the production. Your responsibilities are limited to promoting and selling tickets to your event.

> Offering a range of ticket prices makes it possible for supporters at different income levels to attend the event.

Special Cautions

Keeping in mind the general cautions listed in the Introduction to Programs, the following special cautions about planning a special performance should be carefully considered as well:

The inherent financial risk in this type of event is that your organization may have to take financial responsibility for any unsold tickets that you purchase.

Up-front money is necessary to purchase the tickets from the theater and to pay for the expenses involved in featuring other activities at the event, such as a cocktail party.

To make a large profit, you will probably have to set some of your ticket prices quite high, particularly if the event includes such additional expensive features as a dinner.

Due to the nature of the entertainment industry, certain performances are scheduled just a couple weeks before their opening date, allowing your organization little time to plan and promote the event.

Theaters may be reluctant to schedule a special performance on a weekend evening—which may be the best time for your organization to hold the event—unless you are willing to buy out the house at the market price.

Expenses

A special performance can entail the following expenses for your organization: purchase of anywhere from a block of tickets to the entire house—costs affiliated with such additional features as a dinner or cast party—purchase of liability insurance—printing costs—postage costs—promotion costs. Underwriting or sponsorship should be sought for these expenses, which are all up-front costs.

Volunteer Requirements

The volunteer leaders needed to plan and present a special performance include the event chairperson, printed materials chairperson, promotions chairperson, reservations chairperson, special features chairperson, sponsorship and underwriting chairperson, ticket-selling chairperson, treasurer, and volunteer coordinator. Their roles are described in the Introduction to Programs. In addition to these leaders, many more volunteers are needed, especially to sell tickets to the event.

Arranging a Special Performance

Contact the owners or business managers at area theaters and ask if they would be willing to arrange a special performance of any of their upcoming productions for your organization—either during a dress rehearsal, preview, or regular performance. Make sure that a production has not received poor reviews, since such reviews may have a negative effect on your attendance. Also, make sure that a production has not been chosen to benefit another organization in your area, since such competition may detract from your attendance.

An interested theater will offer you either the whole house or a block of seats for free, at a discount, or at the regular price. Obviously, the best deal occurs when the theater donates a performance and your organization gets to sell every seat in the house and keep all the money. But this only happens when an organization has unusually close connections with the theater owner or the show's director, producer, or star. Usually the theater will offer the house or a block of seats on a weeknight at a discounted rate per ticket.

A theater that offers the entire house to your organization for a price may give you two options for buying out the house. Under the first and most common option, your organization must pay the theater for every seat in the house at the agreed-upon rate, regardless of the number of tickets you actually sell. This arrangement, which guarantees the theater a certain amount of money and allows the theater to claim a sold-out performance, can be financially risky for your organization. Under the second option, the theater gives your organization a chance to sell every seat in the house, but then the theater takes back any unsold tickets by a certain date to sell at the regular price. This arrangement is not nearly as risky as having to buy out the entire house without a return policy.

Carefully consider how many tickets you can sell to your members, how many they can sell to others, and how many can be sold to the general public. If your organization is hesitant about its ability to sell every seat in the house, then either ask the theater if it would be willing to sell the balance, or purchase just a block of tickets.

Arranging a Movie Premiere or Special Showing

A movie premiere entails convincing a motion picture studio to hold the opening night of a major motion picture at a theater in your area to benefit your organization. The movie may somehow tie into your organization's cause, although such a connection certainly is not necessary for a successful event. Movie premieres are exciting because they involve famous people connected to the film. But they are scarce and extremely difficult to obtain unless you have some unique connections with the film company, producer, director, or star.

One way to arrange a movie premiere is to work through a local theater. An interested theater owner or manager should be able to work with the film industry—either directly or through a national theater chain—on your behalf. Movie premieres are advantageous to theaters, since they provide an enormous amount of publicity. But movie premieres offer limited advantages to film companies. A premiere will not affect a movie's success; it will only give the film company an opportunity to make a gesture of goodwill and receive publicity for that gesture.

Arranging a movie premiere without the assistance of a local theater is also possible but much more difficult. To find out about soon-to-be-released movies, purchase a copy of *Variety* at a newsstand. After you decide which movies you want to pursue, call the motion picture studios directly and ask to speak to the appropriate person in the public relations department regarding a benefit movie premiere. Before placing a single call, however, prepare yourself for an involved process that requires a great deal of determination. You might also want to contact American Multi-Cinema, Inc. at 106 West 14 Street, Suite 1700, Kansas City, Missouri 64105, (816) 221-4000 for assistance in arranging a movie premiere.

A special movie showing entails buying out the house or a block of tickets for a movie that is scheduled to be shown at a local theater. Arranging a special movie showing is much simpler than arranging a movie premiere, since it can be done at the local level, and it entails showing a film that will already be in place. Work directly with a local theater owner or manager in planning a special movie showing, which can feature a first-run film, a second-run film, or a re-released film.

A first-run film is a movie that has already premiered and is about to be shown for the first time in your area. Often first-run films are shown at theaters that are part of national chains. Many national chains offer their theaters for special showings only at the market price, not at a discounted price. If you decide to feature a first-run film at your special movie showing, try to schedule the event as a preview to the opening of the movie in your area. That way you can take advantage of all the publicity for the film, yet avoid the risk of your intended audience seeing the movie prior to your event.

A second-run, return engagement film is a movie that has been out for a while and is now being shown at theaters that show only second-run films at a reduced price. Most second-run film theaters are locally owned and easy to work with. Second-run films can also be used to put together a weekend-long film festival. For example, one organization created a "Family Film Fest" of movies that appealed to children and their parents. The movies were shown in rotation throughout a 3-day holiday weekend.

A re-released film is a film that has been released again, usually a number of years after it first appeared. Re-released films include cult films, classic films, box office hits, and critically acclaimed films. These films are generally shown at locally owned theaters. One organization used a re-released film and recreated a glamorous movie premiere of the 1930s.

A written contract should be drawn up as soon as your organization has reached an agreement with a theater regarding either a special performance or a movie showing. The contract should state all of the theater's responsibilities and all of your organization's responsibilities.

Involving Celebrities

Celebrity involvement in an event adds to the excitement and helps sell tickets. Celebrities are more likely to respond favorably to your organization's request to participate in your event if they are particularly interested in your cause, if their participation will result in a great deal of publicity, or if somebody they know makes the request. Determine if any celebrities would be willing to participate in your event either before or after the show. For example, the cast of a play may be happy to attend your dessert party following the performance, the director of a movie premiere may be willing to attend the dinner before the showing of the film (particularly if the director is being honored by your organization), or the star of a movie may be able to attend your event if the star happens to be on tour promoting the movie anyway.

RESOURCES FOR LOCAL PRODUCTIONS

DeSoto, C. *For fun and funds: Creative fund-raising ideas for your organization.* West Nyack, NY: Parker Publishing Co., 1983, pp. 99–106.
Hay, J. T. *534 ways to raise money.* New York: Simon & Schuster, 1983, pp. 59–61, 68–69.
Pritchard, J. H. *There's plenty of money for nonprofit groups willing to earn their shares— How to do it successfully.* Phoenix: Cornucopia Publications, 1984, pp. 161–167, 195–221, 430–433.

RESOURCES FOR PROFESSIONAL PRODUCTIONS

Babitz, M. Why most benefit concerts lose money. *Grassroots Fundraising Journal,* October 1982, pp. 9–10.
Berson, G. *Making a show of it: A guide to concert production.* Ukiah, CA: Redwood Records, 1980.
Honig, L. Fundraising events, Part two: Getting into the act or finding a performer for your benefit concert. *Grassroots Fundraising Journal,* June 1982, pp. 9–13.

RESOURCES FOR PROFESSIONAL SPONSORSHIPS

Musselman, V. W. *Money raising activities for community groups.* New York: Association Press, 1969, p. 228.

Pritchard, J. H. *There's plenty of money for nonprofit groups willing to earn their shares—How to do it successfully*. Phoenix: Cornucopia Publications, 1984, pp. 403–420.

RESOURCES FOR SPECIAL PERFORMANCES

Alberti, C. E., Macko, G. S., & Whitcomb, N. B. *Money-makers: A systematic approach to special events fund raising*. Ambler, PA: Whitcomb Associates, 1982, Supplement 2, pp. 1–27.

B'nai B'rith Fund Raising Cabinet, *B'nai B'rith Fund Raising Chairman Handbook*. Washington, D.C.: B'nai B'rith Leadership Cabinet, pp. 77–79.

Drotning, P. T. *500 ways for small charities to raise money*. Chicago: Contemporary Books, Inc., 1979, pp. 133–137.

Flanagan, J. *The grass roots fundraising book*. Chicago: Contemporary Books, Inc., 1982, pp. 235–240.

Hay, J. T. *534 ways to raise money*. New York: Simon & Schuster, 1983, pp. 61–67.

Leibert, E. R. & Sheldon, B. E. *Handbook of special events for nonprofit organizations*. New York: Association Press, 1972, pp. 169–187.

Musselman, V. W. *Money raising activities for community groups*. New York: Association Press, 1969, pp. 237–238.

National Council of Jewish Women, Inc., *The raiser's edge*. New York: National Council of Jewish Women, Inc., pp. 23–24.

Pritchard, J. H. *There's plenty of money for nonprofit groups willing to earn their shares—How to do it successfully*. Phoenix: Cornucopia Publications, 1984, pp. 235–238, 377–379.

Sheerin, M. *How to raise top dollars from special events*. New York: Public Service Materials Center, 1984, pp. 63–84.

Chapter 12

GALA EVENTS

Auctions

An auction is a type of sale where the participants bid on items that have been donated. At an oral auction, guests bid on items that are presented by an auctioneer. At a silent auction, guests place written bids on items that are on display. An auction usually offers both oral and silent bidding as well as a sit-down or buffet dinner and other gala features, including entertainment, dancing, door prizes, and a raffle. All features are reflected in the admission price to the event. Sometimes a preview party is held the night before the auction to give special supporters a chance to inspect the auction items in advance. Sometimes an auction is the preview activity for another major event.

Special Advantages

In addition to the general advantages listed in the Introduction to Programs, an auction offers the following special advantages:

> An auction can be fun and exciting for people who support your organization and who like this type of gala event. After all, an auction provides its guests with the chance to buy something they normally might not purchase— and sometimes at a bargain price—while having a great time and contributing to a worthwhile cause all at once.

This type of event offers a good opportunity to promote your organization, as volunteers seek donated items from different segments of the community.

The donor, the buyer, and the organization all benefit from an auction. The donor receives a tax deduction for the donation. The buyer receives a tax deduction for the amount paid for the item that is above its retail value. And the organization profits from the sale of tickets to the event, the sale of the auction items, and unanticipated donations.

People who enjoy gala auction events may attend as a result of the publicity, regardless of the cause.

Any time of the year can be a good time to hold an auction.

Special Cautions

Keeping in mind the general cautions listed in the Introduction to Programs, the following special cautions about an auction should be carefully considered as well:

An experienced auctioneer is usually necessary for the success of an auction.

The items being offered at an auction must correspond to the level of affluence of the audience. If the average income of the audience covers a wide range, then a large variety of items should be offered so that everyone can bid on at least something.

Buyers at an auction can deduct from their income taxes only the amount of their contribution over the retail value of the items they purchase.

An auction involves a great deal of personal contact, since all of the items to be auctioned must be solicited. Some volunteers are reluctant to ask for donations.

Expenses

An auction can entail the following expenses for your organization: facility rental fee—auctioneer's fee—catering costs—purchase of decorations—equipment rental fee—purchase of liquor—liquor licensing fee—storage space rental—purchase of liability insurance—security costs—printing costs—postage costs—promotion costs. Of course, it is possible to have the event underwritten or to have many of these items and services donated. Every effort should be made to seek sponsorship or in-kind contributions.

Volunteer Requirements

The volunteer leaders needed to plan and conduct an auction include the event chairperson, honorary chairpersons, arrangements chairperson, acquisitions chairperson, printed materials chairperson, promotions chairperson, reservations chairperson, special features chairperson, sponsorship and underwriting chairperson, treasurer, and volunteer coordinator. Their roles are described in the Introduction to Programs. In addition to these volunteer leaders, a great number of volunteers are needed, especially for soliciting the auction items. The members of the acquisitions committee are crucial to the success of the auction. They should include persons who have contacts in a variety of segments of the community, and who know the right people to ask for donations of merchandise or service.

Volunteers who serve as spotters, runners, secretaries, cashiers, and table workers at the actual event are equally important. Spotters must station themselves among the audience and direct bidders and bids to the auctioneer's attention, as well as assist bidders who are having trouble hearing or keeping track of the bidding. Runners must carry oral auction items to and from the auction block. At least two sets of runners are needed at the auction block so that while one pair removes an item that has been sold, the other pair can bring in the next item. They must also deliver the auction contracts from the secretaries to the cashiers. Secretaries must record on the auction contracts who bought each item and what amount the item was sold for. After an item has been sold, a runner must transfer the contract to the cashier. Cashiers must be extremely well organized so that the purchasers do not have to wait in long lines to pay for their items. Table workers must assist bidders at the silent auction tables. They should be familiar with their table items so that they can answer bidders' questions.

Obtaining Auction Items

Most of the work in organizing an auction involves soliciting auction items and services from potential donors. Acquisitions for an auction can cover numerous merchandise and service territories, including the following:

> *Wholesale items*—Wholesalers and clearinghouses may have leftover goods, especially after a holiday, that they are happy to give away.

Commercial and retail items—All possible stores should be approached either by location or by type of operation. Stores that are part of national chains should be approached as early as possible since they may need to get permission from their main headquarters before making a donation.

Services—Providers of all possible services that will be of interest to your audience should be approached.

In-house items—Services and merchandise should be donated from your own organization's members and suppliers.

Cash—Donations of cash can be used to complement other items. For example, if you acquire a weekend at someone's summer home, a cash contribution can be used to purchase airplane tickets.

All acquisitions should be obtained at least 2 months before the auction so that the auction catalog can be written and printed. Through brainstorming and creative thinking, volunteers can combine different items into attractive packages.

The best method of solicitation is through personal visits, although telephone calls and letters can also be used successfully. With any solicitation, the following points should be kept in mind:

If possible, a friend or acquaintance of the potential donor should serve as the solicitor.

Volunteers may be more comfortable carrying out their solicitations in pairs.

The solicitor should state all facts pertaining to the auction at the beginning of the visit, phone call, or letter (e.g., what organization the auction is for, when it will be held, and what the proceeds will be used for).

If the solicitor has donated an item to the auction, that fact should be included in the presentation.

When contacting a previous donor, acknowledge the person's most recent gift before asking for another donation.

Contact a potential donor with several suggestions for items in mind. Ask for the most expensive items first.

It may be helpful to show potential donors a sample of last year's program book/catalog. The donors can then visualize what their names and businesses will look like in print. And they can see who else has participated in the auction.

It may be worthwhile to mention to a potential donor the items that the donor's competitors are giving to the auction.

If the donor is going to be a guest at the auction, determine whether the donor would be willing to offer the donation a second time at the event if the item causes exciting bidding during its initial presentation.

Be prepared with alternatives for the potential donor. For example, someone who cannot donate an item for the auction may be able to buy an ad in the program book or underwrite a portion of the auction dinner.

If the auction must purchase an item, try to buy it at the wholesale price. And ask the store manager for another type of donation.

When an auction item is obtained, a contract should be filled out on the spot and, if possible, the item should be given to the solicitor. The contract serves to legitimize and protect the transaction and to control the inventory. At least three copies of the contract are necessary—one for the auction committee, one for the donor, and one for the buyer. The contract should include information about the item (e.g., description, retail value, number of pieces, catalog number, storage, restrictions, delivery/pickup), the donor (e.g., name, business address, phone number, signature, name to be printed in the catalog), and the buyer (e.g., name, address, phone number, amount paid, form of payment). Seek legal advice in developing a contract.

Another way to obtain items for the auction is through a series of gift-giving parties. Usually these are parties sponsored by members of the organization. The price of admission is a gift of a certain value to be donated to the auction.

In addition, certain auction items, such as pieces of art, cars, or trips, may be obtained on commission. This means that the amount paid for the item is split in an agreed-upon way between the donor and the group sponsoring the auction. Through a commission, the auction is actually selling an artist's or merchant's goods and taking a percentage of the sale. A commission should be considered only for very special items that the auction must have. It should not be an option available to every donor, since commissions will decrease your profits, as well as raise questions about your organization's credibility.

Storing Items

The ideal situation is when your auction site includes storage space for the auction items. If this cannot be arranged, then try to store the items at a location that is as close to the auction as possible. As a last resort, members of your organization can store the items at their homes. But this adds risks regarding theft and damage as well as difficulty in transporting the items.

Finding an Auctioneer

An experienced auctioneer is crucial to the success of an oral auction. The auctioneer should be able to keep the auction exciting, know where to start and stop the bidding, possess a lively chant and the ability to conduct a fast-paced sale, be able to create interest and rivalry among the bidders, and make the auction items irresistible. In addition to deriving the maximum income potential from your auction, a professional auctioneer may offer the advantage of bringing a following to your auction. Given the chance to view the auction items before the event, the auctioneer may then notify certain people who would be interested in bidding on specific items.

The chairperson of the auction should provide the auctioneer with as much assistance as possible. This should include written descriptions and selling points of all of the oral auction items, a list of the likely most promising bidders and their interests, indications of the appropriate minimum bids, spotters who will be stationed among the bidders, and the opportunity to test the sound system before the auction begins.

Check the Yellow Pages for a listing of licensed auctioneers in your area, or obtain a list of members from your state or local auctioneers' association. If you cannot find an auctioneer who will donate this expertise to your event, do some comparison shopping. Try to observe each auctioneer's style before making a decision. Then book the auctioneer you select as early in the planning process as possible.

If your organization cannot recruit or afford to hire a professional auctioneer, ask two local celebrities or members from within your own constituency to volunteer to fill the role. Two people are needed so that they can take turns before their voices give out. If possible, the volunteers should interview or observe a professional auctioneer in action before the event. Then the volunteers should rehearse their techniques in front of an audience.

Setting Up the Auction

Try to set up the auction the day before the event. If you must set up on the day of the event, start as early as possible. Line up drivers in station wagons, vans, and pickup trucks to transport the auction items and equipment from storage spaces that are not at the site of the auction. Work according to a floor plan that has been drawn to scale and includes such components as the entrance, cocktail bar, dinner tables, catering accommodations, silent auction item tables, oral auction item displays, auction block, secretaries' area, cashiers' area, sound and lighting equipment, coat check, restrooms, and exits.

Guidelines for auction acoustics include using a good sound system, setting up elevated speakers around the room so that everyone can hear, taping down all loose cords in the way of traffic, having backup equipment on hand in case something fails, testing the sound system before the auction begins, and making sure a technician is present during the auction to monitor the sound and make repairs.

Since people at an auction must be able to see where they are going, what the auction catalog says, and what the items look like, it is important to light the room in a sufficient, comfortable manner. Spotlighting can be used to add to the excitement of the oral auction as long as the light is not in the auctioneer's eyes. Always work with a lighting or electrical expert in setting up a lighting system and determining its limitations.

Presenting the Auction Items

Oral auction items should be the most expensive and impressive donations that have the greatest audience appeal. These crowd pleasers should be described in detail in the auction catalog and presented by the auctioneer in an order that will represent a variety of prices and interests. Similar items should not be bunched together. Of the similar offerings, sell the better ones first, so that bidders will not have already spent their money by the time the most expensive items are offered.

Silent auction items should be less expensive than oral auction items. These items should be arranged and displayed by category and then numerical sequence. They do not require lengthy descriptions, because the bidders can view the items on the silent auction tables.

Signs are needed for oral auction items that are not physically present, silent auction item tables, and cashiers' tables. If your organization can afford it, you may want to rent an electronic sign that can be programmed to make announcements and provide information (e.g., about the amount of time left) during the oral and silent auctions. The electronic sign should be elevated so that everybody can see it. A person who knows how to use a computer keyboard will be needed to operate the sign.

If you are expecting a very large crowd for your oral auction, it may be advantageous to take slide photographs of every item and project them on a large screen as they are presented by the auctioneer. Small items, such as jewelry, particularly benefit from appearing on a large screen so that everyone can clearly see them in detail.

Designing an Auction Catalog

An auction catalog serves the important functions of informing your guests of the auction items being offered, bringing in money through advertising, and providing a model for the next auction. The auction catalog should include the event's agenda, acknowledgments, a precise description of each item to be auctioned, the donor's name, the item's retail value and minimum bid, whether the item is taxable, bidding procedures, an addendum of items that were donated after the catalog was printed, item pickup and delivery instructions, and advertisements. Some organizations mail their auction catalogs about 2 weeks in advance of the event to those people who have purchased tickets. This allows the guests to think about what they want to buy. Remember to have enough catalogs at the door for everyone who comes to the auction, since your guests may not remember to bring their advance copies with them.

Organizing the Oral Auction Bidding Process

Minimum bids on oral auction items should be decided according to the item's retail value, emotional value to the audience, and general appeal. Consider the donor's suggestions in determining the minimum bid, especially if the donation has great emotional value to the donor (e.g., a piece of art donated by the artist). A donor may request that the item be returned to the donor if the minimum bid is not met. Prior to the auction, the chairperson and the auctioneer should agree on the length of time that will be given to each item. Usually 60–90 seconds are allotted for each item. Also, they should determine the amount of bid increments. For instance, on items retailing for up to $100, the increments might be $5 or $10. Bids on items with retail values between $100 and $1,000 might be raised by $20 or $50.

Upon arriving at the auction, each bidder is given a numbered card or paddle. During the actual bidding process, a bidder must hold up high the numbered card or paddle and attract the auctioneer's attention every time the bidder initiates or raises a bid. Each bid legally obligates the bidder to pay the bid in full if it is deemed the high bid for the item.

Some oral auctions include shills, who are persons planted in the audience to bid on items and keep the process exciting and on the increase. Being a shill can be costly, because in some instances the shill or the organization actually ends up buying the item. Depending on the situation, it may be possible to contact the second highest bidder at the end of the auction in an attempt to alter the situation. Of course, the shill could be very happy to purchase the item. The best shill is a risk-taker who is a big supporter of your organization and has a lot of money.

Oral auctions also include syndicates which are members of the audience who join together to bid on an item. For example, four couples may pool their funds to bid on a skiing trip for eight people. Syndication should be described in the auction catalog and mentioned by the auctioneer. Syndication is advantageous to the auction since it usually increases the chances of expensive items being sold and results in higher prices.

Organizing the Silent Bidding Process

Bidding sheets should be taped or stapled in numerical order across the front of the tables where the silent auction items are displayed. The sheets should include the item name, catalog number, description, retail value, minimum bid amount, minimum raise amount, space for the bidders to enter their names and/or numbers and their bids, and closing time for bids.

Usually the minimum bid on a silent auction item is slightly less than one half of its retail value. The minimum raise is a fixed increment raise. Generally 10 percent of the minimum bid should be the smallest raise allowable. The amount of the minimum raise should be written in whole number increments only. For example, if the minimum bid on an item is $35, the minimum raise, based on 10 percent of the minimum bid, should be $4 rather than $3.50. Minimum bids and minimum raises will help you approach retail value sooner. Fewer bids may be written, but you will not have to replace filled-up bidding sheets and bidders will not have to return as often to the items to raise their bids.

The auctioneer should announce the closing of the silent auction tables. The tables can be closed one at a time or all at once. Each table worker should be responsible for making sure that the table actually does shut down at the precise closing time and that there are no last-minute bidding disputes. When the table closes, the table worker should circle the name and/or number of the highest bidder on each bid sheet. This name and/or number will be the last entry if the bidders followed instructions. If two people want the same item at the moment that the table closes, the table should still be closed on time. The bidders can then be taken aside to participate in a single-item oral auction.

Allowing Absentee Bidding

Procedures may be established for supporters who want to participate in the auction but cannot attend the actual event. For example, the supporters should be given an opportunity to preview the auction items—in person or through the catalog—and then submit by mail or telephone their maximum bids, accompanied by a check in the exact amount of the bid. The auctioneer or auction chairperson then bids on the supporter's behalf during the oral and silent auctions. All sales, of course, are final. If the supporter's bid turns out to be too low, the check is then returned.

Arranging for Pickup and Delivery

Many purchasers will take home their items at the close of the auction. If this is not possible, then arrangements should be made with the purchaser for pickup or delivery as soon as possible. Delivery is a nice touch, and your organization should offer the service if possible. Provision of a delivery service may actually increase guests' bids on large items.

Adding Special Attractions

Creative special attractions can be included in an auction event. They will add to the fun for everyone in attendance, especially guests who are hesitant to bid on silent auction items and unlikely to participate in the oral auction. Popular special attractions include balloon surprises, a duck pond, a key club, a bid ticket auction, and an appraisal service.

Balloon surprises consist of bouquets of helium-filled balloons with ticket numbers inside or enclosed in envelopes and attached to the strings. Guests who buy the balloons receive gifts that correspond to the ticket numbers. The gifts can consist of donated auction items of low value, items that were received in large quantities, items that are not particularly tempting, or items that do not fit into any of the silent auction categories. To add to the fun and to entice guests to buy more balloons, a few valuable items can be included in the array of gifts.

A *duck pond* consists of plastic ducks floating in a child's wading pool. Guests pay to pick up one of the ducks. The number on the duck's bottom corresponds to a gift. Like the balloon surprises, the duck pond should feature a few enticing prizes.

A *key club* involves purchasing a key from a container full of keys that will hopefully open the lock affixed to a valuable gift (e.g., a color television or a microwave oven). Purchasers should not be allowed to see if their keys open the lock until the end of the evening, when as many keys as possible have been sold. Any remaining keys just prior to the closing of the key club can be auctioned off as a package by the auctioneer.

At a *bid ticket auction* the auctioneer asks all bidders who are interested in a certain item to buy one or more tickets for the item at a set price (e.g., $1, $5, or $10). The ticket stubs are then placed in a container, one ticket is drawn, and the owner of that ticket wins the item. Bid ticket auctions, which are actually raffles, give the winners good value for what they pay. But they are time-consuming and only permit a limited number of items to be presented within a reasonable period of time.

An *appraisal service* involves representatives of an auction house or other experts who agree to donate their service to your event. They then give verbal appraisals to your guests' hand-carried items or clear photographs of larger items. Your guests pay a set fee for each appraisal with all proceeds going to your cause.

Variations

In addition to auctions of general merchandise, specialized auctions can be presented, including antique or art, book, celebrity, date, entertainment, food media, mystery, radio, services, sports, symbolic, televised, travel, warehouse, and wine auctions.

An *antique or art auction* is often conducted by an auction house that deals in these items or by a gallery that holds auctions. The auction house or gallery generally provides the full exhibit, the auctioneer, catalogs, and promotional material. Your organization only has to provide the audience. Professionally conducted auctions may mean less work for your organization, but they also may mean less profit since your group will only receive a percentage of the proceeds, such as 20 percent. Make sure you know how the percentage is calculated and what other costs your organization will have to incur. A contract with the auction house or gallery is essential. Also, be certain that the auction house or gallery is not offering items that it cannot get rid of any other way. Your guests should not be confronted with second-rate items at inflated prices. The items should match the affluence of your audience. A reputable auction house or gallery can tailor the show to any price range. If your organization decides to hold an antique or art auction on its own, check into getting items on consignment from well-known galleries as well as donations from local artists.

A *book auction* can feature the sale of autographed copies of popular books as well as limited copies of rare books. Requests to authors and publishers for books should be made early, since not every request will be met.

A *celebrity auction* involves contacting local and national celebrities and asking them to donate autographed and personal items to your event. For example, you might receive a scarf worn by a famous actress, an autographed script from a soap opera, slippers from a ballerina, an autographed record album from a musician, a piece of pottery designed by an entertainer, or an autographed ball from a sports team. Many celebrities have items specially created for them to give to charitable events. In addition, certain celebrities may be willing to donate their time and have lunch with the winning bidder, go shopping, or play tennis.

At a *date auction* some of the community's most eligible men and women put together date packages of activities that constitute enjoyable dates. Each person's package is sponsored by a local business and auctioned to the highest bidder.

For an *entertainment auction* contributors can offer such items as a day on their yacht, a party at their pool, a band performance, a dance performance, an opportunity to conduct the orchestra, a behind-the-scenes look at a performance, your name in lights on a theater marquee, and theater subscriptions. Also, entertainment for parents to purchase for their children can be featured, such as a slumber party, an appearance by a juggler at a birthday party, a sleigh ride, and computer games.

A *food auction* can feature a formal dinner in a caterer's home, picnic baskets prepared by local celebrities, a case of wine, fresh fruit and vegetable delivery, and a dessert-a-week delivery service. Cooking classes, subscriptions to food magazines, and restaurant gift certificates are additional possibilities.

A *media auction* can include donations of local prime-time television spots, radio time, newspaper space, bill boards, magazine ads, photography, and graphics. This type of auction might be especially appropriate if your guests include small business owners, corporate executives, and staff of public relations firms.

A *mystery auction* involves inexpensive and unusual items. It can be tied to a standard auction, other event, or meeting. Either each guest brings a gift-wrapped item to the auction or your organization provides the mystery items. The auctioneer entices the audience to bid on the items.

A *radio auction* offers free radio exposure to merchants who make donations. Also, a radio auction can reach a lot of people. Prior to a radio auction, merchants should agree to display the items they have donated in their store windows. During the actual auction, the merchandise is assembled at the auction location—the radio station, or another broadcast site, such as a shopping mall. A block of air time is donated by the station or purchased at a discount by the organization. Spectators can bid in person and listeners can bid by telephone as the items are described. Winning bidders are allowed a specified amount of time (e.g., 24 hours) to come in and pay for and pick up their items.

A *services auction* can include baby-sitting services, consultation from an interior designer, housepainting, dry cleaning, any type of lesson, hairstyling, a car tune-up, a chauffeur for a day, fresh flower delivery, dog walking, financial planning consultation, maid and butler service, snow shoveling, pool maintenance, legal services, plumbing, electrical work, accounting assistance, and typing service.

A *sports auction* can feature a variety of sports equipment, lessons, games with professionals, club memberships, event tickets, excursions such as bicycle outings and cross-country skiing trips, and sports camp reservations.

A *symbolic auction* is more in the tradition of philanthropy, since the items up for bid are for the organization. Possibilities include paying for equipment for a hospital or books for a library. This type of auction is actually a direct solicitation for funds and does not involve collecting items to sell. In return for their contributions, people may receive special recognition or acknowledgment in the organization's annual report.

A *televised auction* involves local celebrity auctioneers presenting auction items during donated or discounted air time to potential bidders who watch the broadcast and call in their bids. Local merchants tend to be generous donors to televised auctions, since they receive good publicity as their items are presented. Telephone line installations and other phone expenses for a televised auction can cost a great deal. Efforts should be made to have these costs underwritten.

A *travel auction* might offer weekend vacation spots, cruises, airplane tickets, and major trips. People who donate use of their condominiums and investment homes to the auction will more readily do so if they are familiar with the group that will be attending the auction. Travel agencies and airlines are often willing to donate accommodations and airfare, or at least offer them to your organization at a reduced fee, if they are assured free publicity.

A *warehouse auction* can be organized if a storage or moving company will donate some of its unclaimed property to your event. You can then auction unopened barrels, boxes, trunks, and crates. The bidders' knowledge as to what is actually inside the containers can be limited to whatever happens to be written on the outside of the container.

A *wine auction* can feature wines that are commonly available, as well as wines that are rarely available at retail. This type of event can include wine tours and wine tastings. In certain states, the rules pertaining to wine auctions are numerous and stringent. Check with your state attorney general's office before planning a wine auction.

BENEFITS

A benefit is an expensive, glamorous, gala event that generally includes dinner, drinks, dancing, entertainment, and other unique features for very high ticket prices. "Glitter," "sparkle," and "dazzle" are words that are often applied to this type of event. Benefits are also referred to as dinner-dances and charity balls.

Special Advantages

In addition to the general advantages listed in the Introduction to Programs, a benefit offers the following special advantages:

> Through high-priced ticket sales and underwriting, a benefit can be an extremely lucrative event.
>
> Social columnists like to write about this type of event.
>
> A benefit offers those attending an exciting event, a great opportunity for socializing, and a tax deduction.

Special Cautions

Keeping in mind the general cautions listed in the Introduction to Programs, the following special cautions about a benefit should be carefully considered as well:

A benefit can be a very expensive event to plan and present. Enormous up-front costs are usually involved.

It may be necessary to hire a consultant to plan a benefit.

Often up to 12 months are required to organize a benefit.

Because benefits are extremely popular events, it may be difficult to think of a unique, appealing approach for your event. After all, a benefit is really just a variation on a theme.

The expectations for a benefit are high, making the event vulnerable to scrutiny and failure, as well as difficult to repeat year after year with consistent success. Every benefit strives to be "the party of the year."

This type of event requires volunteers who are willing to sell tickets on a person-to-person basis.

To make a benefit successful, an organization must be able to reach the appropriate constituency. Generally, that constituency must be affluent, since ticket prices are so high.

People are becoming concerned about the rising costs of planning and attending a benefit. Some feel that the opulence of the event is questionable, considering that the purpose of the event is to support a charity. Often people lose sight of the organization's cause in planning and attending a benefit.

Expenses

A benefit can entail the following expenses for your organization: facility rental fee—consultant's fee—caterer's fee—purchase of decorations —florist's fee—entertainment costs—purchase of liquor—liquor licensing fee—musicians' fees—union labor fees—gratuities—purchase of liability insurance—security costs—printing costs—postage costs— promotion costs. Efforts should be made to seek an underwriter for the event or at least donations for as many expenses as possible. And angel, benefactor, sponsor, and patron price levels of tickets should be sold for additional financial support.

Volunteer Requirements

The volunteer leaders needed to plan and carry out a benefit include the event chairperson, honorary chairpersons, arrangements chairperson, printed materials chairperson, program agenda chairperson, promotions chairperson, reservations chairperson, special features chairperson, sponsorship and underwriting chairperson, ticket-selling chairperson, treasurer, and volunteer coordinator. Their roles are described in the Introduction to Programs. In addition to these volunteer leaders, a huge number of volunteers are needed, particularly to sell tickets to the event.

Selecting a Chairperson

The selection of a chairperson for a benefit is a crucial decision, since the individual will be a key person in the ticket-selling process. A well-known, respected, charismatic, efficient, energetic chairperson with connections throughout the community will be able to recruit people to sell tickets. The chairperson should be the type of individual to whom people cannot say no.

Working with a Caterer

Many facilities require that their own catering services be used and prohibit any outside food and beverages from being brought in. But if the location for your benefit allows you to select your own caterer, shop around for the one that can serve you best, since caterers' services and prices vary greatly. The catering service that you select should provide you with a choice and even tasting samples of several different menus for your event, as well as adapt to your suggestions. For instance, make sure that the caterer is willing to have substitute meals available for people who observe religious and dietary customs.

Catering services charge on the basis of a per-person price. Even if you are serving a buffet-style meal, the caterer should agree to charge you per person rather than per plate, since some people may take more than one plate. The fees vary according to the caterer and the menu. Other factors that affect the price per person include who will do the serving, who will provide the supplies, who will clean up, whether the food can be prepared at the event or whether it must be prepared in advance and brought in, and whether it is a sit-down dinner or a buffet. Once you have chosen a caterer, enter into a written agreement.

Restaurants, hotels, and private caterers require guarantees 48 to 72 hours before the event. The guarantee is the minimum number of meals that you will be billed for. Most restaurants, hotels, and caterers will set and be prepared to serve 5 percent more than your guarantee. To determine your guarantee, consider the number of advance reservations you have, the number of complimentary meals you will be providing, the number of last-minute ticket buyers you expect, and the number of no-shows you anticipate.

Serving Liquor

If you plan to serve liquor at your benefit, you should decide whether to have a cash bar or a free bar. Some organizations arrange for cash bars, to hold down the costs and discourage excessive drinking, while others offer free bars, since the ticket prices are so high. If you go with a cash bar, decide whether guests should pay the bartenders at a cash bar directly or use tickets, which decrease the wait at a bar. Be sure to find out what the caterer's liquor, corkage, and bartender fees are, and whether unopened bottles are returnable. Investigate whether you can provide your own liquor and whether you will need a temporary liquor license for a cash bar. Determine how many bartenders will be needed (usually one for every 50 to 100 people) and whether you can provide them. Note that some organizations offer just wine or champagne, to simplify the provision of alcoholic beverages.

Booking Musicians

Music is an extremely important element in the success of a benefit since it helps set and maintain the mood for the entire event. Search carefully for a good band or orchestra that will play according to the tastes of your audience. To find the type of musicians you are looking for, ask members of your organization for suggestions, look in the Yellow Pages under "Musicians," call local clubs that feature live music, or check with the local musicians' union. Some unions will provide musicians for free to a nonprofit organization.

Bands and orchestras should be auditioned before the final selection is made and booked as early as possible. In addition to the type of music they play, musical groups vary in their playing time, fees (from hundreds of dollars to thousands of dollars), and method of payment. Some benefits feature more than one musical group to play alternately or in different areas of the event facility.

Setting the Ticket Prices

The ticket prices for your benefit should be determined according to how much money the event will cost your organization, the amount that your intended audience can be expected to spend, and the going rate for similar events in your community. Any underwriting or sponsorship that you obtain should not affect the ticket prices.

Generally, benefits offer a number of different ticket options—from a reasonably set price to increasingly higher angel, benefactor, sponsor, and patron categories that indicate special support for the event and result in some sort of recognition, such as a listing in the program book. Higher table prices can be set for corporate support.

Guests who select the higher-priced ticket options that entitle them to a program-book listing should be sent a postcard before the program book is printed saying, "You will be listed as _____ in the program book." If the listing is incorrect, the guest can then return the corrected card by a certain deadline. Great care should be given to producing an accurate listing, since people can become very annoyed when they have paid a considerable amount of money only to have their names misspelled in your well-intentioned efforts to recognize their generosity.

Sending Invitations

A benefit requires formal invitations that include reservation cards and return envelopes. Invitations should be sent to a carefully compiled mailing list. Personal notes that are added to the invitations by trustees and others can have excellent results. Photographs taken at the previous year's event and included in the appropriate guests' invitations can also be effective. Publicity that is scheduled just before and after the date that the invitations are mailed will add to people's interest in the event and desire to attend.

Many organizations mail "hold the date" cards to everybody on the invitation list 1 or 2 months in advance of sending the actual invitations. Usually these are postcards that alert the recipient to the event and its date, time, and location.

Organizing the Ticket-Selling Committee

Printed invitations do not bring in the attendance for a benefit; contacts made by ticket sellers do. In addition to good connections, members of this committee should have a sense of dedication and responsibility. They should not hesitate to seek ticket buyers and to place follow-up phone calls.

Some organizations hold kick-off parties for their ticket sellers, who are sometimes called hosts and hostesses and have their names listed in the program book. The purpose of these parties is to do something that is fun for the volunteers, as well as obtain commitments from them to purchase or at least be responsible for filling tables. An enthusiastic atmosphere must be established for the sales effort. The most successful kick-off parties result in the majority of tables being sold even before a single invitation is mailed.

Table sales are encouraged for a benefit, since they guarantee the best possible attendance and generate the greatest profits. Table sales also make seating arrangements easier. Even if your event is going to be so exciting that people will not want to be seated for more than a few minutes, sell tables.

Many organizations form special committees whose purpose is to attract younger people to the event, often at lower ticket prices, in an effort to build a new constituency for the organization. For instance, you might offer a "night owl" or "latecomer" ticket price category so that young people can attend the dessert and dancing portions of a benefit.

Planning the Seating

Planned seating is important at most benefits. Response cards should include space so that guests can indicate the people they would like to sit with. The first step in planning the seating is to obtain a floor plan/seating chart of the room that includes the layout for all tables and the seating capacities of the tables. Number the tables and assign them as they are sold, setting aside certain tables for special guests. Remember that although everybody wants to sit at a table in the best location and with the right people, most people will be understanding about where they are seated. Keep an alphabetized listing of all people who have reservations and where they will be seated. Tickets indicating seating assignments can be mailed out a week or two before the event or distributed at the door, depending on the nature and size of your event. Tickets that are mailed prior to the event serve as an excellent way to confirm the date, time, and place of the event. Be prepared to have a supply of duplicate tickets on hand for those guests who forget to bring their tickets.

Decorating the Setting

The decorations are crucial at a benefit since they can make the difference between a memorable and a quickly forgotten event. A florist is an important, though expensive, factor in most decorating plans. To cut down on costs, try to negotiate a special deal with the florist (e.g., free labor and cost of materials only) in exchange for goodwill, high visibility, and potential business from those in attendance. Also, consider using balloons or other less expensive decorations. Printed sheets can often be purchased at sales and used as table cloths. Remember that creativity is more effective than extravagance.

Designing the Program Agenda

Benefits are social gatherings where people like to see and be seen. The guests' greatest interests are table-hopping and dancing—not listening to long speeches or watching hours of entertainment. The program for a benefit should therefore be designed to enhance socializing while maintaining a sense of excitement.

Handling the Parking

Do not overlook the parking situation as you consider how best to accommodate your guests, since the atmosphere for a benefit is set the moment guests arrive. If you decide to provide valet parking, make sure that you can park and return your guests' cars without causing huge traffic jams or long waits. Check into obtaining any necessary liability insurance for valet parking.

If you decide to have guests park their own cars, ask volunteers to park far away from the entrance of the facility so that the most convenient spots will be available for the guests. Reserve an area at the main entrance for drivers to drop off their passengers before parking (carpeting and a canopy can add special touches to this area). And provide transportation—from shuttle buses to antique cars—if the parking area is a long distance from the facility. Make sure that the parking area is well lit and guarded.

Organizing a Pre-event

Benefits often feature pre-events for underwriters and purchasers of the most expensive ticket categories. For example, a special cocktail party might be held before a dinner-dance. Although organizing a pre-event involves extra work, it will be worth the effort if this special expression of appreciation helps build continued support for your organization.

DINNERS, LUNCHEONS, AND BREAKFASTS

A dinner, luncheon, or breakfast can be a gala event with its own program and special features, or it can augment another activity. For example, a luncheon is often planned in conjunction with a fashion show, and a dinner is often served before an auction. A meal can range from a simple, $5-per-person pancake breakfast that is prepared by your members to a glamorous, $1,000 per-plate sit-down dinner that is professionally catered —or anything in between. Generally, a breakfast is briefer and cheaper than a luncheon, and a luncheon is shorter and less expensive than a dinner. Refer to the section in this Chapter on "Benefits" for information on planning a meal, including working with a caterer, serving liquor, and planning the seating.

Special Advantages

In addition to the general advantages listed in the Introduction to Programs, a meal offers the following special advantages:

A meal can be planned and presented any time of the year.

It is easy to combine a meal with another special event.

Special Cautions

Keeping in mind the general cautions listed in the Introduction to Programs, the following special cautions about a meal should be carefully considered as well:

Tickets to a meal must be sold to members, business associates, friends, and relatives. This requires recruiting volunteers who are willing to sell tickets.

Corporations that are heavily targeted by nonprofit organizations are beginning to question whether underwriting meals and purchasing table tickets are the best methods for supporting charitable causes.

Expenses

A dinner, luncheon, or breakfast can entail the following expenses for your organization: facility rental fee—purchase or rental of supplies and equipment—food and beverage costs—caterer's fee—gratuities—decorations—purchase of licenses and permits—purchase of liability insurance—security costs—printing costs—postage costs—promotion costs. The range of expenses is wide. For instance, an organization that has its own dining and kitchen facilities, all of the supplies and equipment, and volunteers to do the cooking, will be able to present a meal for much less money than an organization that opts for a catered affair. Of course, the cost of the event is reflected in the price of admission. Try to seek donations or an underwriter to cover the event and thus enhance your profit.

Volunteer Requirements

The volunteer leaders needed to plan and carry out a meal include the event chairperson, arrangements chairperson, printed materials chairperson, program agenda chairperson, promotions chairperson, reservations chairperson, sponsorship and underwriting chairperson, ticket-selling chairperson, treasurer, and volunteer coordinator. Their roles are described in the Introduction to Programs. In addition to these volunteer leaders, many volunteers are needed, especially to sell tickets to the event.

Setting Up a Dais

Many meals include a dais, which is a raised table that is reserved for special guests. Generally the people seated on the dais include the event chairperson, the speaker, honored individuals, certain trustees, certain community leaders, and others. Careful consideration should be given to setting up the dais.

Obtaining a Speaker

Many organizations feature speakers at their meals. A speaker should be a well-known person who is eloquent, entertaining, and inspiring. This person's speech generally should not exceed one-half hour to accommodate to the attention span of most audiences.

Speakers can be booked directly or through their agents. Some can be obtained just a few weeks before the event while others must be scheduled at least a year in advance. Fees or honoraria are required by most speakers, although some will talk for free under certain circumstances or donate payment back to the organization. Traveling expenses are usually covered by the organization.

When contacting a speaker for the first time (by letter or phone call), explain the nature of your organization, the purpose of your event, the composition and size of the expected audience, the subject matter you would like covered, the length of the speech, the location of the event, and the possible dates and times for the event.

Locally, look for speakers through your own members' connections, universities, corporations, the media, the arts, sports, and other organizations. For national-level speakers, check the resources at your local library.

All speaking engagements should be confirmed and reconfirmed in writing. The speaker's resume or biography should be obtained early for publicity purposes and so that an introduction can be prepared.

Providing Entertainment

Entertainment can be an attractive feature for a meal. Many organizations, however, hold these events without entertainment since it can raise costs significantly. Also, entertainment makes it difficult to end an event early.

Variations

In addition to a basic dinner, luncheon, or breakfast, a variety of meals can be presented, including annual meetings, celebrity meals, celebrity roasts, potluck suppers, pre-event and postevent meals, progressive dinners, simultaneous dinners, theme meals, and tributes.

An *annual meeting* can be planned as a meal that raises funds if it features a lively, interesting program that makes people willing to attend year after year. Generally, however, an annual meeting serves to reinforce the interests of your members rather than raise funds.

A *celebrity meal* features the presence of well-known local, regional, or national people. Guests attend because they want the chance to share a meal with and be close to celebrities. When there are more tables than celebrities, the celebrities can eat each course of the meal at a different table so that every table is provided with a star for at least part of the event. An opportunity to be photographed with the celebrities can be especially appealing to your guests.

One organization sponsors an annual "celebrity waiters' luncheon" where local sports figures, media personalities, and community leaders, as well as nationally known special guest stars, serve and entertain those in attendance and collect tips that are then donated to the organization. For an additional fee, guests can have their pictures taken with the celebrities or purchase the celebrity waiters' aprons. In addition to the meal, there is a cash bar, music, and a raffle. Throughout the event the waiters compete for the title of "highest tip collector." Another organization recruits local celebrities to flip pancakes at a communitywide pancake breakfast.

A *celebrity roast* is a meal where a well-known local, regional, or national person agrees to be kidded by peers and colleagues for the benefit of a charitable organization. In addition to being well known, the person to be roasted should be willing, witty, and articulate. Roasters should, of course, be humorous as well.

At a *potluck supper*, each person brings a food dish and pays a certain price for admission. Since all of the food is donated at a potluck supper, the ticket costs can be kept down. Some organizations hold potluck dinners to launch the sale of their cookbooks. Members who submitted recipes to the book prepare their dishes for the event, which the entire community is invited to attend.

A *pre-event meal* takes place before another special event, such as a concert or a play. By offering the meal, it is possible to significantly increase the ticket price for the event. A *postevent meal* also provides a means for raising ticket prices. This type of meal, however, may not be successful if the people in attendance are anxious to get home after the main event.

At a *progressive dinner* each course of the meal is eaten at a different location. To serve a number of people with a progressive dinner, it may be necessary to plan first, second, and third rotations of servings at each stop or to serve each course in many different locations. To keep costs down, try to arrange for the hosts to donate the courses that they sponsor. One organizaion's progressive dinner invitation urged recipients to "join the Progressive Party" and to "speak softly and carry a big appetite."

Simultaneous dinners are offered on the same evening, at numerous locations, and sometimes with many different themes. The invitation describes the options, and guests indicate their choices on their response cards. Slots at each location are filled on a first-come, first-served basis. The dinners may vary according to type of setting featured, kind of food prepared, or celebrity in attendance. For example, one organization offered seven simultaneous international feasts—Country French, Northern Italian, Delectable Scandinavian, East Indian Curry, Sophisticated Spanish, Oriental Elegance, and the Grand Tour of London. The overhead for this type of event can be kept low when each dinner is donated by its host. A grand dessert in a single central location is an excellent way to end an evening of simultaneous dinners.

A *theme meal* that is based on just about any idea imaginable can be planned. The theme should be carried out through the invitations, the menu, the decorations, the publicity, and the entertainment.

At a *tribute*, one or more persons are honored by peers and colleagues at a meal for the benefit of a charitable organization. The guests of honor should be connected with your cause and, most importantly, should be prestigious, influential persons whose friends, relatives, and business associates are likely to purchase tickets to the event.

One organization holds an annual "Career Women of Achievement Awards" luncheon. Nominations for the awards are accepted from throughout the community and judged by a distinguished committee. The winner(s), as well as everyone who was nominated, are honored at the event. Since many of the nominations are made by corporations, those corporations tend to buy tables for the event.

Another organization holds an annual "All-Star Salute to Secretaries" during Secretaries Week. The purpose of the event is to honor secretaries as well as benefit the organization, and local businesses buy tickets and sponsor tables so that their secretaries can attend.

PARTIES

A party is a fun-filled, reasonably priced gala event that includes food, music, dancing, and other features. It differs from a benefit in that it is a less elaborate and certainly less expensive event to plan and attend. A party can easily be combined with another fund-raising event, such as a raffle, an auction, or a contest. Refer to the section in this chapter on "Benefits" for information on planning a party, including working with a caterer, serving liquor, and booking musicians.

Special Advantages

In addition to the general advantages listed in the Introduction to Programs, a party offers the following special advantages:

A party can be given any time of the year.

This type of event can be arranged in a relatively short period of time, if necessary.

It is possible to give a party with little up-front money and to keep expenses down, thereby maintaining reasonably priced tickets and allowing guests to feel that they are getting their money's worth from the event.

In addition to raising funds, a party gives members a chance to know each other better.

A good way to reach people who are unfamiliar with your organization is through a party.

Special Cautions

Keeping in mind the general cautions listed in the Introduction to Programs, the following special cautions about a party should be carefully considered as well:

Good party attendance requires widespread publicity and many volunteers to sell tickets in advance.

People's motivations for attending a party are often more social than altruistic.

Expenses

A party can entail the following expenses for your organization: facility rental fee—purchase of refreshments—cost of music—purchase of decorations—purchase of prizes or gift items—purchase of liability insurance—security costs—printing costs—postage costs—promotion costs. Try to have as many of these expenses as possible donated.

Volunteer Requirements

The volunteer leaders needed to throw a party include the event chairperson, arrangements chairperson, printed materials chairperson, program agenda chairperson, promotions chairperson, ticket-selling chairperson, treasurer, and volunteer coordinator. Their roles are decribed in the Introduction to Programs. In addition to these volunteer leaders, the volunteer involvement for a party varies according to the nature and size of the event. Generally, the greatest volunteer involvement is required for selling tickets.

Choosing a Location

The location you select for your party should accommodate the features of your event. For example, if you are having a dance, you will need a place that has a hard floor. If you are serving refreshments, you will need a setting that has a food preparation area. A unique location, such as a museum, warehouse, mansion, shopping mall, aquarium, or park, will add greatly to the appeal of your event.

Sometimes the location for a party leads to the creation of the event's theme. For instance, one organization decided to hold a party in a new building at the county airport, since the person who owned the building was a trustee of the organization. This location led to the development of a "Fly Away" party with the following features: underwriting by a major airline in exchange for a lot of free publicity and visibility; decorations consisting of items from the airline; invitations that looked like airplane tickets: luggage as the door prizes; and airplane food, including packets of peanuts, as the refreshments. A "standby" option was included on the invitation for people who could not attend the party but still wanted to make a contribution.

Including Unique Features

Any party can be special if it includes unique features that are well advertised to attract people's attention and draw them to the event. Unusual, appealing elements will add to a party's potential for success.

For example, if your organization decides to hold a *dance*, you might consider having a *sock hop* and featuring clothes from the 1950s, a dance contest, jitterbug dance lessons, a name-that-tune contest, a 1950s midnight movie, and other creative activities.

Rather than a *cocktail party*, your organization might decide to have a *wine-tasting party*. You could contact distributors or representatives of popular brands of domestic and imported wines to furnish a selection of their best products, as well as a brief talk about the wines.

Instead of a *masquerade*, you might plan a *whodunit party*. This type of party involves hiring a local troupe consisting of professional actors, a director, and a scriptwriter for an evening (or weekend) who come up with a custom-made murder mystery for the event. Guests work in teams of two or more people and try to solve the crime. A form of participation theater, whodunit parties are becoming increasingly popular across the country.

In place of an *annual winter wonderland party*, your organization might opt for a *beach party* held inside a huge facility, such as a sports arena. The party might include a sand-filled area, hot tubs, a tanning salon, volleyball games, beer, hot dogs, soda, chips, and ice-cream bars.

If you want to take advantage of professional talent at the local level, you might organize an "All Stars Night." This event could include short performances by members of your community's ballet, orchestra, opera, and playhouse.

Planning a Non-Event Party

A non-event party is an event that will never happen. It raises money through contributions from people who will never attend the event that will never take place. Invitations to a non-event can be cleverly designed to attract an unusual amount of attention from the surprised and amused recipients. Usually a non-event is held following a number of years of presenting an annual event with a good reputation. This type of event can only be held once, since it is a gimmick. Also, it can only be held if the constituency is familiar with the cause, since the invitation does not allow space to make a strong case for giving.

One organization held a "Stay-at-Home-Tea." Thousands of potential supporters were sent an invitation that included a teabag, and invited to have tea at home by themselves for an admission fee that could be mailed back to the organization.

Another organization held a "No Dance Prom." The invitation included an itemized list of how much each guest would save by not attending, including the costs of purchasing the tickets, buying a dress, renting a tuxedo, and paying for a baby-sitter. The invitation then requested each recipient to send a donation in the total amount.

A "New Year's Eve Gala" was the theme for an organization's non-event that invited potential supporters not to leave the comfort of their homes on New Year's Eve. Invitees were given a variety of packages to choose from, such as no cocktails, no four-course dinner, no champagne dessert, and no dancing until dawn. This non-event was not held in a building that was not yet built.

The invitation to an organization's annual gourmet "Party in the Park" that was not going to be held announced who would not be cooking, who would not be serving, who would not be providing the music, and who would not be showing up. The names of the committee members were listed under the heading of people who were planning to stay happily at home on the date of the non-event. The fact that tickets prices were not raised during the year of the non-event was highlighted.

RESOURCES FOR AUCTIONS

Alberti, C. E., Macko, G. S., & Whitcomb, N. B. *Money-makers: A systematic approach to special events fund raising.* Ambler, PA: Whitcomb Associates, 1982, pp. 5.1–5.23.

Ardman P. & Ardman, H. *Woman's Day book of fund raising.* New York: St. Martin's Press, 1980, pp. 206–208.

Beatty, B. & Kirkpatrick, L. *The auction book.* Denver: Auction Press, 1984.

Beatty, B. & Kirkpatrick, L. Why an auction may be the right "event" for you. *Fund Raising Management,* January 1985, pp. 18–25.

B'nai B'rith Fund Raising Cabinet, *B'nai B'rith fund raising chairman handbook.* Washington, D.C.: B'nai B'rith Leadership Cabinet, pp. 71–74.

DeSoto, C. *For fund and funds: Creative fund-raising ideas for your organization.* West Nyack, NY: Parker Publishing Co., 1983, pp. 63–65.

Drotning, P. T. *500 ways for small charities to raise money.* Chicago: Contemporary Books, Inc., 1979, pp. 101–104.

Flanagan, J. *The grass roots fundraising book.* Chicago: Contemporary Books, Inc., 1982, pp. 208–216.

Hay, J. T. *534 ways to raise money.* New York: Simon & Schuster, 1983, pp. 25–30.

Mirkin, H. R. *The complete fund raising guide.* New York: Public Service Materials Center, 1981, pp. 111–112.

Musselman, V. *Money raising activities for community groups.* New York: Association Press, 1969, pp. 193–204.

National Council of Jewish Women, Inc., *The raiser's edge.* New York: National Council of Jewish Women, Inc., pp. 14–20, 29–30.

Pritchard, J. H. *There's plenty of money for nonprofit groups willing to earn their shares —How to do it successfully.* Phoenix: Cornucopia Publications, 1984, pp. 265–276.

Warner, I. R. *The art of fund raising.* New York: Bantam Books, Inc., 1984, pp. 80–82.

RESOURCES FOR BENEFITS

Adler, J. & Kasindorf, M. Giving when it doesn't hurt. *Newsweek,* May 26, 1986, p. 23.

Alberti, C. E., Macko, G. S., & Whitcomb, N. B. *Money-makers: A systematic approach to special events fund raising.* Ambler, PA: Whitcomb Associates, 1982, Supplement 3, pp. 1–37.

Beatty, B. & Kirkpatrick, L. *The auction book.* Denver: Auction Press, 1984, pp. 104, 108, 109.

Berger, S. Ten steps to a million dollar fund raiser. *The Grantsmanship Center News,* December–January 1975, p. 15.

B'nai B'rith Fund Raising Cabinet, *B'nai B'rith fund raising chairman handbook.* Washington, D.C.: B'nai B'rith Leadership Cabinet, pp. 54–58.

Flanagan, J. *The grass roots fundraising book.* Chicago: Contemporary Books, Inc., 1982, pp. 225–226.

Gaby, P. V. & Gaby, D. M. *Nonprofit organization handbook.* Englewood Cliffs, NJ: Prentice-Hall, Inc., 1979, pp. 88–89.

Hopkins, E., Our Ladies of Charity. *New York Magazine,* October 13, 1986, pp. 46–53.

Kiechel, W. On the charity circuit. *Fortune*, October 1985.

Leibert, E. R. & Sheldon, B. E. *Handbook of special events for nonprofit organizations.* New York: Association Press, 1972, pp. 125–134.

Mahon, G. The grand gala. *Town & Country*, September 1985, pp. 198–199, 241–243, 249–254.

Musselman, V. W. *Money raising activities for community groups.* New York: Association Press, 1969, pp. 220–222.

National Council of Jewish Women, Inc., *The raiser's edge.* New York: National Council of Jewish Women, Inc., pp. 39–40, 54–58.

Ruth, N. Party for a (Non) Profit, *Your Share*, December 1985.

Sheerin, M. *How to raise top dollars from special events.* New York: Public Service Materials Center, 1984, pp. 53–61.

Sheerin, M. Planning the special event: Negotiating the do's and don'ts. *Fund Raising Management*, January 1985, pp. 44–49.

Warner, I. R. *The art of fund raising.* New York: Bantam Books, Inc., 1984, pp. 90–91.

Weiss, J. M. The making of a benefit. *Northern Ohio Live*, February 1986, pp. 32–38, 49–59.

Resources for Dinners, Luncheons, and Breakfasts

Alberti, C. E., Macko, G. S., & Whitcomb, N. B. *Money-makers: A systematic approach to special events fund raising.* Ambler, PA: Whitcomb Associates, 1982, pp. 2.1–2.10, Supplement 1, pp. 1–22.

Ardman, P. & Ardman, H. *Woman's Day book of fund raising.* New York: St. Martin's Press, 1980, pp. 191–195.

Beatty, B. & Kirkpatrick, L. *The auction book.* Denver: Auction Press, 1984, pp. 124–128.

DeMarco, N. J. The fund raising dinner. *In-Sight*, March 1979, pp. 1–4.

Desoto, C. *For fun and funds: Creative fund-raising ideas for your organization* (West Nyack, NY: Parker Publishing Co., 1983), pp. 171–196.

Drotning, P. T. *500 ways for small charities to raise money.* Chicago: Contemporary Books, Inc., 1979, pp. 117–122, 126–131.

Flanagan, J. *The grass roots fundraising book.* Chicago: Contemporary Books, Inc., 1982, pp. 195–201, 251–255.

Gaby, P. V. & Gaby, D. M. *Nonprofit organization handbook.* Englewood Cliffs, NJ: Prentice-Hall, Inc., 1979, pp. 79–82, 92–93.

Hay, J. T. *534 ways to raise money.* New York: Simon & Schuster, 1983, pp. 33, 92–104.

Honig, L. Food for thought—Fundraising luncheons. *Grassroots Fundraising Journal*, June/July 1984, pp. 6–8.

Honig, L. The time it takes—Fundraising luncheons. *Grassroots Fundraising Journal*, August/September 1984, pp. 3–8.

Johnston, D. Fund-Raising Dinners are "Way Out of Hand," *Los Angles Times*, September 22, 1985.

Kiechel, W. On the charity circuit. *Fortune*. October 14, 1985.

Leibert, E. R. & Sheldon, B. E. *Handbook of special events for nonprofit organizations.* New York: Association Press, 1972, pp. 54–60, 110–123.

McCandless, K. Cleveland's celebrity waiters raise funds by collecting tips. *Fund Raising Management*, September 1985, pp. 22–28, 72.

Musselman, V. W. *Money raising activities for community groups.* New York: Association Press, 1969, pp. 59–61, 163–192, 239–240.

National Council of Jewish Women, Inc., *The raiser's edge.* New York: National Council of Jewish Women, Inc., pp. 50, 52–54, 80–84.

Phillips, S. How to get a celebrity to attend your special event. *Fund Raising Management*, September 1985, pp. 59–62.

Pritchard, J. H. *There's plenty of money for nonprofit groups willing to earn their shares —How to do it successfully.* Phoenix: Cornucopia Publications, 1984, pp. 239–246, 385–386.

Sainsbury, J. A. Put the "special" back in special events. *Fund Raising Management*, May 1983, pp. 40–43.

Sainsbury, J. A. *The beginner's guide to advanced fund raising.* New York: Jan Arthur Sainsbury, 1985, pp. 14–18.

Sheerin, M. *How to raise top dollars from special events.* New York: Public Service Materials Center, 1984, pp. 24–29, 37–51.

Warner, I. R. *The art of fund raising.* New York: Bantam Books, 1984, pp. 86–87, 97, 104, 106–107.

RESOURCES FOR PARTIES

Ardman, P. & Ardman, H. *Woman's Day book of fund raising.* New York: St. Martin's Press, 1980, pp. 208–211.

Drotning, P. T. *500 ways for small charities to raise money.* Chicago: Contemporary Books, Inc., 1979, pp. 87–88, 123–126.

Flanagan, J. *The grass roots fundraising book.* Chicago: Contemporary Books, Inc., 1982, pp. 192–195, 225–231, 244–251.

Fund-Raising Institute. Non-Events: The invitation is all you need. *FRI Monthly Portfolio*, March 1984.

Hay, J. T. *534 ways to raise money.* New York: Simon & Schuster, 1983, pp. 49–51, 104–112.

Hopkins, E. Cruising for a cause. *New York Magazine*, August 18, 1986, p. 16.

Leibert, E. R. & Sheldon, B. E. *Handbook of special events for nonprofit organizations.* New York: Association Press, 1972, p. 202.

Mirkin, H. *The complete fund raising guide.* New York: Public Service Materials Center, 1981, pp. 114–116.

National Council of Jewish Women, Inc., *The raiser's edge.* New York: National Council of Jewish Women, Inc., pp. 32, 51, 107.

Pritchard, J. H. *There's plenty of money for nonprofit groups willing to earn their shares —How to do it successfully*, Phoenix: Cornucopia Publications, 1984, pp. 323–327.

Roberts, J. Causes and effects. *New York Magazine*, June 24, 1985.

Sullivan, E. Some parties are murder. *The Plain Dealer*, May 31, 1986, p. 3-A.

Chapter 13

GAMBLING EVENTS

BINGO GAMES

Bingo is a game of chance in which players buy bingo cards, each with a grid of 25 spaces arranged in five horizontal and five vertical rows. Every space is designated by a combination of a letter and a number, except for a free space in the center. Each card is different. A bingo caller announces letter-number combinations that are selected at random—either manually or mechanically—from a receptacle containing 75 combinations. The first person to cover five spaces in a row (either horizontally, vertically, or diagonally) on a card yells "Bingo!" and wins a prize—usually cash. Many nonprofit organizations run profitable bingo games in their local communities on a regular basis.

Special Advantages

In addition to the general advantages listed in the Introduction to Programs, bingo offers the following special advantages:

> Bingo can be an ongoing event that, with a loyal following from throughout the community and over a period of time, can provide a continuing source of significant income to your organization.
>
> It is easy to publicize bingo games with posters, by word of mouth, and through special local bingo magazines.

Playing bingo is fun. Even losers can rationalize the
expense of participating by acknowledging that their
money is going to a good cause.

Special Cautions

Keeping in mind the general cautions listed in the Introduction to
Programs, the following special cautions about bingo should be carefully
considered as well:

Certain states prohibit bingo. Those states that do allow
it require the sponsoring organization to have a bingo
license.

At least 6 to 12 months are needed to plan a bingo program, since obtaining a license requires a good deal of
time and detailed preparation. Also, raising enough
money to meet all of the up-front expenses for supplies
and equipment, finding a facility that can be used on a
regular basis, and recruiting a sufficient number of volunteers can be a lengthy process.

Bingo should be offered on a regular basis (e.g., weekly) so
that a loyal following can be developed.

Many volunteers are required to conduct a bingo program
that is held on a regular basis.

A number of months may be required to build up the large,
consistent following necessary to make your bingo program profitable.

Some members of your organization may object to sponsoring bingo since it is a gambling event.

Expenses

Bingo can entail the following expenses for your organization: license
fee—purchase, rental, or leasing of equipment and supplies—facility
rental fee—purchase of refreshments—purchase of paper serving products—purchase of door prizes—purchase of liability insurance—security
costs—printing costs—postage costs—promotion costs. The purchase of
bingo equipment can run into thousands of dollars. If your organization
cannot afford such an expenditure, then try to arrange to rent or lease the
equipment.

Volunteer Requirements

The volunteer leaders who are needed to plan and conduct a bingo
program include the program chairperson, arrangements chairperson,

printed materials chairperson, promotions chairperson, treasurer, and volunteer coordinator. Their roles are described in the Introduction to Programs. In addition to these volunteer leaders, the volunteer involvement for a bingo program that is held on a regular basis is enormous. There are numerous roles to be filled, and for most bingo programs they must be filled at least weekly. Volunteers for bingo games that are held on a regular basis should be given the opportunity to sign up for the dates of their choice. And assignments should be rotated. The greatest number of volunteers are needed to serve as monitors. Their role is to circulate among the players and sell cards, offer assistance, and verify bingos. These volunteers must be friendly, patient, and willing to do all that they can to help build and encourage the loyal following that a successful bingo program depends on. Under most state laws compensation cannot be paid to persons providing consultation to or volunteering at charitable bingo games.

Obtaining a Bingo License

An annual application for a license to conduct bingo along with the license fee must be submitted to the office of your state attorney general. Generally, the application requires the following information: the name and address of the applicant, a statement that the applicant is a charitable organization that has been in continuous existence for a certain number of years, the location where the bingo games will be conducted and whether the organization owns or leases the premises, the days of the week and times of those days that the bingo games will be conducted, and a statement of the charitable purpose for the bingo proceeds. The attorney general then notifies the applicant of acceptance or rejection.

Complying with Regulations

Generally, bingo regulations, which are very strict, pertain to the following issues: places where the equipment can be purchased or leased, how the gross receipts from the bingo game may be used, the types of premises where the bingo game may be held and the maximum rental rate that may be paid, how the bingo license must be displayed, how often bingo games may be conducted, the maximum amount of prize money that may be paid out at any one session, and the times of day that bingo may be conducted. Do not deviate from the regulations in any way, since the state is likely to inspect your bingo program closely. Violations can range from misdemeanors to felonies and can result in both prison terms and fines.

If your organization is approached by a bingo operator to run a program for you and give you a percentage of the profits, investigate the proposal closely. In many states such operators are illegal. Also, even if the operator is legitimate, your organization could make much more money by running its own program.

Choosing a Facility

A good-sized facility is needed to run a bingo program, since a large number of people must be accommodated. The facility must also be available on a regular basis. Possibilities include a convenient school gym or cafeteria, a church social hall, a lodge, a party room, or even a skating rink. The facility should be able to provide the necessary tables and chairs; otherwise, you will have to rent them. And it should have a good public address system as well as good ventilation.

You might want to check out well-established bingo programs at various facilities in your community to determine what works best and to investigate the possibility of using the facility and the equipment of an existing group during an open period of the week.

Selecting a Time

Bingo programs are usually offered weekly and held on weeknights or Sunday afternoons. Choose a day and a time that will not conflict with other weekly games in your area.

Obtaining Equipment and Supplies

Bingo equipment and supplies can include an electronic bingo blower, a manual bingo cage, bingo balls, a flashboard to indicate the numbers called, bingo cards, bingo chips, instant bingo cards, markers, and aprons. Bingo equipment and supplies can be purchased, leased, or rented. In some states it is illegal to obtain bingo equipment and supplies from anywhere but a charitable organization. So, first check with your state attorney general's office to determine if there is a designated charitable bingo consultant in your area who is linked with a purchasing agent (e. g., the Central Purchasing Office of the Catholic Diocese). Otherwise, contact game suppliers that are listed in your local Yellow Pages. You might also consider trying to work out a deal with other charitable organizations that run bingo programs with their own equipment. Just be sure to do comparison shopping.

Offering Cash and Other Prizes

Usually cash is offered as the prize at bingo games, since money has the greatest audience appeal. At most bingo events the total amount of money that can be offered is divided up among the games, and the amount gradually builds up so that the biggest cash prize is awarded at the last game. This adds to the excitement and serves as an incentive to keep people involved throughout the event. To attract as many people as possible to your game, you should probably offer the maximum amount of prize money that, in your state, can legally be given away during any one bingo program.

Door prizes of merchandise can also be given away during the event. Solicit local businesses for donations in exchange for publicity and recognition at the event.

Recruiting a Caller

The person who calls out the numbers during a bingo game can influence the success of the event, since appealing callers who run fair games often build followings. Because state law sets the ceiling on prize money, it is often the caller and that person's gimmicks that distinguish one organization's bingo program from other organizations' programs. Make sure that the caller you recruit is able to work a large crowd, handle hecklers, joke with regulars, and sustain the suspense of the game.

Selling Cards

Generally, players pay admission fees at the door and receive a certain number of playing cards to start with. Additional cards must be purchased singly or in packages at prices that depend on the particular game. A special table should be set up to sell bingo cards, and volunteers should be able to sell cards on the floor throughout the program. Verification sheets of the number of cards each person purchases should be used so that people do not bring in their own cards or fail to return yours.

Selling Refreshments

Refreshments are often sold at bingo games, since players like to have snacks and drinks throughout the event. First check with your bingo supplier, since concessions may be available through the supplier. Otherwise, contact the regular food vendors of the facility where you will be holding the games and try to work out an arrangement. Or check with local food and drink suppliers as listed in the Yellow Pages. Consider selling candy, chips, pretzels, popcorn, baked goods, soda pop, and coffee. Offer the refreshments at a price that is profitable for your organization, yet reasonable for the purchasers.

Handling the Money

Since a large amount of cash is handled during a bingo program, it may be wise to hire a security guard at an hourly rate to protect the money during the games and safely deliver it to the bank. The volunteers running the bingo bank must be extremely accurate and trustworthy. If possible, consider purchasing a cash register to eliminate errors.

Keeping Records

Detailed records must be kept for a number of years (usually 3) from the date that a bingo program is conducted. Generally, the records should include the following information: an itemized list of gross receipts of each game, an itemized list of all expenses, a list of all prizes awarded, a list of all winners, an itemized list of how the proceeds are used, the number of persons who participated, and a list of receipts from the sale of food and beverages. The state attorney general or local law enforcement agency may at any time investigate your organization, examine the accounts and records, and conduct inspections, audits, and observations.

Dealing with the Players

Volunteers must be able to patiently handle the players, many of whom will have their own routines during the games. For instance, some may race for what they consider to be the best seats—near the caller, the exit, the smoke ventilators, the refreshment stand, or the restrooms. Others may hurry toward a particular table that they feel is lucky. When picking bingo cards, some players may look for lucky numbers, while others use their own unique systems for making the selections. Many players will arrange their lucky charms on the tables. Volunteers must be able to deal with these and other player idiosyncrasies.

Variations

Although the procedures of a bingo game are standard, certain gimmicks can be featured to distinguish your program from another organization's games. Ideas include the following:

Friendship Bingo—The people sitting on either side of the person who gets bingo also win prizes.

Bingo Drawing—Players enter a drawing for the following week where they can win free cards, prizes, and cash if they are present. This is a good way of building regular attendance.

Progressive Numbers—One number is called per week until somebody wins. This also builds regular attendance.

Instant Bingo—These special cards are sold throughout the program. Portions are peeled off to indicate instant winners.

Letter Game—The first person who covers spaces on a card in the shape of a particular letter (e. g., T or X) is the winner.

Four Corners Game—The first person who covers all four corners of a card is the winner.

Picture Frame Game—The first person who covers the spaces around the entire border of a card is the winner.

Fill-Up Game—The first person who covers every space on a card is the winner. This game is usually played for a very large cash prize.

Talk to experienced bingo players for additional suggestions of ways to make your bingo program special.

CASINO NIGHTS

A casino night offers players the opportunity to pay to participate in games of chance in the hope of winning prizes. Generally, admission tickets are sold in advance at a price that depends on the nature of the audience and the other features that are included in the event, such as dinner, entertainment, a raffle, and a certain amount of chips or play money to start out with. Casino nights are also referred to as Las Vegas nights, Monte Carlo nights, and Atlantic City nights.

Special Advantages

In addition to the general advantages listed in the Introduction to Programs, a casino night offers the following special advantages:

A casino night is a fun, exciting event and very appealing to people who enjoy gambling.

With the rental of the appropriate games and equipment, a casino night is relatively easy to organize.

This type of event can be conducted any time of the year.

Special Cautions

Keeping in mind the general cautions listed in the Introduction to Programs, the following special cautions about a casino night should be carefully considered as well:

Some states and cities do not allow gambling—even if it is for a charitable cause. Check all laws before proceeding.

Up-front money is needed to rent the games and equipment.

If there is not a nearby location that rents the games and equipment, then everything must be transported from a distant location. This can be costly and difficult.

Volunteers are needed who are experienced in running gambling games and using gambling equipment so that the event will run smoothly. Otherwise an experienced croupier may have to be hired to train the volunteers and supervise the event.

All monetary transactions during a casino night must be tightly controlled.

A casino night may not be appropriate for the image of your organization, since it is a gambling event.

Expenses

A casino night can entail the following expenses for your organization: facility rental fee—games and equipment rental fees and transportation costs—croupier's fee—purchase of food and drinks—entertainment costs—purchase of decorations—purchase of prizes—purchase of licenses and permits—purchase of liability insurance—printing costs—postage costs—promotion costs. Expenses can be kept down by using your own facility if you have one, by renting less expensive games and equipment (e.g., card games are cheaper to rent than wheel games), and by convincing an experienced croupier to donate any expertise and service.

Volunteer Requirements

The volunteer leaders needed to plan and conduct a casino night include the event chairperson, arrangements chairperson, acquisitions chairperson, printed materials chairperson, promotions chairperson, special features chairperson, ticket-selling chairperson, treasurer, and volunteer coordinator. Their roles are described in the Introduction to Programs. In addition to these volunteer leaders, numerous volunteers are needed at a casino night to operate the games, serve as cashiers, and act as hosts and hostesses. Volunteers who run the games should be scheduled to work in shifts throughout the night. Select your most vivacious volunteers for this role or recruit local celebrities. Cashiers should be able to quickly accept players' money and accurately give them playing chips or play money as well as pay off players who are finished for the night and want to cash in their remaining chips for prizes. Great care should be taken in selecting the volunteers who will serve as cashiers. Hosts and hostesses should be willing to greet guests, serve food and drinks, and keep the casino area clean.

Considering State and Local Laws

Check your state and local laws before planning a casino night. Some areas do not allow gambling at all, while other areas do. In certain instances, gambling for prizes but not cash may be permitted.

Choosing a Facility

A casino night requires a large facility that can be easily decorated and can accommodate the many different aspects of the event—gambling, eating, dancing, socializing, and prize display or auction. Gyms, halls, arenas, clubs, shopping malls, and huge tents are possible locations.

Creating the Proper Atmosphere

The proper atmosphere will add to the success of a casino night. Players should feel that they are part of an exciting, fast-paced event. Costumes and decorations reflecting modern casinos, the Roaring Twenties, the Old West, or any other appropriate theme can help create a mood that will stimulate action at the game tables.

Recuiting a Head Croupier

A croupier is the person who runs a gambling casino table, collecting bets and paying out winnings. Unless one of your volunteers is an expert at running gambling games, you will need to recruit an experienced croupier to train your volunteers and supervise your event. Try to obtain this person's services for free or at least at a reasonable rate.

Deciding Which Games to Feature

The games that you decide to feature at your casino night will depend on what is legal in your area, what might be most appealing to your intended audience, and what the rental fees are for the various games. Possibilities include keno, poker, blackjack, dice tables, and roulette wheels.

In deciding which games to feature, it is also very important to consider the house odds on the different types of games. Talk to an expert or borrow the appropriate gambling books from the library. After all, a game with poor house odds that is being run by a novice and played by a sharp gambler could be a money loser for your event.

Determining the Number of Games to Offer

The number of games necessary to keep a casino night exciting depends on the number of players you expect to have at the event. In turn, the number of games that you decide on will affect your rental costs and volunteer requirements. A carnival or casino company that rents gambling equipment should be able to advise you regarding how many games you will need. Also, check with other organizations that have conducted successful casino nights.

Establishing the Rules

Although the rules for each game are somewhat standard, they must be formally established in writing by your head croupier and strictly adhered to by all game operators and players. The rules should include the maximum number of players permitted to participate in any one game at any one time, the minimum and maximum betting limits for each game, and the actual playing procedures. Printed copies of the rules should be posted or distributed to each person participating in the event.

Obtaining Prizes

Most organizations that conduct casino nights offer merchandise prizes rather than cash to the winners. Although cash generally has greater audience appeal than prizes, by offering cash an organization reduces its profit. Donated prizes, however, cost the organization nothing and do not affect profits.

Donations of prizes ranging from clock-radios to VCRs, from dinners to trips, and from bicycles to cars should be sought from local merchants. Donors should be assured that their contributions will be highly publicized both before and at the event. If you feel that it will increase attendance at your event, consider asking merchants who donate valuable prizes to display the items in their store windows for a period of time before the event. The display should explain to whom the donation is being made, why it is being made, and where to purchase tickets.

If it is not possible to get all prizes donated, then try to borrow items from local merchants. Agree that you will either pay for the item if it is selected as a prize or return the item if it is not taken. Any prizes that must be purchased should be obtained at a discounted rate.

As another option, you might consider entering into an arrangement with a small number of local shops or boutiques to set up displays of their merchandise at the event. Players would then be able to purchase items from the merchants with their winnings. After the event your organization would exchange the merchant's play money or chips for cash—less an agreed upon percentage of the gross sales that would go to your organization.

Setting Up a Bank

A bank should be set up in a central location so players can easily purchase chips or play money as well as turn in chips for prizes or cash. When playing for cash, the bank should open with sufficient funds to pay off players who decide to quit early and cash in their chips or play money before the other players have sufficiently built up the bank with their purchases.

Generally, in an effort to establish a big-time spender atmosphere where everybody feels rich, a certain amount of real money purchases a much larger amount of play money (e.g., $10 in cash is worth $1,000 in play money). Your actual rate of exchange will depend of the nature of your audience, your ultimate fund-raising goal, the number of prizes you have to offer, the nature of those prizes, whether the prizes were donated or you had to pay for them, the amount of your other expenses, and your anticipated income from such other sources as admission tickets. Do not underprice your money.

Awarding Prizes

Players can use their chips or play money either to purchase prizes throughout the evening or to bid on prizes that are auctioned off at the end of the evening—depending on the format of your event. Players should be allowed to purchase additional chips or play money so that they can pay for or bid on a prize that they really want. The grand prize of the event may be set aside from the sale or auction and awarded to the big winner of the night.

All prizes should be put on display at the event and clearly marked as to who donated them. The number of chips or amount of play money needed to purchase them should be noted, or the opening suggested bid amounts should be indicated.

NIGHTS AT THE RACES

A night at the races is a gambling event that involves organizing an evening at a local racetrack for a group of people. Usually a bus is chartered to transport guests to and from the racetrack, a reception is held or dinner is served in the track clubhouse, and an added attraction, such as a raffle or a tour of the stables and paddock area, is offered.

Special Advantages

In addition to the general advantages listed in the Introduction to Programs, a night at the races can offer the following special advantages:

A night at the races is an exciting and entertaining event.

A relatively short period of time is required to organize this type of event.

The volunteer requirements are not overwhelming for a night at the races.

Special Cautions

Keeping in mind the general cautions listed in the Introduction to Programs, the following special cautions about a night at the races should be carefully considered as well:

Since a night at the races is a gambling event, it may not be appropriate for your organization.

This type of event can only be scheduled during the racing season in your area.

Expenses

A night at the races can entail the following expenses for your organization: purchase of food and drinks—fees for chartering one or more buses—printing costs—postage costs—promotion costs. Most of these expenses must be paid for up-front.

Volunteer Requirements

The volunteer leaders needed to plan and conduct a night at the races include the event chairperson, arrangements chairperson, printed materials chairperson, promotions chairperson, special features chairperson, ticket-selling chairperson, treasurer, and volunteer coordinator. Their roles are described in the Introduction to Programs. In addition to these volunteer leaders, volunteers are needed to assist them, particularly with selling tickets to the event.

Working with the Race Track

It is important to visit the racetrack and meet with the manager to go over the details of using the facility for your event. You will want to determine the costs involved, available dates, attendance limits, and other issues. A racetrack will often offer discount admission tickets for large groups and provide predesigned party and meal plans. After all, catering to groups makes up a good portion of a racetrack's business. Once an agreement has been reached, a contract with the track should be drawn up and signed.

Designing a Special Program Book

A major component of a night at the races is a special program book that lists all the races, includes betting instructions, and features advertising. Check with other organizations that have held nights at the races for program book ideas.

Variations

Instead of a night at the racetrack, your organization might consider organizing an evening of videotaped horse races or planning a trip to see dog races.

Videotaped races are actual horse races that are shown on 16 mm color and sound films. They can be part of an exciting event when the fun includes betting on the races and an auction at the end of the evening so that participants can use their winnings to bid on prizes.

Once you have determined that this type of event is legal in your area and obtained any necessary permits or licenses, contact a legitimate local or national organization that specializes in arranging this type of event. The organization should be able to provide you with everything you need, including audiovisual equipment, films, betting tickets, programs, play money, instructions, and promotional materials. You will have to locate an appropriate facility to hold the event.

A *trip to the dog races* in your state or a nearby state can be a novel, fun, and exciting event. Plan a bus trip to the dog racetrack and keep everybody on the buses busy to and from the track with auctions, raffles, and other activities.

RAFFLES

A raffle involves raising money by selling numbered tickets as chances to win valuable prizes. A raffle can be an excellent fund-raising event itself, or it can work well in conjunction with another event, such as a dinner-dance. Raffles are also called drawings, sweepstakes, and lotteries.

Special Advantages

In addition to the general advantages listed in the Introduction to Programs, a raffle offers the following special advantages:

If the prizes are donated, then a raffle has few up-front costs.

A raffle is a good way to publicize the name of your organization and its cause through the ticket-selling process.

Everyone can get involved in a raffle, since it is not possible to have too many volunteer ticket sellers or buyers.

This type of event can be conducted any time of the year.

There is usually room for another raffle in a community.

It is possible to organize a raffle in a relatively short period of time.

Special Cautions

Keeping in mind the general cautions listed in the Introduction to Programs, the following special cautions about a raffle should be carefully considered as well:

It is important to make sure that running a raffle is legal in your area.

The time and effort of numerous volunteers are needed to sell raffle tickets.

The grand prize must be able to attract many ticket buyers.

Certain trustees or other members of your organization may object to a raffle since it is a form of gambling.

Expenses

A raffle can entail the following expenses for your organization: purchase of the grand prize—purchase of smaller prizes—purchase of refreshments to be served at the drawing—facility rental fee for the drawing—purchase of licenses and permits—printing costs—postage costs—promotion costs. The total cost of the event will depend on how successful you are at getting the prizes and other expenses donated.

Volunteer Requirements

The volunteer leaders needed to plan and conduct a raffle include the event chairperson, arrangements chairperson, acquisitions chairperson, printed materials chairperson, promotions chairperson, ticket-selling chairperson, treasurer, and volunteer coordinator. Their roles are described in the Introduction to Programs. In addition to these volunteer leaders, numerous additional volunteers are needed, particularly for the ticket-selling effort. Ticket sellers should have a lot of contacts, and they should not be shy. The number of volunteers needed to sell tickets will depend on the number of tickets to be sold and how many tickets each volunteer can reasonably be expected to sell.

Consulting State and Local Laws

Before you begin planning a raffle, it is crucial that you determine whether your state and local laws permit raffles. Many governments prohibit or restrict such events. Often a city or state license must be purchased to conduct a raffle.

If you intend to conduct a raffle through the mail, first check the postal regulations. They are extremely strict regarding the sale of chance tickets through the mail.

Determining the Rules

It is very important to establish written rules for a raffle regarding all regulations, limitations, and restrictions for ticket buyers, winners, and your organization. For example, as discussed in Chapter 3, the purchasers of tickets should be informed that the IRS does not allow the price of a raffle ticket to be a charitable tax deduction (donors of prizes to the raffle are, however, entitled to a tax deduction for their gift). Ticket buyers should also be told that any taxes on the prizes are the sole responsibility of the winner. Eligibility requirements and entry deadlines should be stated in writing as well.

Selecting and Obtaining the Prizes

The prizes you decide to offer in your raffle will depend on how much time and money you can invest in obtaining them. The prizes you feature will also depend on how much money you want to earn from the raffle, since the prizes offered can influence the price of your tickets and the number of tickets you sell.

A grand prize should be exciting, innovative, and valuable. It should not be offbeat, since that would require too much explanation in the publicity. It should reflect the organization's image (an animal rights organization would not give away a fur coat). And it should appeal to the target audience (a raffle intended for an upper-income audience might feature a Mercedes, while a raffle intended for a middle-income audience might feature two Fords). Remember that cash is a favorite prize. A cash prize can even be advantageous to your organization if the winner decides to donate back a portion of the money.

Try to obtain all prizes for free or at least at a discounted rate, since the less money spent on prizes, the greater the profit. If you must pay for an expensive grand prize, try to avoid committing yourself to the actual purchase until you are sure you will sell enough tickets to cover the expense. After all, as embarrassing as it might be to have to cancel the raffle and return the ticket money, it would be much worse to have to suffer a large financial loss only to save face. In deciding how many prizes to feature, consider whether your intended audience would be more interested in winning one extremely valuable prize or, at somewhat better odds, one of a number of more moderate prizes.

Setting the Ticket Price

The price you decide to charge for each raffle ticket will depend on the value of the prizes, how much money (if any) it cost you to obtain the prizes, the makeup and size of your intended audience, and the number of volunteers you can recruit to sell tickets. Many communitywide raffles that feature moderate prizes (e.g., VCRs, color televisions, personal computers) charge $1 per ticket since it is much easier to sell a lot of tickets to a large audience at this price than at higher prices. Of course, raffles that feature very valuable prizes (e.g., luxury cars) and appeal to a more specialized, affluent audience can sell expensive tickets (e.g., $150 each).

Inexpensive raffle tickets are often sold in books. For example, a person might be able to purchase a book of six $1 tickets for $5. This type of packaging can be appealing to ticket buyers. The ticket book must state the number of tickets it contains and the amount for which it is being sold. To otherwise adjust the printed ticket price and offer random discounts or special deals is illegal.

Selling the Tickets

The success of your raffle will depend on your volunteers' ability to sell as many tickets as possible within a limited time period. You must have a sufficiently large, highly committed volunteer force to sell individual as well as books of tickets.

Some organizations turn the ticket-selling effort into a contest itself by offering prizes to the top ticket sellers. As another incentive, you might tell ticket sellers to write their own names on the back of every ticket they sell. That way, the person who sells the winning ticket will win a prize as well.

Actual tickets usually consist of two parts. One part is the numbered stub where the purchaser's name, address, and phone number are printed.

This part is turned in for the raffle and then used later to compile a mailing list for the organization. The other part has a number that matches the stub. The purchaser holds onto this part so that if the person is a winner, the prize can be claimed.

Running the Drawing

If the raffle is not part of another event, such as a dinner-dance, it can be conducted within a very brief time frame of just an hour or so. You can invite people to have refreshments, listen to music, and socialize for a while. You might have drawings for smaller prizes every 15 minutes. Then you can hold the drawing for the grand prize. The person who draws the winning tickets can be someone from your organization or, for added glamor and excitement, a local celebrity. A glass bowl or other visible container should be used to hold the tickets. The container should be the appropriate size so that it looks full. All ticket stubs should be kept and used as the basis for future contacts.

Variations

A number of variations of a raffle can be organized, including a 50-50 raffle, house raffle, limited raffle, reverse raffle, shopping spree, sideboards, sweepstakes, theme raffle, and year-round raffle.

A *50-50 raffle* is usually conducted at a meeting or other regular gathering of an organization. It involves selling raffle tickets before the meeting and conducting the raffle at the end of the meeting. Half of the money collected from the sale of the tickets goes to the winner. The other half goes to the organization. A 50-50 raffle is generally held on a regular basis (e.g., monthly). Each raffle alone may not result in much money, but the amounts can add up over a period of time.

In a *house raffle*, a homeowner enters into a contract with an organization. The contract allows the organization to buy the home for an agreed-upon price if it manages to sell a certain number of raffle tickets by a specific date. The raffle prize, of course, is the house. If not enough tickets are sold to make the raffle profitable, the deal is cancelled and the ticket money is returned to the purchasers. Ticket prices for a house raffle are generally quite high. House raffles are easy to publicize as they almost automatically attract media attention. Note, however, that this type of raffle is illegal in certain states.

In a *limited raffle*, only a certain number of tickets are sold. Generally they are sold at a high price (e.g., 250 tickets at $150 each) and for an expensive grand prize, such as a new car, a trip, or cash. Leading up to the grand prize drawing are several other drawings for more moderate prizes. Although it is more expensive than other raffles, a limited raffle is attractive to the people who can afford it, since it offers better odds of winning due to the small number of tickets sold. A limited raffle is often held in conjunction with a dinner-dance so that the guests feel they are at least getting something for their money, even if they do not win the grand prize. Note that a limited raffle offers no financial risk to the organization when the grand prize is 50 percent of the total cash collected from the ticket sales (the other 50 percent goes to the organization).

In a *reverse raffle* the winner of the grand prize is the person who holds the ticket that is drawn last. Raffle tickets are drawn throughout the event and every tenth ticket (another number may be used, of course) is declared the winner of a small prize. The prizes become more valuable and the excitement builds as the drawing continues. Sometimes guests use scorecards to keep tally of which tickets have been drawn. Sometimes the holders of the last tickets are given the chance to decide whether they want to split the grand prize (if it is cash) evenly among themselves or take their chances on just one winner. All nonwinning tickets can be placed in a separate hopper for a consolation-prize drawing. A reverse raffle is usually held in conjunction with a dinner-dance or reception since the tickets, which may be limited in number, tend to be expensive.

A *shopping spree* can be an attractive grand prize for a raffle. The holder of the winning ticket is given the chance to spend a certain amount of time (e.g., 5 minutes) gathering items in a store worth up to a certain amount of money (e.g., $1,000). Shopping sprees generally take place in supermarkets. Try to get the supermarket to donate the spree in exchange for a good deal of free publicity. Or at least ask the supermarket to give your organization a discount on the winner's final shopping bill and to help you publicize the event.

Sideboards are inexpensive raffles that are conducted as a special feature at a reverse or regular raffle event. A sideboard consists of a display of numbers. People purchase numbered tickets off the different priced sideboards (e.g., $2, $5, $10). The same drawing is used for both the reverse or regular raffle and the sideboards. In a reverse raffle, as numbers are called off eliminating tickets the same numbered tickets from the sideboards are eliminated as well. The person holding the last ticket from each side-board wins half of the money taken in at that sideboard. The other half goes to the organization. In a regular raffle, the person holding the numbered ticket from each sideboard that matches the winning raffle ticket wins that sideboard pot. Sideboards can add significantly to the profit made from a raffle since the excitement of the event prompts people to purchase numerous relatively inexpensive sideboard tickets.

A *sweepstakes* is a raffle that is conducted through the mail. People are sent tickets approximately 6 weeks before the drawing and urged to return the stubs along with a contribution, such as $10. The contribution, however, is suggested—it is not required (if it were required, the sweepstakes would not be legal). An entry deadline date as well as a drawing date for appealing prizes are printed on the tickets. An enormous mailing should be organized for this type of effort since the return is usually very small.

A *theme raffle* adds an unusual twist to a raffle event by including unique decorations, costumes, refreshments, and additional activities in a festive setting. For instance, one university holds an annual raffle in the winter called "Bahamas or Bust." The grand prize is a free trip to the Bahamas for two people. All ticket holders must be present at the drawing— dressed in beach clothes with packed suitcases—since the winners leave for their trip directly from the site of the drawing. All other ticket holders remain for a party.

A *year-round raffle* is a limited raffle in which each person purchases one number that is their number for weekly and monthly drawings throughout the year. In one community, 300 numbers are sold for $50 each. Weekly drawings are held for small cash prizes, monthly drawings are held for larger cash prizes, and a grand prize drawing is held at the end of the year during a dinner-dance. Since a year-round raffle includes a limited number of tickets and regularly held drawings, people feel that they have better-than-usual chances of winning in this type of event.

RESOURCES FOR BINGO GAMES

Alberti, C. E., Macko, G. S., & Whitcomb, N. B. *Money-makers: A systematic approach to special events fund raising.* Ambler, PA: Whitcomb Associates, 1982, Supplement 1, pp. 1–12.

Fernbacher, M. Bingo. *The Plain Dealer Friday Magazine*, November 8, 1985, p. 23.

Flanagan, J. *The grass roots fundraising book.* Chicago: Contemporary Books, Inc., 1982, pp. 118–120.

Ohio Revised Code, Chapter 2915: Gambling.

Woodward, K. L., Underwood, A., & Raine, G. Is bingo's number up? *Newsweek*, August 26, 1986, p. 54.

RESOURCES FOR CASINO NIGHTS

Alberti, C. E., Macko, G. S., & Whitcomb, N. B. *Money-makers: A systematic approach to special events fund raising.* Ambler, PA: Whitcomb Associates, 1982, pp. 10.1– 10.11.

Ardman, P. & Ardman, H. *Woman's Day book of fund raising.* New York: St. Martin's Press, 1980, pp. 189–191.

B'nai B'rith Fund Raising Cabinet, *B'nai B'rith Fund Raising Chairman Handbook* Washington, D.C.: B'nai B'rith Leadership Cabinet, pp. 59–65.

Drotning, P. T. *500 ways for small charities to raise money*. Chicago: Contemporary Books, Inc., 1979, pp. 92–94.

Jensen, C. Las Vegas: As close as your neighborhood church. *Plain Dealer Friday Magazine*, February 7, 1986, pp. 36–37.

National Council of Jewish Women, Inc., *The raiser's edge*. New York: National Council of Jewish Women, Inc., pp. 45–46.

Pritchard, J. H. *There's plenty of money for nonprofit groups willing to earn their shares— How to do it successfully*. Phoenix: Cornucopia Publications, 1984, pp. 301–306.

RESOURCES FOR NIGHTS AT THE RACES

Alberti, C. E., Macko, G. S., & Whitcomb, N. B. *Money-makers: A systematic approach to special events fund raising*. Ambler, PA: Whitcomb Associates, 1982, Supplement 3, pp. 1–15.

B'nai B'rith Fund Raising Cabinet, *B'nai B'rith fund raising chairman handbook*. Washington, D.C.: B'nai B'rith Leadership Cabinet, pp. 67–68.

Hay, J. T. *534 ways to raise money*. New York: Simon & Schuster, 1983, pp. 23–24.

RESOURCES FOR RAFFLES

Alberti, C. E., Macko, G. S. & Whitcomb, N. B. *Money-makers: A systematic approach to special events fund raising*. Ambler, PA: Whitcomb Associates, 1982, pp. 11.1–11.13.

Ardman, P. & Ardman, H. *Woman's Day book of fund raising*. New York: St. Martin's Press, 1980, pp. 184–189.

B'nai B'rith Fund Raising Cabinet. *B'nai B'rith fund raising chairman handbook*. Washington, D.C.: B'nai B'rith Leadership Cabinet, pp. 75–76.

Flanagan, J. *The grass roots fundraising book*. Chicago: Contemporary Books, Inc., 1982, pp. 201–206.

Hay, J. T. *534 ways to raise money*. New York: Simon & Schuster, 1983, pp. 120–122.

Kanner, B. Swept Away. *New York Magazine*, January 1, 1986, pp. 10–11.

Pritchard, J. H. *There's plenty of money for nonprofit groups willing to earn their shares— How to do it successfully*. Phoenix: Cornucopia Publications, 1984, pp. 307–313.

Sheerin, M. *How to raise top dollars from special events*. New York: Public Service Materials Center, 1984, pp. 105–108.

CODA

Fund-raising events are constantly evolving and changing. The programs presented in this book are current successes. New and innovative ideas are continually being developed as volunteers and staff of nonprofit organizations strive to attract more people to their events. This dynamic, ever-changing process is what makes planning and implementing fund-raising events a challenge. Have fun!

BIBLIOGRAPHY

Adler, J. & Kasindorf, M. Giving when it doesn't hurt. *Newsweek*, May 26, 1986, p. 23.

Alberti, C. E., Macko, G. S., & Whitcomb, N. B. *Money-makers: A systematic approach to special events fund raising*. Ambler, PA: Whitcomb Associates, 1982.

Ardman, P. & Ardman, H. *Woman's Day book of fund raising*. New York: St. Martin's Press, 1980.

Babitz, M. Why most benefit concerts lose money. *Grassroots Fundraising Journal*, October 1982, pp. 9–10.

Beatty, B. & Kirkpatrick, L. *The auction book*. Denver, Colorado: Auction Press, 1984.

Beatty, B. & Kirkpatrick, L. Why an auction may be the right "Event" for you. *Fund Raising Management*, January 1985, pp. 18–25.

Berger, S. Ten steps to a million dollar fund raiser. *The Grantsmanship Center News*, December–January 1975, p. 15.

Berson, G. *Making a show of it: A guide to concert production*. Ukiah, California: Redwood Records, 1980.

B'nai B'rith Fund Raising Cabinet. *B'nai B'rith fund raising chairman handbook*. Washington, D.C.: B'nai B'rith Leadership Cabinet (no date).

Brody, R. *Problem solving: Concepts and methods for community organizations*. New York: Human Sciences Press, Inc., 1982.

Brody, R., Goodman, M., & Ferrante, J. *The legislative process: An action handbook for Ohio citizens groups*. Cleveland, Ohio: Federation for Community Planning, 1985.

Brody, R., Goodman, M., & Josephs, S. *Tax levies and other ballot issues: A campaign handbook*. Cleveland, Ohio: Federation for Community Planning, 1984.

Cobb, L. M. Fund raising's revolving door: How it can be stopped. *Fund Raising Management*, March 1985.

Colwell, P. T. The use of charts: A tool for management. *Fund Raising Management*, August 1984, p. 52.

Connors, T. D., Editor-in-Chief. *The nonprofit organization handbook*. New York: Mc-Graw-Hill, Inc., 1980.

Contact Center, Inc. *Getting yours: A publicity and funding primer for nonprofit and voluntary organizations*. Lincoln, Nebraska: Contact Publications (no date).

Council of Better Business Bureaus, Inc.—Philanthropic Advisory Services. Special events and charitable contribution deductions. *In-Sight*, March 1979.

DeBono, E. *Po: Beyond yes and no*. New York: Penguin Books, 1983.

DeMarco, N. J. The fund raising dinner. *In-Sight*, March 1979, pp. 1–4.

DeSoto, C. *For fun and funds: Creative fund-raising ideas for your organization*. West Nyack, New York: Parker Publishing Co., 1983.

Drotning, P. T. *500 ways for small charities to raise money*. Chicago, Illinois. Contemporary Books, Inc., 1979.

Federation for Community Planning. *Publicity guide*. Cleveland, Ohio: Federation for Community Planning, 1987.

Fernbacher, M. Bingo. *Plain Dealer Friday Magazine*, November 8, 1985, p. 23.

Flanagan, J. *The grass roots fundraising book*. Chicago, Illinois: Contemporary Books, Inc., 1982.

Fottler, M. D. & Fottler, C. A. The management of volunteers in nonprofit organisations. *The Nonprofit World Report*, September–October 1984.

Fox, H. W. Astute pricing for nonprofits. *The Nonprofit World Report*, May–June 1985.

Fund-Raising Institute. Non-events: The invitation is all you need. *FRI Monthly Portfolio*, March 1984.

Fund-Raising Institute. Pothole club raises funds for Columbus. *FRI Monthly Portfolio*, July 1984.

Fund-Raising Institute. Risk-free "Dream Home" tour raises gifts and publicity for hospital. *FRI Monthly Portfolio*, June 1981.

Gaby, P. V. & Gaby, D. M. *Nonprofit organization handbook*. Englewood Cliffs, New Jersey. Prentice-Hall, Inc., 1979.

Grambs, M. & Miller, P. *Dollars and sense: A community fundraising manual for women's shelters and other non-profit organizations*. San Francisco, California: Western States Shelter Network, 1982.

Groman, J. E. Growing through donor acquisition. *The Nonprofit World Report*, May–June 1985.

Guercio, G. F. Festival of trees brightens hospital's fund raising year. *Fund Raising Management*, January 1985, pp. 38–43.

Hay, J. T. *534 ways to raise money*. New York: Simon & Schuster, 1983.

Honig, L. Food for thought—Fundraising luncheons. *Grassroots Fundraising Journal*, June/July 1984, pp. 6–8.

Honig, L. Fundraising events, Part Four: Starting at home. *Grassroots Fundraising Journal*, December 1982.

Honig, L. Fundraising events, Part Three. Budgeting. *Grassroots Fundraising Journal*, August 1982.

Honig, L. Fundraising events, Part Two. Getting into the act or finding a performer for your benefit concert. *Grassroots Fundraising Journal*, June 1982, pp. 9–13.

Honig, L. The cost of people—Evaluating fundraising events. *Grassroots Fundraising Journal*, October 1983.

Honig, L. The time it takes—Fundraising luncheons. *Grassroots Fundraising Journal*, August/September 1984, pp. 3–8.

Hopkins, E. Cruising for a cause. *New York Magazine*, August 18, 1986, p. 16.

Hopkins, E., Our Ladies of Charity, *New York Magazine*, October 13, 1986, pp. 46–53.

Hughes, T. M. Horse shows raise funds, promote civic cooperation. *Fund Raising Management*, February 1985, pp. 70–78.

Jaffe, L. Gifts-in-kind organization gives something for nothing. *Fund Raising Management*, January 1985, pp. 50–51.

Jensen, C. Las Vegas: As close as your neighborhood church. *Plain Dealer Friday Magazine*, February 7, 1986, pp. 36–37.

Johnston, David. Fund-raising dinners are "Way Out of Hand". *Los Angeles Times*, September 22, 1985.

Kaiser, L. Fund raising's future lies with creative visionaries. *Fund Raising Management*, March 1985, pp. 34–39.

Kanner, B. Swept away. *New York Magazine*, January 1, 1986, pp. 10–11.

Kiechel, W. On the charity circuit. *Fortune*, October 14, 1985.

Kotler, P. *Marketing for nonprofit organizations.* Englewood Cliffs, New Jersey: Prentice-Hall, Inc., 1982.

Kotler, P. *Marketing management—Analysis, planning, and control.* Englewood Cliffs, New Jersey: Prentice-Hall, Inc., 1980.

Leibert, E. R., & Sheldon, B. E. *Handbook of special events for nonprofit organizations.* New York: Association Press, 1972.

London, M. Effective use of volunteers: Who, why, when and how. *Fund Raising Management*, August 1985, pp. 18–20.

Lord, J. G. Marketing nonprofits. *The Grantsmanship Center Reprint Series on Management*, 1981.

Lord, J. D. Thirty-five essentials every trustee should know. *The raising of money.* Cleveland, Ohio: Third Sector Press, 1983.

Lord, J. G. The marketplace perspective: A new approach to the development of institutions. *Philanthropy and marketing.* Cleveland, Ohio: Third Sector Press, 1983.

Lovelock, C. H. & Weinberg, C. B. *Marketing for public and nonprofit managers.* New York: John Wiley & Sons, 1984.

Loykovich, J. Special events in the 80's: A case for marketing approach. *Fund Raising Management*, January 1985, pp. 26–35, 49.

Mahon, G. The grand gala. *Town & Country*, September 1985, pp. 198–199, 241–243, 249–254.

Martinez, B. F. & Weiner, R. Guide to public relations for nonprofit organizations and public agencies. *The Grantsmanship Center Reprint Series on Management*, 1979, pp. 1–15.

McCandless, K. Cleveland's celebrity waiters raise funds by collecting tips. *Fund Raising Management*, September 1985, pp. 22–28, 72.

Metsker, R. How to produce a profitable walk-a-thon. *FRI Bulletin*, May 1982.

Miller, A. & Williams, E. Peddling a social cause. *Newsweek*, September 1, 1986, pp. 58–59.

Mirkin, H. R. *The complete fund raising guide*. New York: Public Service Materials Center, 1981.

Mulford, C. *Guide to student fundraising: 129 ways to raise money*. Reston, Virginia: Future Homemakers of America, 1984.

Musselman, V. W. *Money raising activities for community groups*. New York: Association Press. 1969.

National Council of Jewish Women, Inc. *The raiser's edge*. New York: National Council of Jewish Women, Inc. (no date).

Nonprofit Executive. Syndicate arrangement helps raise funds. *Nonprofit Executive*, September 1984, p. 5.

Ohio Revised Code. Chapter 2915: Gambling.

Olney, J. The last word. *Chocolatier*, Summer 1985, p. 97.

Phillips, S. How to get a celebrity to attend your special event. *Fund Raising Management*, September 1985, pp. 59–62.

Plessner, G. M., Golf Management Manual. In *The Encyclopedia of Fund Raising* (vol. 2). Arcadia, CA: Fund Raisers, Inc., 1986, pp. 7–108.

Pritchard, J. H. *There's plenty of money for nonprofit groups willing to earn their shares— How to do it successfully*. Phoenix, Arizona: Cornucopia Publications, 1984.

Raebel, J. Volunteers from business. *The Grantsmanship Center Reprint Series on Corporate Funding*, 1980.

Reid, R. Monopoly turns fifty. *Republic*, September 1985, pp. 82–91.

Roberts, J. Causes and effects. *New York Magazine*, June 24, 1985.

Ruth, N. Party for a (Non)Profit. *Your Share*, December 1985.

Saasta, T. Grass roots fund raising. *The Grantsmanship Center News*, October–December 1977.

Sainsbury, J. A. Put the "special" back in special events. *Fund Raising Management*, May 1983, pp. 40–43.

Sainsbury, J. A. *The beginner's guide to advanced fund raising*. New York: Jan Authur Sainsbury, 1985.

Schleck, R. S. Building a quality board. *Nonprofit World*, September –October 1985.

Schneiter, P. H. & Nelson, D. T. *The thirteen most common fund-raising mistakes and how to avoid them*. Washington, D.C.: Taft Corporation, 1982.

Shakely, J. Exploring the elusive world of corporate giving. *The Grantsmanship Center News*, July–September 1977.

Sheerin, M. *How to raise top dollars from special events.* New York: Public Service Materials Center, 1984.

Sheerin, M. Planning the special event: Negotiating the do's and don'ts. *Fund Raising Management,* January 1985.

Stevens, S. K. A reflective budget means you'll never have to say you're sorry. *Fund Raising Management,* December 1984.

Strawhecker, P. The process of developing innovation and leadership. *Fund Raising Management,* March 1985, pp. 26–32.

Sullivan, E. Some parties are murder. *Plain Dealer,* May 31, 1986, p. 3-A.

Swanson, A. *Building a better board: A guide to effective leadership.* Washington, D.C: Taft Corporation, 1984.

Sweeney, T. & Seltzer, M. Survival planning for the 80's: Fundraising strategies for grassroots organizations. *Community Jobs Reprint,* 1982.

United Way of America. Guidelines for organizing special events. *Community Magazine,* July 1985.

Vapnar, G. S. Fundraising: A common sense approach.: *Family Resource Coalition Report,* 1985, pp. 4–5.

Vogel, C. Show Business. *New York Times Magazine,* April 28, 1985, pp. 78–80.

Von Oech, R. *A whack on the side of the head.* New York: Warner Books, 1983.

Warner, I. R. *The art of fund raising.* New York: Bantam Books, Inc., 1984.

Weiss, J. M. The making of a benefit. *Northern Ohio Live,* February 1986, pp. 32–28, 49–59.

Woodward, K. L., Underwood, A., & Raine, G. Is bingo's number up? *Newsweek,* August 25, 1986, p. 54.

Zein, L. Tao House calendar. *Grassroots Fundraising Journal,* February 1985, pp. 10–12.

INDEX